Praise for Mennonite Cobbler

...excellent therapy for the insomniac...
Sleepless Weekly

MENNONITE COBBLER

Balancing Faith and Tradition
in a
Turbulent World

Kenneth David Brubacher

AuthorHouse™
1663 Liberty Drive
Bloomington, IN 47403
www.authorhouse.com
Phone: 1 (800) 839-8640

Published by AuthorHouse   12/11/2015

ISBN: 978-1-5049-5390-0 (sc)
ISBN: 978-1-5049-5388-7 (hc)
ISBN: 978-1-5049-5389-4 (e)

Library of Congress Control Number: 2015917744

Print information available on the last page.

Special thanks to Rick & Kathy Blacow,
whose eagle eyes and sharpened pens skewered scores of wriggling demonic errata
to these pages. They then ably applied saintly precision and patience in the
naming of the demons, thus facilitating their exorcism.

ALSO BY KENNETH DAVID BRUBACHER

The Watcher

The Poor Shoemaker

Fly

There's An Angel Under My Bed

Leafy and Sprucy

Fire Dragon Moon

The Book of Truth and Wisdom

Amos and Salina Go To Town

Commotion in the ManureYard

ERRATA

Because I am poor there was no money for expensive professional editing, so the reader is welcome to draw my attention to any errors found. I will then send a copy of the DVD of my stage play by the same name as this book to the first five people who send in a faux pas. I say 'five' because there is a high degree of probability I may quickly run out of DVD's. This is also, of course, a shameless plug for other of my (equally boring) works. Or just send a note and tell me how if you liked the book. I cry easily, but it's ok… ken@mennonitecobbler.com

Table of Contents

Appendices

This book is dedicated to my darling daughters

Angela Rose Brubacher Ishaka

and

Genevieve Rebecca Brubacher Hiller

Who, as of this writing, have yet to completely disown their dad
But by the time they are finished the book
This may well have happened

INTRODUCTION

You will find the introduction at the end of the book where it belongs. Most introductions are much given to inconsequential blithering codswallup, palpably designed to augment the author's endless superiority complex in the expostulation of the trivial nature of the matters to hand. At this juncture the reader is normally instructed to laboriously circumnavigate copious piles of that which emanates from the south end of a north-bound horse in anticipation of potentially meatier matters beyond, but in reality supplying enormous quantities of literary rediculosis to keep the reader from getting down to the real business at hand which is Reading the Blessed Book!

So instead of boring you to death on *Why I did It* and other such crappiolla, herewith

A Note of Mennonite Wisdom

Quality

Quality is like buying oats.

If you want nice, clean, fresh oats

It is necessary to either grow and harvest them yourself

Or pay a fair price.

However

If you are willing to settle for oats

Which have already been through the horse

That comes somewhat cheaper

Art by
Graeme MacKay
who consented to illustrate this book primarily due to the author's knowledge of
where to find the very best in Mennonite summer sausage
to feed his addiction to same.

MENNONITE COBBLER

Kenneth David Brubacher

A HAT & HAMMER PRODUCTION

VISIT: mennonitecobbler.com

CHAPTER 2

Bastard

One of my earliest memories is of my brother Freddie and me playing in the sandbox hard by the driveway of the old house on the top of the hill east of Elmira. I was four and he was six. It was a nice summer's day and Mother was hanging out the wash nearby when, for no apparent reason, Freddie – he of the golden hair, brilliant blue eyes, and cherubic countenance – took it upon himself to fling a shovelful of sand at Mother and to cheerfully inform her that she was a bastard.

When the yowling had pretty much subsided, it was determined that Freddie had been put up to this by the heathen Lutheran boys who lived across the road. They had apparently taught Brother Freddie that antics of this nature were signs of endearment that would put him right solid in the affections of his mother.

Everyone knew that these heathen boys' property backed onto the chemical plant, and every day or two, black slag was dumped onto the property adjoining the house of these boys. Rumor also had it that there was a very high degree of probability their property had a poisoned well, and so it was no wonder that these boys behaved in the manner described.

So what did we learn from this? What to take home? Well, for one thing, it was clearly evident that the teachings of the heathen boys across the road were not to be trusted. Also, it was not a good idea to fling shovelfuls of aggregate at one's mother. And, last but not least, it was a seriously bad idea to call into open question the legality of the nuptials of one's maternal grandparents.

Mother's Pet Thistle

Soon after the episode of the flying aggregate, we moved down into the town proper, about a block from the far west side of Elmira. Dad had taken the polio and didn't walk anymore, so he caused to be built a house that was friendlier to a wheelchair.

Looking back on it, ours was a peaceful and quiet neighborhood, and one with many gardens. Every house had at least two, one for vegetables, and at least one more for flowers, with few exceptions.

My mother planted a variety of flowers on the east and south sides of the house. The west side was guarded by large maple trees, so that this and the north side got little direct sunlight. There was, however, a swath of annuals located beyond the shaded grass on the north side of the property separating the lawn from the vegetable garden, featuring mostly marigolds, gladiolas, and evening scented stalk. On certain still nights, it was a delight to inhale the fragrance of those particular flowers.

Most of rest of that substantial back yard was reserved for the vegetable garden. In the Mennonite traditions, in which I was raised, it was pretty much sacrilege to buy something in the store that you could plant or create yourself. This not only applied to food-stuffs, like veggies and such, but also to clothes. Mother was always sewing something for us to wear.

I grew up in the middle of the "war-time houses" – originally subsidized housing for returning veterans of WWII. These were small two-story frame slate-clad homes without basements set on fairly large lots. Ours, on the other hand, was a new house which father caused to be built on a large vacant lot in 1956, on account of him now being in the wheel-chair from the polio. It had wide doors, hard floors, and everything he needed on the ground floor. Needless to say, he did no gardening. That would have been mother's domain in any case, polio or no.

Gardening was serious business. The loudest matter of the year occurred when, each spring, Mr. Sauder appeared with his rotor-tiller to churn the garden into fine soil. He pulled the starter cord on the tiller, which then farted into smoking noisy life to do the honors. When he was done, rows were laid out with stakes and the ball of butcher cord from the drawer in the kitchen. Packages of seed appeared. The lettuce and onions and other salad greens went in first, followed by carrots, squash and the rest. Last was corn – never before May 24 – and even then, one of us boys was dispatched to sit with a bare butt on the soil. If that went ok, the corn was planted. If there was miscellaneous cold-assed yowling and yelping, mother waited for a warmer day.

Our next door neighbor was one Oscar Ritter. He was an older gentleman who doubtless yearned for quiet enjoyment but had to deal with three rambunctious boys. Sort of like a Mister Wilson with three (count 'em, three) Dennis the Menaces next door. He was rather portly, in the manner of retired farmers of the time, and wore farmer's bib overalls, a white shirt, and shabby six-inch work boots made by the Hydro City Shoe Company in Kitchener that he bought from father in our shoe store.

He was a bit shrill by expression and strenuously objected to small boys who, he was certain, went out of their way to make his life miserable. They (we) ran around, laughed, shouted, and played games at all hours until dark. On warm summer's days he sat in his badly screened front porch, fuming, and swatting flies, which were doubtless seen vicariously as small boys in disguise sent by the Lord of the Gardens for his smiting and revenge because, horror on horror, we small boys played games with balls, which inevitably found their way into his garden.

Mr. Ritter's garden was a prize winner. Pretty much the only time he ever ventured from his house or porch was to tend his yard or garden. This he did with fervor only comparable to the single-minded dedication seen today in religious fanatics. Indeed, for Mr. Ritter, gardening was not a hobby or food-stuff necessity at all. It was religion.

Mr. Ritter's garden started every spring same as all gardens. Somebody came with a tiller and chewed the soil into tiny baby bite-sized bits. Then out came the stakes and string to mark the rows. Every seed was personally pressed into the ground with precision only a machinist with micrometer in hand could fully appreciate. Each seed in exactly the depth and spacing required – each seed potato section lovingly placed so the eyes were closest to the sunshine. All rows were staked out with a surveyor's eye. Thus Generalissimo Ritter executed his garden war campaign, with seedling troops to the ready, row upon row positioned in silence, awaiting the command of the sun and the gentle rains of an Elmira Spring to blossom forth, to do the bidding of the Master, He who called life to the dormant, and arrayed all forces of the earth to His good pleasure.

The season waxed, and, under his TLC, Mr. Ritter's garden always prospered. Today, the term for this is "micro-management". Nary a weed escaped excision. Hills of earth surrounding his corn and potatoes manicured just so. The weakest siblings were culled to allow the strongest to flourish. Tomato plants were tied lovingly to carefully selected sticks skewered adjacent to their roots to support the heavy crop to come. All was in order – everything in place and subject to the command of his almighty green-thumb-man-ship.

Throughout the neighborhood, the crops were harvested in their season. Our salad greens were plucked and washed to receive the homemade creamy dressing made from milk delivered daily by Mr. Holling from the Purity Dairy. It was delivered in a covered wagon pulled by an old sway-backed nag that knew the whole route. It stopped at every house as needed (but took several weeks to learn a new stop if one occurred). The milk was meant for our cups at table, but the bottles first passed through mother's hands for the removal of the cream on top, thence to dressings and other creamy delights.

In corn season, mother would put the large pot to the boil, and then several of us children would trail her out into the garden. She peeled aside the husks to determine the ripeness, and, once plucked from the stalk, the corn was shucked on the spot and run back into the kitchen. Then it was put into the pot for corn on the cob, about fifteen minutes from stalk to mouth. With butter, salt, and pepper, that was supper, and it was all we needed or wanted.

Corn was the herald of squash, and squash foretold snows to come. The gardens were by this time pretty much bereft of crop, their spoor strewn about the violated soil awaiting winter. When all the crops were off, a farmer would appear with a spreader loaded with cow manure, which was mechanically distributed over mother's whole garden. The next day a small tractor came to plow it all under, to await the winter blast; sleep, sleep, and awake again the next time the sun sent the icy crusts away, warming Mother Earth, and commencing the cycle once again.

But that's not exactly how it all went at Mr. Ritter's place next door. Indeed, the crops were plucked and put away – nobody really knew where. He lived with his wife, Mrs. Ritter, a grey anonymity of no word or opinion on any matter that anybody had ever heard. We boys were pretty sure she didn't even have a first name. The garden appeared to produce much more food than the two of them could ever consume by themselves. Rarely were any family observed to call, and seldom a visitor. Just the two of them in that old grey slate house with the Insulbrick clad garage, wherein resided the sand-colored car they seldom used. Each Saturday, Mr. Ritter backed it out onto his gravel driveway, washed it with no soap, and then shut it back up into that garage again. Maybe they fed the car potatoes as well. We didn't know.

Each autumn about the time the last of the squash were plucked from their moorings and transported to new digs, a large pile of very rancid pig manure appeared on Mr. Ritter's garden, which was placed on the very edge of his side of the border between us. This location also happened to be almost exactly under mother's wash line.

Mr. Ritter did not get somebody in to spread the manure and plow his garden, he dug his garden each fall by his own hand and put the manure in with a shovel. He did it all himself. Wheelbarrow after wheelbarrow of this rancid crud was dug from the pile and taken to the digging portion of the garden, allowing the fragrance to flow freely. Not a perfume you could readily peddle downtown. This always took weeks.

In those days the only way mother had of drying clothes was to hang them on a wash line, mostly outside, though there were a few strings rigged up in the cellar. For example, in winter father's white shirts were hung out to basically "freeze-dry" on a sunny day and then were subjected to a repeat performance in the cellar until ready. There were no electric or otherwise driers in the house. Pretty much all laundry was hung outside on that line bordering the two properties.

It shall be further understood that the pig manure Oscar Ritter acquired was not fresh. In point of fact it had been sitting in somebody's manure yard for probably most of the summer and so had become "ripe", to term the matter with great charity. So, when the pile appeared under Mother's wash line, it was not a source of massive rejoicing in the Brubacher household. Only a reader who has donned supposedly fresh clothing that seems to have been washed in pig manure will completely appreciate the matter.

Mother was not by nature a vindictive person, insofar as I could, from a lifetime of observation, determine. Nevertheless, I also learned that if you repeatedly pissed her off, you did so at your peril. It's not that she went out and bought a gun or yelled and screamed or manifested her displeasure in any immediately obvious manner, but eventually she would put the matter in order.

One year when I was enjoying my eighth or ninth summer, I noticed that about a foot inside the property line between ours and Mr. Ritter's gardens, a Scotch thistle started to grow. Normally mother would have commended us boys for its removal to the Thistle Happy Hunting Grounds, but this time was different. She told us in no uncertain terms that this thistle was to be left alone. No plucking, walking over, running over, bumping against, squashing down upon, bouncing of balls thereon, or in any way shape or form were we to disturb the equilibrium and progress of this "Thrice-Blessed Thistle". This was a matter of no small puzzlement to us, but when mother spoke, she Spoke. And beware the wrath of mother when she Spoke.

The summer grew, and the thistle with it. It was a beauty. By mid-June it was 3-foot tall, by July, 4-foot and change. It just grew and grew and came out with wonderful flowers and then pods with crowning glories of purple to make a Scotsman reach for another jar to celebrate the wonder of that solo plant. We also noted that mother actually watered it!

Mr. Ritter was not amused. He admonished mother that, as our place was generally windward of his, if the pods exploded, spoor of that plant would cover his garden, his prize-winning pride and joy. His weeding exertions would treble, if not more, for years to come. It was unthinkable.

All that summer, when Mother was out tending her own garden, Mr. Ritter berated her with all manner of dire tales of thistle infestations and the dangers attached. Could she not please cut down that blasted plant and be done with it?

Mother held her peace for a long while, but then, one time only, so far as I know, she responded. *Now Mr. Ritter, just look at that plant. That is one of God's creatures too. It doesn't have to have fur or feathers or fins to be a wonderful creation. Just look at it! Healthy! Strong! Beautiful! And observe all those purple-crowned pods! I'll bet you that the amethysts in the crowns of the Apostles sitting at the feet of Jesus and praising the Lord are not more gorgeous than the purple in those pods!*

And besides, Mother calmly let him know that she had heard that the fragrance and aura from the Scotch thistle was a powerful antidote to the odor of pig manure. Every year her wash had a problem with the smell from Mr. Ritter's pig manure, and while she didn't want to be un-neighborly, or interfere with his business, she had to look after the daily needs of her family. So, if she could counteract the problem of the manure in such a simple way, everybody should be in perfect accord in the matter, and wouldn't Mr. Ritter agree? And besides, she said it would appear that pig manure is excellent food for Scotch thistles—simply look at that plant! Well, Mr. Ritter could do nothing but fume and rail against the evils of the inevitable explosions of the pods, and the dispersal of the Thistle Demons throughout his whole garden.

Late in that summer, when those pods looked like they may well explode any day, or maybe even any minute, mother said, *Kenny, fetch a six-quart basket and come along out to the garden.* There was mother at the thistle, armed with leather gloves and a set of wicked-looking pruning clippers. Then, one by one, and way slower than she would have needed to do it, all the pods of that thistle were clipped and put into the basket while Mr. Ritter did his hoeing at the far side of his garden, pretending not to notice. Then mother carefully placed that osier cage, now full of pods, at the base of the plant, and left the stalk standing.

That autumn Mr. Ritter's manure came from cows – fresh. Not only that, but the pile was placed as far away from mother's wash line as possible.

For Christmas that year, dad bought mother an electric clothes dryer.

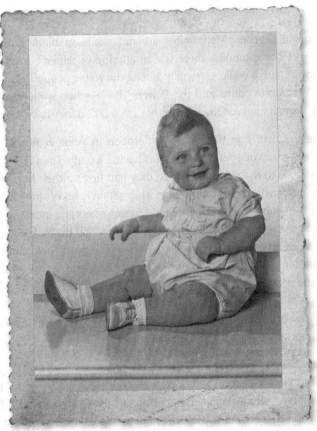

The author rejoicing in the best year of his life. Also, the *only* year of his life.

𝕳𝖔𝖗𝖘𝖎𝖓𝖌 𝕬𝖗𝖔𝖚𝖓𝖉

Contrary to popular belief, Mennonites are not saints in black hats: they are humans too. And, being human, there is a smattering of rather human behaviour that wanders by once in a while, especially among the young people. It is understood amongst the Mennonite adults and the Powers That Be that, while young, people need to let off steam. However, the minute they get married they have to toe the line.

Walking along the river one fine Sunday afternoon in summer not so long ago, I chanced upon a group of young Mennonites having a party. The party place was a clearing pretty close to the side road where they had tied up their horses and then dragged their stuff down to the water's edge. They sat on bales of straw and blankets on the ground, partaking of all manner of food from baskets and imbibing fluids that were far away from mother's milk. Except for the horses and the garb, I might just as well have stumbled onto an Italian wedding. There was a boom-box hammering out country and western music to which they were dancing, and several of them were swimming in the nearby swirling pool. This was the first time I ever saw Mennonite co-ed skinny-dipping – quite a sight. When I greeted them in their own tongue, one of the boys replied in English, *Buddy, have a beer!* It was one of those times when you pretty much shoot yourself for not packing a camera.

Also most every Sunday evening after the chores are done there is an aggregation of teenaged Mennonites in somebody's barn. A clearing is made on the threshing floor and a perimeter of bales of hay or straw are set up. Out comes a fiddle and/or a mouth organ and there is music and sometimes square dancing. Almost always a bottle appears. The festivities can go quite late and nothing is said about the matter so long as the individuals involved are up and about their chores and responsibilities at the appropriate time early the next morning.

In Elmira some years back, there was a couple who lived on the main street of the town north of the traffic lights where the road goes down to the river. They were entertaining guests on the Sunday evening after participating in a music concert and the guests had parked their car on the street while they all partook of a late dinner. Suddenly there was this great commotion and clanging crashing from the street. A team of horses pulling a carriage load of young Mennonites had collided violently with the car parked on the street. There were young folk flung in all directions, a carriage pretty much trashed, and horses in a very bad way. It was also clearly evident that no small few of the riders in the carriage had been partaking rather heroically of the contents of bottles of fluid that were not sold at the grocery store.

Before long, other carriages and wagons appeared, more or less like magic, with the parents of the young folk involved. The remains of the carriage were loaded onto a wagon, horses were shot and loaded onto other wagons, the whole mess was cleaned up, the street washed, and there was a cheque in the hands of the owner of the car for a sum considerably greater than what would normally have been paid.

The police were also in attendance. They stood there like everybody else and watched in amazement at the speed with which the matter was contained. What to do about it? With what were they going to charge anybody? Impaired driving of a horse? So the whole thing simply disappeared. Nothing made the papers, nothing made the newscasts. It all simply went away without much of any trace. Their parents and elders just dealt with it.

Few words were said, but when they all got home it's pretty certain that there was instruction via the business end of a horse whip. Those kids were not likely to do that again any time soon.

There is no law on the books that spells out how old a person must be to drive a horse and buggy. It is not uncommon for a 14-year-old boy to have the reins in his hands, and those horses are often really fast – race horses that did not quite make it to the big time. Old Order youngsters are no different than kids the world over. Let There Be Speed! The faster the horses the better, and some were very high-strung to boot.

One such time a young lad drove to town and his horse was spooked by a loud noise,

maybe a truck or an engine backfiring or some such. At any rate the horse bolted, and when all was brought under control again, the horse sported a large gash on a haunch. The young lad didn't know what to do about it, until somebody told him, *Go over to yonder drug store and get some tape and tampons.*

So, while others held the horse, he went into the drugstore and asked the young lady at the counter for tampons. Now, as you can imagine, this is not your average request in anybody's drugstore from a young fellow wearing a straw hat. If you instructed a young Mennonite man to scribe a book on tampons, it would with great certainty be a very slender volume.

Nonplussed, the attendant at the counter asked, *What size would you like?* The lad replied, spreading wide his little finger and thumb, *Ach vell, I'm not chust exactly sure, but the slit is about this long...*

Grampa (Josiah Martin) Brubacher (1885-1977) with his second wife (the widow Snyder), taken looking out the kitchen window c. 1963. Pictures of their faces were not allowed.

CHAPTER 🐢🐢🐢

Boots and Such

I grew up working in my father's shoe repair shop and shoe store. I don't remember learning to fix shoes. I suppose I was doing it along about the time that I was in kindergarten. I was always in the shop rather than the store if at all possible, because I liked working with my hands. The store meant dusting shoeboxes or dragging normal shoes out to fit impossible feet. For example, if a lady came in with a hammer-toe, the shoes of the time were not equipped to handle an animal of that nature. We tried to stretch the leather in the offending area with miscellaneous instruments which looked for all the world like they came out of a medieval torture chamber, but many times they just plain did not work. So there was no help for it but to mark the lumpy spot with a piece of chalk, cut a hole about the size of a looney, and then cover the area with a piece of kid leather, thus forming a tent. It's all we had. There was nothing, not even a concept of the stretchy and other user-friendly materials of today.

My first so-called formal job in the shoe repair shop consisted of patching rubber overshoes. Every Friday afternoon, a bag of stinking boots would be brought around by Westgate Acres, who bred turkeys just east of Elmira. These boots were often very full of holes, and while they had been given a rudimentary cleaning, there was still much work to be done before they could be patched. You cannot patch a wet rubber boot. It just plain does not work. The boot has to be clean and dry, inside and out, or the glue will not attach and the patch will fall off. So before you can start sanding the gloss off the offending area surrounding the hole, it was absolutely necessary to get things clean and dry.

Now I don't know what exactly the employees of this turkey establishment did to the birds in the daily course of events, but I am pretty sure that these birds did not appreciate it. There were great gaping holes, and sometimes pretty much an entire

toe was ripped out of a boot. So, to facilitate the cleanliness aspect of the matter, it was up to me to clean them.

As we had no proper facilities or anything resembling a washtub, I had to drag them, sometimes a dozen or more, downstairs to the bathroom and wash them in the toilet. We all know that there are milestones in life. I'm sure we can all look to circumstances in our existence where we said, *Yes, that was a watershed. That was where I was when that happened, and I am a changed person on account of that.* Well, in my case I suppose you could say that the toilet was a watershed, in a manner of speaking, because life is just not the same until you have rescued a rubber boot from the swirling suction of a flushing toilet.

To dry the boots I would line them up on top of the furnace, where they looked and smelled for all the world like a murder of stinking crows. The furnace, of course, circulated the air through the entire store, so that by morning not only the basement but the whole upstairs as well smelled plenty ripe. On Saturday mornings, the first person in had to open the doors front and back, even in winter, and try to exorcise that odoriferous demon, Turkey Manure.

However, I got very good at patching rubber boots.

HAND SHOEMAKING

During my teen years, I worked in the shoe repair shop a fair deal and had a pretty good idea of which end was which. But doing it for a living was a matter entirely different. Pretty soon I realized that banging on heels and soles was not going to take me very far. I started dabbling in tearing shoes down further and further to rebuild them, especially cowboy boots. I discovered that people would pay a very serious premium for the restoration of their badly worn cowboy boots if I retained the flavor of the fit. Also there was an increasing amount of build-ups to be put on shoes, because hip surgeries were not all that great in those days and people ended up with one leg a fair deal shorter than the other one. If you banged on a block of stuff and people went clump, clump, clump, you had one kind of a result. But if you shaped the addition to the sole in such a manner that folks could have their elevation and also facilitate the rocking and rolling – think Elvis – they were much more appreciative of the matter. And so I was in the medical business and I didn't even realize it.

Along about that time there came in a man with a pair of work boots in his hand. These boots had been made by the Hydro City Shoe Company in Kitchener, a company already out of business. The boots were all leather, and Mr. Bauman from Wallenstein greatly enjoyed this cool leather comfort. Shoes with rubber bottoms burnt up his feet and he wanted his cool shoes restored. However, they were so badly beaten up that you could practically read the newspaper through the soles. I indicated to him that the resurrection department was a little bit thin, and if he wanted new shoes like that, they would have to be handmade. *Fine*, said he, *you go ahead and do that then*. Being unwilling to admit that I did not know how, I told him to come back in a week. I didn't even know enough to measure his feet. He told me he was size 9½, and in my great and glorious wisdom – read ignorance – I assumed that 9½ meant nine and a half. He left the old boots with me and I went to work.

One of my suppliers in the shoe repair department previously had worked for a shoe company in Galt and knew of people who took the old shoe molds (called lasts) home when they switched from making them of maple to polyethylene. I have a theory that the good Lord Almighty when He was here on earth, our Lord Jesus Christ, may well not have been a carpenter at all. He told everybody *The last shall be first*, and thus He may well have actually been a shoemaker. Nevertheless, I was taken to a friend's cellar in Galt where there were barrels of old wooden lasts. We blew the dust off of some until we found a set that said 9½ F. The 'F' did not then compute, but later I learned that it meant double E, or one width wider than a single E.

I took the old shoes apart to use the pieces as patterns. I had a half a skin of oil tanned leather, which was used to patch the cracking and wearing portions of the breakpoint of work shoes, and I reasoned, accurately, that if it was good enough for the wear points, it was good enough for the whole shoe. I used the dismembered bits of the old boots and traced out the new pieces. Then I cut and stitched them together with the old Singer foot-operated sewing machine until I had some raw uppers in my hand.

Then there was a problem. The making of shoes consists of turning flat leather into round leather. Okay, I now had the last around which to facilitate this, but the methodology was a mystery. I tried to pull things into shape with this kind of implement and that sort of pliers but nothing really worked. Then I spied what we called the gluing pliers. They had curved jaws and a knob stuck to the bottom. We had no idea why that knob was there. Then I discovered that if I used the knob as a lever, pulled the leather into place, and then used the knob again to drive a nail, viola! So I employed this method until the upper and the lining were pegged into position.

I proceeded to nail a midsole onto the bottom of this semi-shoe. I left the edge wide so that I could stitch two more soles onto the shoe, then I applied hob nails, horseshoe plates, shovel plates, and toe plates. These shoes were of substantial matter. They weighed in at 5¾ pounds for the pair. Even a slender man could stand up in a pretty strong wind wearing this foot gear.

On Saturday morning Mr. Bauman came in and, while I held my breath, he tried on his shoes. He walked about, marking up the wood floors. Then he cleared his throat and declared, *Yup! These will do! How much money?* We had not discussed that bit, and so with great fear and trembling I asked for 60 bucks. Evidently I should've asked for a lot more because he pulled a wad of 20's out of his pocket that would have choked a hippo, peeled off three, and left. I never saw him again, and figured that this was the end of it.

But he told one of his co-workers who had a bunion on his foot, and after a while, this chap came into the shop and said, *I've got this knob on my foot.* I replied, looking down at his feet, that I could see that. *And by the time that nob's wore in there comfortable like,* he continued, *me shoes is near enough right wore out. I hear you are shoemaker.*

Well by then I had made – well, sort of – a pair of shoes, and so now I was a shoemaker. What I had actually done was *copy* a pair of boots. But he wanted shoes made with the knob wore in there comfortable like, and I didn't see any reason why I couldn't do it. This time however, I traced his feet.

I went back to my buddy with the lasts and got a set that was close. Then, after superimposing the last onto the tracing, I piled a bunch of junk onto the bunion area, which I learned later was called *leathering up the last.* But this time I didn't have any old shoes to go by for upper patterns, so I got out a pair of ratty old blue jeans, the kind you would now probably pay 600 bucks to buy in the store, all ragged with holes in the knees, cut them into chunks, and started to shape them to the modified last. I cut and pasted and tucked until the denim sat fairly tightly on the surface of the last. Then I got out a marker and proceeded to draw the style lines onto the denim, after which I cut the pieces apart, made allowance for seams and lasting and, in short, taught myself to make patterns. Crude, mind you, but patterns nonetheless. Trace the pieces onto leather, sew, tug, and pull and nail, and *Violliolla!* A pair of boots complete with bunion knobs!

So then another miracle happened. This chap came back for his shoes and was happy as well. He put on his boots, walked around, declared that his bunions no longer hurt, and gave me some money. Praises be! Another miracle! But to this day I do not know whether the matter was actually properly successful, or whether none of us had the skill and experience to make that judgment.

But that's how it started and, as they say, the rest is history. Word got around. People would show up at the shop looking somewhat shell-shocked. *I hear you are a shoemaker.* Um, ah, okay yes I suppose so. *Thank goodness. My shoemaker is dead.* Or gone or both. *Can you make me shoes like this?* Okay sure. I can do that. And then I'd figure out how.

People have asked me over the decades, who is my teacher? Well, I suppose my teacher is fixing my mistakes late at night for free. That is a stern master. You pay attention to that guy.

For a pictorial hand shoe-making demo please visit www.mennonitecobbler.com and click on Shoemaking 1915.

Mennonite Origins
(Insomniac Therapy, Part 1)

Mennonites come from an area of Europe which is today roughly in the environs of south Germany and Switzerland. They were originally known as Anabaptists. The name Anabaptist means *against baptism*. The Roman Catholic Church would sprinkle a newborn with so-called holy water and baptize that infant into Catholicism. The Anabaptists did not agree with this practice. They reasoned that baptism was something initiated and sanctioned by our Lord Jesus Christ when He was on earth and, as an adult, when you were baptized you went under the water and come back up again, symbolically identifying yourself with the death and resurrection of Jesus Christ. It was thus a public statement by an adult that there was commitment to Christian living and in the dedication of oneself to the teachings and practice of faith in Jesus. (I, myself, was baptized by being immersed in the Conestoga River one fine Sunday afternoon while the cow patties floated by – perhaps a sign. *Hold your breath, baby Christian! Sometimes schiteola is close to home, and at eye level!*)

Anabaptists were also the original peaceniks. The National Sport of the day was to take up arms and go trash the neighbors. They didn't want to do that. They were pacifists and believed in peace and harmony with your neighbors. The practices of peacery and dry babies were not well received by those in power. After all, the Lord of the Manor needed soldiers. And so, while I doubt very much whether these peaceniks quilted flowers in their hair or smoked dope, the peace movement was not large on the agenda of the gentry. Also if you preached and practiced theology which ran counter to that promulgated by the Roman Catholic Church, they had this habit of sending some people around to sit down with you and have a cup of tea and ask you some questions. This questionnaire came to be known as the Spanish Inquisition, and was more often than not a very effective method of having you become well-done steak at the stake.

So, the Anabaptists had to flee. Some fled to parts of south Germany where they were welcome on account of not only the Thirty Year's War but also the plague having wiped out large portions of the farmers. Seems the Anabaptists mostly bested that disease. Many took boats down the Rhine River to what is present day Holland where there was much more tolerance of religion than elsewhere in the European world. They were welcomed as good farmers, stayed under the radar and kept their noses clean, worshiping in a manner that was pleasing to them. They became associated with a renegade Dutch catholic priest, one Menno Simons, took him as their mentor, teacher, and leader (1535) and thus became known as Mennonites.

Then in 1693 they became subject to the National Sport of Churchianity – they split up. In this case the split was over a matter which we shall call shunning. A portion of the Mennonites believed that if a brother is taken in a fault he should be shunned and shut away until such time as his sins were confessed in public and then he could, at the sole discretion of the Powers that Be, be restored to the faith. The other side to this dispute said *No, the Lord Jesus Christ while on this tired old earth taught us concepts such as love, compassion, and forgiveness. So there is no room in there for shunning.* To paraphrase Garrison Keillor, (may he live forever), *We are supposed to love and forgive all sinners even if they are one of our own, and we are not going to talk to you shunners again until you change your mind, and when you change your mind then you let us know and we will take it under advisement.* So they split up. The shunners side went to be followers of a fellow named Jacob Amman and thus today are known as the Amish. The loving side then called themselves the Old Order Mennonites. The Amish and Mennonites have thus lived side by each in awesome silence for more than 300 years. You can tell them apart even today by noting that the Amish wear beards and the Mennonites are clean shaven.

Then, about 150 years or so after the Anabaptists went to Holland, along came the Spanish and conquered the low lands on account of and being as they had all this loot from the New World. They had doubloons and triploons and quadruploons and pieces of eight and gold and silver bars and such truck in great abundance, with which they were able to raise armies and go trash the neighbors. They brought their

Spanish Inquisition along with them, so our Mennonite brethren had to flee again. Some went to Russia, some to South America and Mexico, and some to Pennsylvania starting around 1700. In Pennsylvania it was guaranteed that they would never have to take up arms and that they could practice their religion peacefully and without any interference from the authorities. They cleared the land and got down to the business of farming. Also to the business of creating more Mennonites. Lots and lots and lots more Mennonites. Consider that if your parents didn't have late night TV and the pill, you may well come from a much larger family too. So they ran out of farm land.

The Mennonites and Amish started to come to Canada around 1790. They first crossed the border into the Niagara Peninsula and set up colonies, all the while pushing further west and then north. In 1802 a large parcel of land known as German Tract Block One was purchased (20,000 acres) in what is now the southern portion of Waterloo County. A couple of years later Block Two, north of there, and Block Three in present-day Woolwich Township, collectively known as the German Company Tract, in total about 60,000 more acres were also purchased. Meanwhile others had carried on to the area today called Markham set up shop. So Ontario then had three general groupings: the Niagara Peninsula, Waterloo County, and the Markham area.

This was all virgin hardwood forest. It took an average of 30 years to clear 50% of the land. This was brutally hard work and there were often fairly large distances between farms, so that neighbors saw each other only every 2 to 4 weeks when church services were held. Many times of the year such crude roads as existed were practically impassable. Slowly the forests were pushed back, roads established, and communications improved.

And with better communications, the Mennonites got to celebrate what surely must be the national sport of All Churchianity, by which I refer, of course, to the penchant for every religion under the sun to sprout an internal quarrel, feed it, water it, have it grow to its full glory, and then reap its fruit in great abundance. The fruit is called *'Let's split up and form two Churches. Or maybe even three, if our quarrel is weighty enough'*.

Mennonites were and still are very good at this, maybe even the best ever. They split up over every conceivable item of doctrine and theology available and also separated over the use, or otherwise, of tractors, cars, electricity, items of clothing, telephones, rubber buggy rims, zippers versus buttons, to name a very few. In Ontario as of this writing there have been at least 102 different divisions of Mennonites. I think they should change their name to Baskin Robbinsites – they now come in so many flavors. When I was a boy in Elmira, Ontario, there were four flavors of Mennonites in the area.

The first were the Old Order Mennonites who were the descendants of the original split with the Amish and who held to their name and traditions pretty much since their inception. They drove horse and buggy, but some of them by now had tractors and electricity in the barn but not in the house. No radio or TV or any such heathen truck was allowed. They met in white wooden meeting houses every two weeks.

The second flavor were the Markham Mennonites, who drove black cars, had tractors, electricity and telephones, but who were otherwise pretty much as plain as the Old Order. No radios or TVs, no drink, no smoke, and aside from the cars and the shape of their hats and slightly more modern black suits, one might confuse them with the Old Order. They divided from the Old Order about 1907 in Markham, thus the name Markham Mennonites.

This same division soon occurred in Waterloo County as well, and it was an amicable split. In point of fact they still share their meeting houses. In Waterloo County there are nine meeting houses. Five of those are horse and buggy Mennonites every Sunday and four of them are for the Markham Mennonites. I didn't know, when going to church on Sunday up the hill west of Elmira, if I was going to see cars or horses and buggies at the white meeting house.

The third flavor is called the Red Brick Mennonites, so-called because their meeting houses were (wait for it… drum roll…) all made out of red brick. I later learned that they were Conference Mennonites, adherents to a brand of the Mennonite faith whose central committee is in Goshen, Indiana. This flavor of Mennonite you cannot tell from any other person on the street. They are modern of dress, drive colored cars, have radios and TV and phones, and aside from keeping their noses somewhat cleaner then the surrounding heathen, are pretty much like everybody else.

The Old Order Church was taken in another division almost 100 years ago. There was an Old Order Bishop named David Martin who, in 1918, decided that the Mennonites were becoming too modern. The word 'tractor' was starting to enter the conversation and there were other modern gizmos which started to rear their ugly heads: gizmos such as zippers and rubber rims on your buggy wheels instead of steel, and so forth. Also there was a theological matter called *zeichness* which is not only non-translatable but also very difficult to talk about, so we just plain won't. Nevertheless, this was a very major division in the Old Order Mennonite Church. Families were split down the middle and they pretty much never talked to each other again.

One time my brother Freddie was doing some flatbed trucking and was sent up country to get the slabs of a silo that had been torn down. He took these silo slabs up a lane at the end of which were two farms, one on either side. Freddie pulled into the farm indicated and there were three or four men waiting there to help offload these 80-pound slabs. It was heavy work on a hot day. Freddie could see that on the other side of the lane, lounging around, were 30 or 40 men who were clearly waiting for building materials to put up some manner of edifice such as a pole barn. So Freddie said to the guys unloading with him, *How about we get them fellows over there to help, they're not doing anything.* And the answer came back, *Oh, you wouldn't want to have their sort of help.* On the one side the farm was Old Order and on the other side they were from the David Martin group. They had split up and are very much separate to this day.

Since that time, however, there have been a huge bunch of other divisions of Mennonites scattered about the landscape. There is a brand called the Conservatives who are sort of partway between the Markham and the Red Brick, loosely speaking. They are all identified by their manner of dress. For example, the Conservatives do not wear neckties, and the dress and headgear of the womenfolk are different than any others in the neighborhood. Some Mennonites also decided to go plainer than even the Dave Martin or *Newborn* Mennonites. They split off from them in 1954 under David Hoover, and then another division under Elam Martin in1956. These two joined to become the Orthodox Mennonites in 1962. They went en masse to Howick, Ontario and were nick-named Beardo's on account of and being as they believed that the Good Lord in His infinite wisdom gave them facial hair and to scrape it off like a naked scalded pig was not the thing to do. They also do not do things like use chainsaws or other engine devices and are an extremely plain people indeed. Then, of course, they split up in 1974 over the beards and …. yawn… back to the David Martin … zzzzzzzzz…

My grandparents and parents were all Old Order Mennonites, on my mother's side living in Floradale, and Grampa Brubacher just east of Elmira hard by Balsam Grove School. And even though dad and mom ostensibly left the Old Order Church in 1939, they never really shook it. In later years I told my dad that he is still an Old Order Mennonite—only now he wears a funnier-looking hat and drives a green car.

And as billed right off the top, this part of our festivities is especially geared to the relief of the insomniac.

MENNONITE JOKE:

What do you call an Old Order Mennonite with the horse stuck out in a cedar swamp on a warm evening, hollering for help? Hoarse and buggy!

CHAPTER 👣👣👣
At Johnson's

It always smelled great in Johnson's barber shop. It smelled like talcum powder, shaving cream, and aftershave, all infused with an undertone much as if these flavors were all aged in a barrel which had spent its entire lifetime smoking cigars. It was delicious. A small boy could almost eat it. There was, and is, no smell like that of an old-fashioned barber shop.

My father which art in heaven needed his hair cut, just like most other men. His options were limited in Elmira because he was in a wheelchair on account of the polio, and Johnson's Barber Shop and Billiards Emporium had no stairs. This establishment, owned and operated by Jack Johnson, was situated about a block and a half down the street from Brubacher's Shoes, my dad's store, *Step In For Comfort* above the door. So from time to time we three boys would push father down the street to Johnson's. Dad really did not want to go there but the problem of stairs was very real, and Johnson's was the only hair game in town level with the sidewalk. So to Johnson's we went.

We pushed dad in there, and while they attended to him we boys went and sat down on the bench to wait. Mostly Jack Johnson cut dad's hair and, as was the custom of the time, at the end of the administrations of the clippers and scissors, there was the foaming cream hand-brushed around the ears and then the straight razor came out. This wicked looking device was smoothed on the leather strop and applied to the areas around the ears and down the neck. The operative terms were to be still of recipient head and smooth and sure of operating hand.

At one time, Jack's helper was, looking back on it, either an alcoholic or a man with Parkinson's – or both. When it came time to do the shaving, this worthy approached dad's throat with the straight razor in a very shaky hand, whereupon

dad firmly pushed that hand to one side and said, *That will be all, Thank you very much.*

But there was a problem. This problem was the pool hall out the back. The pool hall rejoiced in three regular pool tables, two full-sized billiards tables, and four pinball machines scattered into the corners.

While Jack Johnson or his helper were administering to the necessities of our father's hair, we three boys were seated on the only bench available which was just outside the door to that Den of Sin, Vice, and Iniquity known as the Pool Hall. We were adjured in no uncertain terms, *Thou shalt never listen to nor ever look at whatever was going on back there in the pool hall. The devil is in there and if you look in there the devil will surely come out and bite hard down on your nether regions and drag you down into the flaming pit of hell and maybe even right today!*

So, naturally, we boys would take every opportunity to peek back in there when dad couldn't see us. It was fascinating. We waited until dad's chair was turned away from us and then drank in the sins of that iniquitous back room. There were evils like the clanking of balls on green felt-covered tables, of words which we did not learn in Sunday school, bottles of the Demon Drink, and the smoke. If you had a machete you may well have been able to venture in there and hack out a chunk of atmosphere to take home as a souvenir. It was intoxicating. So I bided my time, and eventually I learned to play pool in Johnson's pool hall.

I suppose I might have been about 12 or so when I first ventured solo into that Den of Sin, Vice, and Iniquity. Ostensibly the library had called to me in the matter of homework. The Carnegie Free Library was situated two doors down from the pool hall, so no problem to go in that direction. I have no memory of how I paid for time on the tables, but I suppose it was a combo of charity and pecuniary assets *borrowed* from the proceeds of my paper route. In any case the smoke smell on my clothes had to be explained. It was clearly evident that there was no tell-tale breath, so the explanation that the research area of encyclopedia books could only be read at one table, and there was a chap there smoking a cigar. So what could I do? This excuse was accepted, but I do not know if it was totally believed.

In this manner I absorbed the fundamentals of becoming a fluent liar. I have since repented of this iniquity. I cannot anymore embellish any sort of event nor contribute additions or subtractions to what actually has happened. Today, if I tried to alter the truth, no doubt my tongue would dry up and stick to the roof of my mouth, and only arid urking sounds would emanate therefrom. The truth, the whole truth, and nothing but the truth. That be me.

But let us tell of any sort of scene; take the painting as opposed to the camera in describing the same matter. The photo of the story is that which you get with what the eye and lens of the camera records. Nothing but the truth insofar as the device is able to depict.

But the painter does something different. There always needs to be quite a bit of shading to bring the right coloring and texture to the canvas of the story. The painting will take on tonal inflexions that the camera cannot hope to affect, and all because the artist can imbue the result with opinions and emotions of personal opinion.

As time filters the memory of the story in the same manner as the painter shades the camera, the teller of the story can, with complete honesty, portray the event as slightly more, shall we say, *colorful* than the original. So I recollect and recount these incidents to you with complete confidence of the original facts, but with perhaps a trifle of the filtration of time.

A few summers ago I went to my barber shop in Stayner and there he was – gone. So I drove up Mosley Street in Wasaga Beach and chanced upon an establishment rejoicing in – what else? – the Wasaga Beach Barber Shop. It had the obligatory striped pole, so in I went.

It was the first day of summer, hot and humid, and I was doing my sweating dying act. I hate the heat and especially hate the humid heat. When my turn came and I was decorated with the white cloth designed to choke a camel, the lady asked how I wanted it. *Summer cut*, I said, and she then asked, *Shall that be a 2 or 3 or what?* Facetiously I responded, *2 and 3*, pretending to know what that was. *Oh Good choice*, said she, *We will do a 2 on the sides and a 3 on top*. Then she snapped a do-dad onto the buzzer-gig and went to work. OMG. Pretty soon I looked like a poster-boy for geriatric boot camp.

But it felt amazing. Freedom from heat and combs and brushes and all such. It brought back memories of a small boy having undergone the shearing of the retired farmer where father sent us down the way, hair about a tenth of an inch of fuzz. No matter how much cavorting in the sandbox or mud, before supper just peel off the shirt, bend over and then mother would hose us down in the yard. Rub a towel over the top a time or two and viola! – ready for supper. One seldom feels so *alive* as when cold hosed down with almost no hair.

So now every time I decide I need attention to my hair I go over to The Beach. You see, whether it is Sammy (who is slightly more Italian than Marco Polo) doing the honors, or Michelle, who created the boot camp boy, or Alda, who zealously guards chair number one closest to the door, or the lady I have named The Hair-Witch because she cruises the floor with her broom, I am always made to feel welcome. They don't try to give me a coiffeur. They remove hair. I tell them to make me look rich and handsome, and they laugh and they laugh… They know I have a perfect face for radio.

When they too, just like for my dad, are done with the snippers and the buzzers, out comes the cream and the razor. These days there are changeable blades instead of all that stropping, but the hands are steady. Ears lowered, neck free from foliage. Application of the aftershave. Feels so cool a man could slow down the chillies in a hot tamale.

But what I most like about it is the smell when I get inside the door – the smell of shaving cream and talcum powder and the rubbing alcohol of the aftershave. They have unfortunately lost the flavor of the smoke, but the place brings back memories of Johnson's pool hall, together with other dens of sin, vice, and iniquity of a similar nature where colored balls on green tables gleefully cavort.

CHAPTER

Barn Raising

The National Sport of Mennonite comes in three divisions: *Hard Work, Eating Heartily* and, of course, *Making Lots More Mennonites.*

First Sport: Hard Work. Mennonites work hard. I found out about this the summer I was 14, when my father sold me into Mennonite slavery. I hated the shoe business and everything it stood for. I hated being there, and I hated dusting shoeboxes with a passion. Dusting was done to no avail because, as soon as you were done, the first batch was dusty again and then you had to start all over. Besides, other boys were fishing and swimming and playing outside, while I was dusting shoeboxes. I suppose I created enough of a ruckus and near enough rebellion that my father thought he would fix my little red wagon. He found a Mennonite farmer that would take me for the summer. And so I went. Anything but dusting shoeboxes was just fine with me. Or so I thought.

I pretty much immediately learned what *hard work* was all about. Each morning at dawn, seven days a week, found me up in the silo forking down cow feed. When a sufficient pile had accumulated at the bottom, my next job was to shovel it into a wheelbarrow and distribute it into the troughs to feed the cows. I carried pails of milk. They were heavy. I shovelled cobs from the corn crib into a wagon and fed them through the hammer mill to make pig feed. Then I piled that into a wheelbarrow to slop the hogs. Something I learned very early was that *when you slop the hogs they quiet right down.* This also applies to a family reunion or church supper. Could be pretty nearly any noisy matter, when you put food in front of them and a method with which to wash it down, the decibel level descends accordingly. Life is like a pig barn.

The most all-pervading chore (besides the feeding of the animals) was dealing with what came out of the south end of every north-facing animal. There was always lots of it, in fact, much more than any town boy could imagine. Mostly this had to be done in very warm weather. When it just lay there with the straw or whatever bedding was to hand, that was one matter. But when it was disturbed it was quite another. Nevertheless I was not dusting shoeboxes, and even this was an improvement on that occupation.

A few weeks after I started work there, a barn down the road burned. The farmer put in hay that was too tough (wet) and there was spontaneous combustion. So the barn went up in smoke. Every day after breakfast I was sent over on my bicycle to help with the cleanup. There I learned what *hard and dirty work* was all about. A lot of moldering hay and so forth lurked in the embers among the foundations of the barn and my job was to help get it out of there so that a new barn could be raised. Most of the time, a forkful of the residue pulled from its moorings would burst into smoky oily flame. As we had no masks or any other form of protection, this was a whole gang of no fun. Nevertheless there was no help for it. It was evil, dirty work, and I was mightily glad for the proximity of the river. After supper and chores I could go down there and swim. That was as near to heaven as I could have imagined at that time. Grab the rope tied to the tree branch overhanging the pool and take the plunge.

So while we were cleaning up, many wagons of timbers and lumber came up the lane and were deposited in the barnyard and the orchard in preparation for the raising of the new barn. It was clearly evident that the designer and engineer of the new structure was one Eli Shirk, a tall spare man of few words. How he did it I have no idea to this day. His weaponry consisted of a measuring tape and a piece of chalk and nothing else. The rest was in his head. He walked around the beams and posts deposited on the ground, measured, and drew on them. A line meant cut here. A rectangle called for a mortise (an oblong hole designed to receive a support). A circle meant drill here. So men with hammers and chisels and saws went to work and the timbers were prepared. All by hand – there was no electricity or chainsaws.

Then came the day of the barn raising. About 150 large families in horses and wagons descended on that property. Pretty much immediately the men were like a swarm of bees erecting posts and beams and buttress supports, all under the direction of Eli Shirk. He spoke little – but the words were heavy. When he called for bars, men jumped to his command and beams were erected into position. No cranes or other

lifting devices, just men with pike poles and ropes and pulleys. Many men working hard. It was amazing. By noon the skeleton of that structure was in place, including the rafters for the roof. I wish I had a video of that. I was treated to a matter of no small consequence, a chapter of a book from a by-gone era, and wish mightily that I could see it again. My job was to clean up the scraps. I was not big and strong enough to help with the actual construction, but I could clear away sawed-off ends of lumber because these people knew that a messy workplace is a dangerous workplace. So I cleaned up and threw the shards of lumber onto a pile in the corner of the manure-yard.

Second Sport: *Eating Heartily*. Along about noon, some form of silent signal went forth. The men finished what they were doing for the immediate moment and then washed up for the dinner. Rows of basins and towels had been set up on the edge of the yard and the men washed their hands and faces and went and sat down at improvised trestle tables made from barn lumber. You have heard the expression *the groaning table* – well, this was it.

There was silent prayer. All heads bowed, and all eyes closed in silence and thanks for the sustenance about to be consumed. After a minute or so, one of the elders said *Amen*. All heads upped periscope and I have never before or since seen food disappear with such gusto and rapidity as I beheld that day. And all in awesome silence. It was amazing. There was little if any conversation, even to the asking of another dish to be brought within reach. The women were in charge and saw to it that every dish was replaced or filled as needed. Then came dessert, which included pie and cake and tarts and muffins and fruit. Canned fruit preserves. There were no separate fruit dishes for the men, they simply took bread, mopped up their gravy, and laid on desert. Much great food consumed with the joyful vigor only an appetite born of hard work can create. When the meal was pretty much exhausted they pushed back their chairs and then there was some moderate conversation.

Now all this time there was a city-slicker reporter sent from some newspaper or other to cover the proceedings. He had been adjured in no uncertain terms, *Thou shalt not take any pictures*. The Mennonites believed that graven images and iconoclastic claptrap was not for them so you don't take pictures. However, he had a tape recorder over his shoulder and, when the meal was done and the men had pushed back their chairs, he more or less accosted Eli Shirk to get an interview. He had determined that Eli was straw boss and headquarters had decreed that he needed to evince some cogent comment from the head honcho.

Sir, it is absolutely amazing that the men work like this. I have never seen anything like it in my life and could you care to comment on the work ethic of these people. Now as I said, Eli Shirk was a man of few words. He digested this request at some length, and eventually ponderously spoke. *Yes, the men like to work.* The reporter, however, needed to get the matter further involved. *But the men work so hard! How is it that they like to work so hard? Yes,* said Eli, *Yes, the men like to work hard.* So our roving reporter was dying. He tried a different tack. *So what do the men do for entertainment? Hmmm,* pondered Eli, *Entertainment, um, entertainment...* You could very nearly see smoke coming out of his ears by this time. *Well, for entertainment they just work a little harder.*

Pretty soon after, the men were busy proving just exactly that. By the time the sun was shading from yellow to late afternoon orange, the roof was on and the sides clad. Two of the three National Sports well proven: *Hard Work and Eating Heartily.* However, the third was also manifest in abundance: *Making Lots More Mennonites.* This last Sport required no demo – just count the kids.

Brubacher Origins
(Insomniac Therapy, Part 11)

The name Brubacher comes from two old German words Brugge and Bach. The Brugge is the bridge and the Bach is a fast-moving mountain river, in this case one that enters Lake Zurich in Switzerland. If Johann Sebastian Bach were with us today he may well be called Johnny River. It is of interest to me (but to few others) that I come from a long line of doctors and teachers and take the family name back to 1580. Or 1530 – take your pick. After all, what's a half century between friends anyway?

Before that date the name goes back to c. 1335 but the records are incomplete due to the fires of the Reformation. It is recorded that my namesake was a surgeon on the field of battle and saved the life of the Head Honcho during a big fight, presumably by sawing off his leg and tying up the left-overs or some such, then slinging him over his shoulder to take back to mommy for the heal-up. For this act of brave butchery he was awarded the big house by the bridge over the river.

In the manner of the day, he took his name from his position or occupation and so he became the BruggeBacher, that is, the dude who controlled traffic and the tolls over that bridge. He had two pockets: one for the grand Pooh Bah and one for himself. Someplace along the line the name lost the *e* in the middle and he was the BruggBacher, and further on down the line they blew off the *g's* and he became the Brubacher.

Consider the Brubacher coat of arms attached and on the back cover. It is clearly evident that they were (and still are) a very horny people. At the top is a unicorn

Bruggebacher

Brubacher

rampant, which not only signifies that they had the equipment to do the job but also that they were ready and willing to get it on *RFN*! (The *R* is short for Right and the *N* is for Now and you can fill in the middle for yourself.) Not only is there a unicorn *rampant* at the top, but, plastered below onto the shield buckler, just in case you missed it, is another rampant (meaning seriously horny) dude. This chap's cornishness is somewhat less *up*, if you catch the drift, and supposedly represents family Brouhaha up top's marriage with another less noble family from up the mountain pass someplace. But not as rampant.

Note then also the plumage-like foliage busting out all around these horny worthies. All this leafage and such represents the multitude of off-spring which was the result of the horny-corny Bruggebachers. The family tree to this day has many leaves and branches, and the offspring in number are much like the flies on a manure pile on a warm summer's day. Also worthy of note is the buckler's straps on the bottom, which means that this coat of arms was worn over just that: a breastplate of armor.

The Bruggebacher descendants got caught up with the Anabaptists and had to get out of there. Some records show they travelled down the Rhine River to Holland and then to England and America. Somewhere along the line the name lost the "gge" in the middle and we became Brubacher, amongst many other spellings. Other accounts have the Brubacher clan going from Switzerland to Germany for a while, and thence directly to Pennsylvania where they settled in Lancaster County. Recently I made a sojourn there, joined the Mennonite Historical Society, did the research recorded there on my name, and proudly found myself standing on the turf where the first Brubacher took an axe to the trees. The brass engraving on the stone foundation of the house reads Johannes Brubacher 1717. For me this was a proud moment indeed. They were and are a prolific people and when they ran out of farmland they loaded up their Conestoga wagons and ended up in Waterloo County, Ontario.

The first wave of Mennonites to southern Waterloo County in Ontario, in 1810, bore names like Bechtel, Schneider, Eby, Bricker, and Erb and settled around present day Kitchener. About 10 years later another Pennsylvania bunch bought 60 thousand acres of crown land in northern Waterloo County for the sum of 10,000 British pounds. This was known as The German Tract and the immigrants rejoiced in names such as Martin, Bauman, Frey, and Brubacher. Thus my people cleared the land and settled the region, bringing their traditions of peace and tolerance (and don't forget their cornishness) with them. My mom comes from 12 kids, dad from 13.

Mom and Dad on their wedding day, January 1, 1940. Another time and place he could have been a rock star, she an operatic soprano.

CHAPTER

Father O'Brien

The Good Lord Almighty is merciful and gracious, and from time to time allows even us sinners to do good works in spite of ourselves. Once in a while you can get some excellent wine from misshapen bottles.

Foot trouble is no respecter of persons. It comes in all shapes and sizes, all ages and colors and, if you will pardon an expression dear to my heart, from all walks of life. Once in a while I have the privilege of collecting a VIP, a very interesting person with bad feet.

One such was Father O'Brien, a Roman Catholic priest of advancing years. He was a big man and had a ton of arthritic problems with his feet and ankles. These had evidently been badly broken many years ago and so, if he was to walk at all anymore, he was obligated to come to us in Elmira to have special boots made which incorporated ankle bracing.

Father O'Brien, I soon discovered, was not your average Roman Catholic priest. From time to time his manner of speech betrayed an upbringing which I am pretty sure had not included a whole pile of time in the church choir. He also emitted words that were normally not learned in Sunday School. He was very appreciative of our efforts and came from the wilds of Toronto to obtain services which had largely dried up in his neck of the woods.

Every couple of years or so he got a new pair of boots, which had to be continually upgraded on account of the osteoarthritic deterioration of his underpinnings. Eventually he spent a fair bit of time in a wheelchair, which made it very difficult for him to travel. There was no help for it but for me to go to Toronto and serve as best

I could at arm's-length, wherever he happened to be. This was no great hardship because Father O'Brien was, as I say, a very interesting person. I now wish that I had taken a Dictaphone and recorded some of our conversations.

As it turned out Father O'Brien did not enter the priesthood in the usual fashion. He did not go from the choir to seminary to cloth and to heaven. It was exactly the opposite. He started his spiritual journey in the heavens and ended up on earth.

He was a paratrooper with the Canadian military in the Second World War. Along about 1942 he, together with a pile of his buddies, jumped out of airplanes someplace over North Africa. It was soon evident that his parachute did not properly deploy, so he had a fast word with the Almighty on the way down, promising that if he were spared and survived the war, he would join the priesthood. The Almighty said, **You're on, boy!**, landed him on the side of a steep sand dune or some such where he badly broke his feet and ankles. He crawled across the burning sands how many miles and was rescued. Eventually Corporal O'Brien was true to his word and joined the priesthood.

One time late in our relationship, as he had grown quite old and infirm by then, I was routed down to Toronto to his new digs, bearing new footwear with me. I was shown to his little apartment in quite a large building, and I could not help but notice that nearly all of the denizens of this lair where old ladies. Piles of them. As I was fitting his new shoes I made inquiry on the matter and learned that Father O'Brien was here in this building in the capacity of father confessor to this whole raft of retired nuns. And from his description of the circumstances I could tell that his enthusiasm for his situation was less than one of ecstasy. Nevertheless, *a parachute promise is a parachute promise*, so here he was.

Anyway, the boots having been fitted, he said, *Ken, Ken, may I call you Ken?* (he asked me this every time we met for about 15 years) *it's time for lunch.* He had a voice like a gravel crusher. *Would you honor us by joining me for lunch downstairs?* Well, it was lunchtime anyway, I was hungry, and so down we went. He and I sat at a table together and we were surrounded by a sea of gray and white heads. *Ken, he said, just look around you at all these decrepit old nuns. It's so depressing. Every day I have to listen to them come to me with their imagined sins – Father, forgive me for I have sinned. It has been – well now let me see – two days, or is it three, or was it... it was yesterday! Yes, yesterday since I made confession. But I have sinned father, I was envious of Sister Mabel's new hairdo. How many rosaries... and on and on... – Ken, it's so damned depressing! Why can't they come to me with nice big juicy sins once in a while, something to keep me awake in the confessional, like, I've started to practice voodoo, or, me and sister Rose and sister Mildred have been engaged in a lesbian ménage à trois since last Christmas. Something to actually require penance! It's so damned depressing!*

I was trying not to pee myself laughing, and in the containment of my mirth I let fly a fart like a small clap of thunder. Heads turned in our direction, and I turned my head and looked over at Father O'Brien, who was somewhat hard of hearing, thus passing the farting buck onto the innocent, reverend... *Father, forgive me, for I have sinned...*

The author boning up on his Lone Ranger act, 1957.
Note the enthusiastic expression on the face of the pony.

Black Shoes

So I realize that a fair few times in the recent history of your drab, dull, tired, unfulfilled existence, you wake up and commune within yourself, saying, *I would feel far more fulfilled as a human if I could have more black shoes, and yet I do not have the budget to go out and purchase a whole new wardrobe of footwear of Stygian hue.* I feel your pain. I really do.

And you wonder why these feelings of monumental consequence are upon you. No mystery there – you are a closet Mennonite. It may well be that, if you investigate your linage with sufficient diligence, you will find a life-style of snarfing that which comes from the south end of a north-bound horse while you are wearing a black hat. Not to mention shoes. I totally sympathise. Been there. Done that.

Early on when I got back into the shoe business or, more properly, the shoe repair business, a well-dressed gentleman in a business suit came in with a pair of expensive brown dress shoes in his hand. He wanted them dyed black but, *Not*, quoth he, *Not Mennonite Black*. Well, I had to meditate on that kind of fast-like. Not sure from where this came but I said to him, *Not a problem Sir, here we dye shoes Rich Black.* So he left the shoes, I died them Mennonite Black, he came and picked up his Rich Black shoes and went away happy. To this day I am not sure exactly what was going on in his head. It may be that he had taken a pair of shoes to a Mennonite farmer who had set up shop in the driving shed of his son's farm, dad now relegated to the *doddy haus* or grampa domain attached to the main domicile where the next generation was now ensconced. Gramma helping with the kids and garden, grampa with the chores but with time left over.

People were starting to live much longer than they did 100 years ago. In 1900 a man lived on average to 47 years, the women much less, on account of birthing problems and little modern medicine to deal with most of the problems we take today to be of little mortal account. Along about 1960, grampa might well take over a corner of the driving shed next to the barn and fix harness and shoes. The harness of a horse was always leather and needed to be oiled. Leather is a natural skin and under the not-so-tender administrations of the elements such as sun and rain and so forth, not to mention the sweat of the horse, it needed to have a drink. Into the oil bath it went.

I am not exactly sure, but with considerable confidence I think that the purveyor of these brown shoes had been subject to the tender administrations of one such grampa. Another pair of his shoes to be dyed black had been slung into the viscous oily morass with the harness. The result would well have been anything but satisfactory.

We dyed a lot of shoes black in those days. It was the Mennonite rule that all shoes, especially Sunday shoes, had to be black and they had to have laces. Lots of times the women folk would find a suitable pair of shoes but maybe they were brown, and they were brought to the shop to receive the Mennonite Black Treatment.

Another gentleman who, as I recall, was a Mr. Shantz who hailed from the environs of St. Jacobs, brought in some expensive shoes to have dyed black. But this time they were white. Along about those days the wearing of white shoes in summer was dying out, if you will pardon an expression. The front portion of these white shoes was woven leather with no lining, to give maximum coolness. Black was requested.

I got out the usual accoutrement, including the dye remover, stripped these shoes, stuffed them with newspaper, brushed them with liquid dye a couple of times, let them sit overnight to dry, and then sprayed them with a final glossy finish. Presently Mr. Shantz picked up his newly blackened shoes, appeared well satisfied with the matter, paid, and left.

Some days later he was back, shoes in one hand and a pair of (formerly) white socks in the other. These socks now rejoiced in a lovely crisscross black pattern. It did not take a whole pile of rocket scientists to figure out what had transpired. I certainly didn't like it much but I said, *I guess maybe I owe you a pair of shoes.* He replied, *Son, that was the correct answer. The making of the man is not whether he makes mistakes, but rather how he goes about trying to correct them. You've passed the test. We all learned something.*

So what did we all learn? Well, I learned when not to dye shoes black. And he learned when not to wear white socks.

Mother and her 7 surviving siblings c. 1924. Mom was the baby.

CHAPTER ☙❧❦

𝖘𝖕𝖊𝖊𝖉𝖎𝖓𝖌

I love speed. Always have. I remember my first time on the AutoBahn in Germany in 1990 when I went to celebrate my brother Freddy's wedding. Yes, the same Freddy who miraculously survived throwing sand at mother. I had rented a small car at the Dusseldorf airport and, after a pit stop nearby to visit a company which sold pretty much anything to do with hand making of shoes, I found myself on the open road going north.

But not just any old open road – this one had no speed limits. Go as fast as you please. So I brought this shaky bucket of bolts up to about 160 km/hr which was serious fun, but as it appeared that this Opel Kadet was going to disintegrate at any moment, I backed off. Subsequent trips over there saw me drive faster and faster cars. I loved it! Nothing is like the AutoBahn in a well-engineered German car accelerating through 200 km/hr. That be a rush. Not such a great idea back home though. They put you in jail or a coffin.

This past March I was renting a car in the Orlando airport. I had reserved my usual anonymity of conveyance and, as is the custom, the gal behind the counter did the normal up-sell. Then a demon crawled out from under my shirt, perched himself on my shoulder and asked, *Do you have anything that's fun*? The lady said, *We have Corvette Stingrays! Oh goodie*, said the demon, *I'll have one of those*. She asked, *What color*? The answer came back, *Fire-engine red*.

Pretty soon I was tooling down the 528 in the direction of Cape Canaveral. Did I mention it was a convertible? Top down, wind in my hair, the snarling of 625 horses under the hood, clocked to 225 mph. That's *miles* per hour. And so it was life in the fast lane and GLH. Coming out of the toll booths on this highway was a real joy.

Peddle nowhere close to half down and still, *hang onto your hat!* First car I had ever seen with a HUD (Heads Up Display – Google it) which showed speed, rpm's, gear, and G-forces. That's right, *G-forces!* Gauge went up to 6… So for the next 2 weeks I drove like a racer.

They had told me at the airport to watch my speed because the cops loved to pull over red sports cars and give out speeding tickets. But that is exactly what I wanted! I plotted to get a citation, frame it together with a pic of me in the Vette, and hang it next to my desk. Show everybody that while there be snow on the roof, there's still fire in the furnace!

But I couldn't get a ticket. I drove around South/Central Florida for more than two weeks and never saw a cop. Or if I did, he was writing up somebody else. Normally they are on every street corner and behind every bush – but not this year. Nary a one to be found.

So I said to My Good Lady, *How be we go for a spin*. No asking twice on that one. We went around to the Cocoa Beach Florida police precinct and parked outside. *What are we doing here?* Said I, *Come on in, you will see.* I needed a witness.

I went up to the hole in the bullet-proof glass and said, *I would like to buy a speeding ticket*. I did this in much the same manner as a contestant on Wheel of Fortune would say, *I would like to buy a vowel please.* Except this was a speeding ticket, and not a vowel. The two ladies who manned the fortress looked at me with roughly the same expression as a large pig peeing on a flat rock. *Excuse me?*, they asked! Yes, *May I please buy a speeding ticket.*

Needless to say this was not your average police station request. I told them that I had a guilty conscience in that I had been riding around in a brand new fire-engine red Corvette Stingray convertible and had been contravening the speeding laws in no small measure. Therefore I deemed it advisable that in good Christian manner I should confess and pay my debts.

This did not compute.

I then offered to provide a sizable donation to the local Police Association if I could persuade one of the constabulary to write up a citation for my crimes, and could there please be a photograph of the same recorded for posterity.

My motive, I must confess, was not so much that I felt very guilty for my crimes, but that I wanted a framed picture of me in the Corvette and the speeding ticket attached on the wall of my office.

There was clearly no small amount of consternation amongst the hallowed ranks of the administration of this particular Police Department behind that bulletproof glass. Telephones were employed, and after a considerable while I was informed that one of their colleagues in Community Relations would speak with me. Meanwhile My Good Lady was also about ready to summon the boys who bring those tight little jackets.

We waited approximately 20 minutes and then a big burly uniformed man, bristling with all manner of weaponry, restraining paraphernalia, and communications devices, came through the door and wondered what this was all about. I explained that I had been driving this very hot Corvette on the streets and roads in the environs of this Most August Establishment for the better part of two weeks now, and in many cases in clear contravention of the laws of the road regarding the limits placed upon the speed of the vehicles traveling thereupon. I wanted to pay my debts and obtain clear proof of this contravention and payment, and volunteered to do whatever necessary in a monetary manner to facilitate the introduction of a piece of paper which might serve as evidence. I was also very happy to pay the appropriate fine.

Again, this did not compute. First of all, he explained, they had to physically catch me at the scene of the crime and accost me on the spot. I told him to *follow me down the street about a hundred yards and he would have your catch.* No go. *How be I am told where there is a speed trap and his buddies could catch me as I cruised by?* No go number two. Cannot reveal whereabouts of officers on duty. *How about I make contribution to their charity or some such and get a photo of a blank citation?* Nyet #3. They could not just give me a copy of a citation because if I filled this in erroneously and, say, put in 145 mph in a 50 mph zone, and if it further became known on the Internet or other method of communication that I had not been arrested and incarcerated for this grievous crime then they, the local constabulary, could well be in serious trouble. *Nein. Das is nich gut.*

Further, I was advised that speeding is a serious crime and carries all manner of expensive penalties, up to and including incarceration if I was caught exceeding the

speed limit to any point where I was doing 100 mph . Disappointed, I left the precinct and proceeded to break the law at every possible opportunity.

Previous to this I had been, as is my habit thereabouts, driving down Highway US 1 between Cocoa and Melbourne, Florida. It can be a very busy road or, equally, be nearly devoid of traffic. On this particular occasion it was the latter. I came up to a set of stop-lights at Barnes Avenue and was waiting for the green. A hotted-up black Ford Mustang pulled up beside me. This was a seriously modified car with rumbling noises and ¾ camshafts which would hardly let the engine idle. There were two young men in this Mustang and one called down to me, *Hey Gramps Nice ride! Want to give her a go?* What choice is that! I gave these young fellows a thumbs-up and waited for the green.

Let me first explain that I am a grandpa and I normally drive a grandpa-mobile. It is a Chevy Silverado and about as hot as your eighty-five year old maiden aunt. I had never done any drag racing or any other sort of street racing in my entire life, but when these two youngsters offered to race, a flag went up. At the green signal off we went.

The driver of this Mustang knew his vehicle very well He must have had a Hearst shifter and a five-speed manual transmission and a very hot engine. He got two car lengths on me with rubber in the first three gears. Then the 625 hp of the Corvette kicked in and it was quite a show. I passed him at 140 mph and that Vette continued accelerating through 195 mph whereupon I left the kids in the dust and then backed off. Little did I realize at the time that, had I been in the cross-hairs of a state trooper, I would automatically have gone to jail. But it was still the most fun I ever had on four wheels, and might well have been worth it. I was shaking for about 15 or 20 minutes afterwards. I realized after the fact I didn't even have my seat-belt on, not that it would have much mattered at those speeds if a tree had walked out onto the road.

So what manners of sin are to be attached to the circumstance? Well, the first would easily be identified with the sin of extravagance. I blush to expostulate upon what that vehicle cost me for the two weeks, and that I was residing at my condo in Florida. But you never saw a hearse pulling a safe. Just going down to my condo in Florida, examined in the correct light, could well be viewed as an unnecessary luxury. After all, that money could have been given to the poor. Then, renting a fire engine red

Corvette Stingray convertible could easily be construed as extravagant and therefore sinful. A plain brown sedan would have done the job easily as well.

Driving around the streets in this red beauty in no small measure turned heads. Attached to this is the sin of pride and also evinced sins of envy from the passersby. Then we have iniquities such as waste by using the highest-priced fuel for no good reason other than to drive about and show off.

Last but not least is the crime of just plain having fun in a fast car, which is the epitome of the American Dream. The young aspire to it but cannot afford it. The older yearn for it but either do not dare or are so stiff and sore that they can hardly get in or out because it sits so low to the ground. But to the lucky few, it is a powerful magnet. Gotta get me one of them thar sinful cars.

Driving down the streets without exception turned heads, brought whistles, thumbs-up, shouts of joy, *go for it Gramps, sweet ride,* and all manner of honking of horns and appreciation for the pure sweet joy of observing the best on the open road tooling down the street. It was a ball.

So I joyfully and deliberately sinned in the matter of that wonderful fire engine red convertible Corvette and, as of this writing, have one more half-day to continue my iniquitous activity until the flight back to the sleet and slush. It is still in late March but so hot and humid in Florida that, while I was tempted put up the top of this car it seemed sacrilegious to do so. I just pile on more sunscreen, turn the AC to max and activate the seat coolers. Yes! It has cooled seats too! I simply rode about in this wonderful manifestation of beautiful technology and the American Dream and smiled. And while I have to take it back to the airport tomorrow whence it came, and then take a flight back to the white crappeola of my native land, I shall on the way to the airport press the peddle down and hunt for one last chance of getting a speeding ticket.

CHAPTER

At Amos Hoffman's Place

Amos Hoffman was an elder in our church and thus one of father's henchbuddies. He was also by far the richest man in the church. He had a very nice farm just outside of Heidelberg, Ontario, but the real source of his wealth was the animal feed mill just up the hill toward town from his farm. He seemed to have a knack for making money but was not ostentatious about his wealth. While it was true that every two years or so he got a new car, it was a Ford Fairlane, or automobile of that nature, and not a Mercedes or Maserati or any vehicle of that sort. From my recollection of the matter he was a very pleasant man.

It was clearly evident that Mr. Hoffman greatly enjoyed children, but as happenstance had it he had none of his own. As long as I can remember he taught a Sunday school class and always had a smile and a kind word for us children. I am not sure exactly how the arrangement happened to come into fruition, but for several summers when I was a tad going on a whippersnapper, I and my brothers went and stayed with Mr. Hoffman at his place on the farm for a week or so. This was seriously cool as we got to do things under his administrations that we would never have been able to at home.

For example, Amos took us to a lake not so far away that had a beach and we could go swimming. He would also buy us lunch from a hot dog stand on the beach and then get us ice cream cones. This was as close to heaven as I could have imagined at that time. Also, we got to play in the barn and go up to the feed mill to run around and, I am sure, get in the way of the workers there. Great times.

The keeper of the farm was one Arthur Brubacher, no relation that I know of. He was a man of prodigious strength and few teeth. Also few words. It was apparent that his philosophy was, when faced with a problem, to employ his favorite adage, *Before fetching another tool, apply all possible muscle.* He was not a big man, but very strong and wiry. I wish I had a video (besides that in my head) of him chinning himself with one hand seven times in a row from the overhead bucket track.

He rose early each morning to milk the cows and do the necessary chores to feed and water the other animals around the barn. I thought this was pretty cool and got up early to help him, though I suspect if the truth is known, I was more underfoot then help. He seemed to take this in good stride as it was probably a semi-welcome diversion from his daily routine.

When the first portion of the chores was done we went in for breakfast. It was a serious farmer breakfast and nothing at all like the porridge and apple that I routinely got at home. There was bacon and eggs and toast and lots of it. We never ever got that at home. Then there was fruit and, unbelievably, pie! Whoever thought of eating pie for breakfast! The kicker was the honey-dip doughnut. I had never seen a honey-dip doughnut nor ever the method with which Art treated its consumption.

Now let me explain that when we got maple syrup at home it was kind of like liquid gold served out by the teaspoon. Generally we each got maybe two teaspoons worth on our ice cream or whatever if there was a very special occasion. I wasn't sure whether lightning would strike when, for the first time, I observed Art putting his honey-dip doughnut into a fruit dish and then pouring maple syrup onto the doughnut until it floated. *Actually floated!* Consider the extravagance! This was a matter of no small astonishment at the time, and I suppose it still is. There was no question concerning him growing fat on such a diet because he was built out of whip-cord and a nearly fat-less man. Nevertheless I have sometimes wondered how many calories that man consumed in a day. He worked very hard.

Mr. Hoffman's wife Mary liked to cook. As I recall the matter she cooked very well. When I was there it was often supper for a dozen or so, not only itinerant children such as me, but also extra farmhands and other invited guests who happened to have been there. When the bowls had been passed and the main course largely consumed, Mary would ask everybody by name in turn whether they wanted more. Gordon, Frederick, Kenneth, Anne, Esther, Ruth, Amos, Naomi, Amanda, and Art... Also the onus was on Art to pass judgment on any new dish. I am pretty sure that Mary did not watch the food channel on account of and being as the food channel was far into the future. From where she got the notions of a new circumstance in culinary cuisine I have no idea. But they appeared. So when it got time for judgment on this new dish, Mary would ask Art whether or not he liked it.

Art, from long and perilous experience, had learned that if he said he didn't like it, he would never see it again. Equally, if he declared that he did like it, then it would likely be served every evening meal for several weeks. Therefore Art, being a Mennonite pacifist and diplomat far beyond his ken would say, *Its edible. Yup. Its edible.*

I one time only chanced upon Art on a Sunday when his mouth was rejoicing in the influx of his false teeth. At first I didn't recognize the man. My Art had bib overalls and most of his front teeth missing due to a quarrel with a cow. Art with a full set of teeth and a Sunday suit just barely computed.

Art would also take it upon himself to take us boys for an outing. We all piled into his small red Ford Falcon which seldom left the driving shed except on Sundays when he went to church. But at least once every sojourn at the Amos Hoffman farm we went with Art to A&W situated in Waterloo at the corner of King and Weber streets. In those days we drove up to the central spine in the A&W parking lot and partly rolled down a window. The waitresses came out on roller-skates and took our order. Art always asked us each *Could we handle a quart,* evidently the standard unit of root beer which he enjoyed. We always said we could indeed handle a quart, and presently our roller skated waitress would come with a tray on which our quarts resided, and hook the tray to the edge of the window. This was as close to heaven as we were able to rejoice in those days. However, for a relatively small boy to consume a quart of root beer at a sitting was probably impossible. Perhaps it was a pint, or half a quart. Whatever. Let's just term it a Cold Unit of Liquid Heaven.

About 10 years later, fresh out of high school, my first job was working at Amos Hoffman's Feed Mill in Heidelberg. It was hard work but I was young and strong. My job was to take the bags into which had been put 100 pounds of product, tie them by hand with binder twine, and throw them onto two-wheeled hand trucks. Thence cart them either into one of the delivery trucks or pile against the wall waiting for an order to come in. One-hundred pound bags are heavy, and I became very sore and my hands were very sore, but then I became strong and my hands became very tough. I don't know how many bags I tied that year but it was a lot, and I can still do it pretty much dead-drunk in the dark.

There were very strong people working in that feed mill, one of whom was Frank. I had joined the night shift because I got a 25 cent per hour shift bonus, which increased my hourly wage to $2.05. At that time, at least for me, this was a big deal. Frank was a tall lean drink of water and a man of deceptively prodigious strength. Maybe a cousin to Art. One time we were loading the 3-ton feed truck which was significantly smaller than the normal 10-ton delivery trucks. We backed trucks up to the loading bays and, depending on how much weight was on the truck, the floor of the truck box would be either above or below the sill of the loading area. A three-ton truck is about 18 inches lower than the sill, and so we piled 500 or 600 pounds of feed onto the 2-wheeled hand cart and ran it out onto this smaller truck. Down you go THUMP with your load and then drive it to the front and dump against the bulkhead of the aluminum box.

One time I observed Frank doing just exactly that, only as soon as he got the loaded cart down onto the floor of the box he realized that it was the wrong stuff. Without even thinking about it he yanked that cart and its contents back up onto the floor of the feed mill, wheeled it away, got the correct bags and plunked it down into the truck. A 2-wheeled feed cart weighs about 100 pounds and there was at least 500 pounds of bags on that thing. So let us say that we have 600 pounds of just snatching right back up and drive away. That is a very strong man.

But he was not as strong as another chap with whom we worked. Sometimes he drove truck and sometimes worked in the mill. He came from a farm family nearby and he was as strong is the proverbial ox. Also roughly as smart. There was very little that he could not do in the way of packing and lifting and carrying, he was just plain built very, very strongly.

Animal feed consists not only of wheat and oats and barley and grains, chopped up and/or pelletized, but also into the batch goes minerals and salts and vitamins and other additives, these to assist in a balanced diet. This was known as *the pre-mix* and came from Baden, the location of the area head office for Maple Leaf Mills. Hoffman's establishment was a registered dealer, so they would send a truck over to Baden to get the pre-mix. It came in bags which were designed for much bulkier feedstuffs such as corn and oats. They never seemed to have smaller bags, so they would put it in bigger ones which were 22 inches across the mouth when they lay flat. Even at 100 pounds of premix, when such a bag lies flat it is only a few inches thick, and hard to handle. This particular time another worker and I were unloading this pre-mix onto feed carts, with our very strong fellow worker taking the loaded carts away. He was as slow as he was strong, ponderously removing a load while we piled the next one onto the alternate 2-wheeled feed cart. We piled on the normal number of bags and waited. And waited some more. When he showed no sign of return, we kept piling on more bags. We got 18 bags on that cart until it was full to the handles at the top.

Finally he came back to exchange the cart. He grabbed the handles and placed the sole of his boot on the axle and pulled. Nothing happened. After all, it now weighed something in the order of 1900 pounds. So he took hold again, and still nothing happened. And then you could see kind of a slow stirring behind the eyeballs – where things normally didn't stir very often – he clamped his huge hands around the cart handles, hunched those great shoulders and puuulllllled! The truck tipped back. He didn't utter a sound or change expression one iota. Pulled back that cart and then pushed it creak, creak, creak away across the floor, propelling the better portion of a ton of stuff. A very strong man.

Working the night shift in the feed mill in winter was a very cold job. The doors were not properly sealed where the trucks backed to the loading bays on all four sides of that square building, so the wind would often whistle right through. My job was tying and carting off large quantities of 100 pound feed bags with my bare hands, and I grew to be very tough in that department. Working hard in those conditions required a lot of energy, so I took on much fuel. Every day mother made eight double sandwiches for me plus a big thermos of stew, together with apples and cookies and anything else available for transport. I went to work at about 4:30 in the afternoon, prior to which she made me a big pile of fried potatoes and eggs or leftovers from the previous night's dinner, so I didn't go to work hungry.

But pretty soon, with that heavy work, I was hungry. About 6 o'clock was first break and I ate half my sandwiches. Next stop at 8:30 or 9 o'clock and I ate the rest of the contents of my lunch-box. By midnight, hungry again! So we jumped into somebody's jalopy and went up to the Heidelberg Hotel where I would eat another hot hamburger

sandwich full dinner. That generally finished me through the shift. Yet on the way home there was very often a stop at Wagner's Corners and buy some chocolate bars for the rest of the drive. I'm not sure what the caloric intake of that was, but I will let the reader do the math. Didn't put on an ounce other than muscle. We worked hard.

Then one day in autumn during first break (the night shift started at about 5 o'clock) around eight or so I was having a bottle of pop with Pete Metzger, the pellet mill operator. We were sitting on the loading dock that faced the road. It was a beautiful evening and I was drinking Schweppes ginger ale. Pete said if you can drink a Schweppes ginger ale, that stuff is so awful, that you could stand to drink beer. Well, I had never had a beer, so I had to wait for rejoicing in the matter of beer until a later time.

As we were sitting there the little brother of our immensely strong cart-wielding fellow came up the lane on a bicycle. This kid would have been about 12 or 13 and he was built like his brother, that is, he was constructed from slightly flexible bricks. He had a steel 45-gallon drum perched on his shoulder held with one arm while he peddled his one-speed bike up the lane, somewhat uphill from their farm down by river. We couldn't believe our eyes. Here's this kid with *at least* 100 pounds on his shoulder and controlling his bike with one hand. As he got closer it was evident that it had been filled with molasses, residue of which still smeared the spigot and down the sides. We also knew, in the manner of such barrels everywhere, a fair bit of residue still lurked therein. It was heavy.

But this kid didn't even blink. He crossed the road, got up to the loading dock and without stopping the bike he flung the barrel onto the dock and said *mallosich* (molasses). He knew we would deliver it, full, back to the farm probably the next day. So Pete said to the kid (this all in German) he said to him, *Isn't that a bit heavy?*, and the kid replied, *Ach, ess ist yusht a baal.* It's just a barrel. Just a barrel indeed. That kid was going to be a very, very strong man. Like his brother, who could push 1900 pounds of feed around in a 2-wheeled hand cart designed to carry 600.

CHAPTER

Skunks and Such

The old farmhouse in which I live is clearly a highly desirable habitation for many critters that sport fur – I mean besides me. In the manner of my dad and grampa, I am a pretty hairy guy, but not quite in the league of the denizens seeking shelter within the confines of this very old house. Over the years it has played host to a great many such critters. This has not occurred by any sort of overt invitation, unless of course the lack of due diligence paid to miscellaneous apertures through which they pass can be construed as a multiple welcome mat.

Chief of these of course, is mice. When I first moved here it was late winter and the problem was not too bad. But as the snow melted and the greenery appeared, there was a pretty serious influx of small gray furry rodents. I could never be sure from where they all came, but the fact that just yonder is a very old barn with a lot of straw still on the threshing floor upstairs, I suppose it doesn't take a whole lot in the way of deductive reasoning to figure out that the barn might be prominently featured in the matter. At any rate, in they came. They came with triple G – that is with Great Glee and Gusto. Pretty soon not only was I finding the spoor of their passing and inhabitation in a whole lot of places, but also, especially in the night when dead silence reigns, I didn't have to reach for a hearing aid to pick up on the gritcha gritcha gritcha of tiny teeth munching on the woodwork. Also, every so often, I could see one scurrying past out of the corner of my eye.

This of course necessitated trips to the hardware store where I soon became the proud possessor of a fair number of mousetraps. While mice will eat pretty much anything in the line of cheese, I am pretty sure that their favorite is Havarti. It seemed to work better than anything else, possibly because it has a rather sharp odor to it, which can be picked up upon at greater distances, or perhaps it is because of my mice are not country mice at all. They perhaps migrated from the city and, like many of the two-footed inhabitants around here who moved North for better prospects and entertainment, brought with them their love of cheeses other than medium cheddar. Genteel mice if you will. At any rate the traps yielded a fairly voluminous quantity of result.

When the grandchildren came to visit, one of the first things they did was to check my traps. They would start behind the kitchen door, move to the toe kick by the door to the sunroom, over to the cavity beside my desk, thence to the broom closet under the stairs, then up to my bedroom and bathroom and the spare rooms in the south wing. On this one occasion, there was a particularly big fat specimen, deceased, in the broom closet. With me on this trap line inspection were my two oldest grandchildren, Micah, aged six, with Elise, then four. I asked Micah if he wanted to grab the carcass by the tail and then take it out and fling it into the lilac bushes. He blanched and retreated at the prospect, whereupon his little sister cheerfully piped up, *I'll do it grandpa!* And so she did. However, halfway across the dining room she was accosted by her mother who was appalled at the sight of her little girl gleefully swinging a dead mouse around her head by the tail in the environs of the table set for dinner. The deceased was duly disposed of and then her mother washed her daughter's hands very carefully indeed.

I categorically deny that I have ever had rats in the house. I am not sure if the mudroom counts as being in the house but one summer there was a fairly interesting odor circulating thereabouts and it was anything but pretty. This went on for quite a while and then diminished. Eventually I moved the dryer and sure enough, there resided the mortal remains of a large rodent. But that was the only time and technically not in the house. Or maybe it was a chipmunk. That was it! A chipmunk! That is my story and I'm going to stick to it, even though there has been report by other guests which suggest otherwise. I deny this. I am like the wet Egyptian – I am in de-nile.

I heat the old farmhouse with wood. Once in a while, because there is no screen on the top of the chimney, a blackbird wanders down in the middle of summer and gets trapped in my stove. It's not that I am overly tender-hearted to the point where I cannot swat a mosquito, but I draw the line at keeping a bird in prison until it succumbs to dehydration. That I cannot do. On the other hand I learned the hard way that just opening up the door to the stove and then the doors to the house is not the answer either. A blackbird can flap around in the house for days and leave residue of its passage in many places. Then the danger is still that it dies, having crawled in to some crack behind the book cabinet or place of that nature, and we have another kind of a problem.

It will be understood that the old farmhouse is also host to cluster flies. Where they come from I don't know, but I am told that larvae spring from eggs that have been laid in the sash maybe many years ago, and in the warmth of the spring sun they come to life and buzz around. They do this in great quantity and eventually it is necessary to vacuum up a whole pile of dead flies. I have a Shop Vac which my buddy Deano swears is powerful enough to suck crows out of the sky. Well, I discovered that he may well be close to the mark in this assessment. One time I was vacuuming flies from the windowsills and it was coincidental with a blackbird loose in the house. It fluttered from window to window trying to get out and came in close proximity to where I was looking after fly business. I swear (sorry – *affirm* – Mennonites don't swear) before the Almighty that I did not even think about it, but that, more or less of its own volition, the business end of the Shop Vac came in proximity to the blackbird. There was a very interesting set of swooshing type slurping noises as the bird disappeared into the maw of the vacuum cleaner. I took it outside and opened it up but the bird was dead. It must've broken its neck on the trip down the hoses. At least I tried.

Subsequently I went to a sporting goods store and bought a good-sized dip net normally used for fishing. Plan was to let a trapped bird loose and immediately snare it in the net and take it back outside. It is written, *The best laid plans of...*, It did not go well. When the door of the stove was opened, the bird saw the net and stayed put. Take away the net and adios bird stage left, all over the house.

The reader will by now have determined that the author is not very bright. But once in a while the Good Lord Almighty allows even us sinners of lesser intelligence a Good Idea. In this case the Good Idea was simply to plug the chimney with a bundle of rags so no birdies got in. Duh... That took only 10 years to figure out. One must remember, however, that the removal of said chimney obstruction in the autumn before firing up the stove is a very necessary item on the To-Do list. Failure to do so will, without fail, result in a house full of smoke.

While I was never able to put a numerical value on the number of mice in the house, the chipmunks are a different matter. I think I have now finally closed all the holes where they used to get in, but back in the early days they seemed to have four-lane highways all through the establishment. I would feed the birds outside, yet I would find birdseed tucked into cracks in the couch, underneath pillows, under mattresses, you about name it. So I went and bought a chipmunk trap. The first one I caught in the live trap I drowned in the rain barrel. This caused no small amount of consternation with the Lady in My Life, so I had to promise I would not do that again. I think the record for catching and releasing chipmunks occurred about four years earlier than this writing when I caught and released 32. I made a rule to release them in a suitable location in neutral territory at least 5 km away from my property. I have no idea whether I kept catching the same ones as they came scurrying back or not. At any rate the numbers seem to have decreased and last summer I was down to two. Same deal with squirrels. If you let these get into your house or your attic there is a lot of nasty mess to deal with, and not an easy matter at all. So it's catch and carry.

Then, of course, there are the raccoons. They dearly love to inhabit any place they possibly can, and that includes the barn, the driving shed, the attic of the house, the attic of the overhang, the attic of the summer kitchen, the mudroom crawlspaces, anyplace at all. And it's not just one or two. They invite their brothers and their sisters and their cousins and their aunts, and then they all make like Mennonites and spawn a whole pile of offspring. They make a big mess and just plain try to take over.

Any reader who gets all bent out of shape about the disposal of vermin is now invited to move on to the next chapter. For those of you who have chosen to stay with me here, let us just say that the good Lord Almighty invented the 12-gauge shotgun for very valid reasons. I think the seasonal record for additions to the raccoon burial plot behind the barn was roughly a dozen or so. Last year I did not see any. But I pen this in early spring, and this year, well, we shall see.

And then, last but not least, there is a critter out there that is black and white. It has a big bushy tail and greatly enjoys taking up residence in and under any sort of crawlspace or similar habitation. I met up with my first skunk in early November of the first year of my residence here. It was a Saturday evening and I opened the door to the summer kitchen to put out some recycling and there stood the answer to a fair few mysteries. You see, the old house had been disused for quite an extended period of time before I moved in. It took a great deal of renovation before it was habitable,

including pretty much the changing of every surface inside the house except the ceilings. Also in various corners, and especially those of the summer kitchen, was a great deal of what I considered to be that which came from the north end of a south-bound cat. And yet it did not quite add up because cats do not normally do their business in some of the places where I found the residue.

So here I came face-to-face with a skunk. We looked at each other for a few moments and then it scurried into the space underneath my deep-freeze. The floor to the old summer kitchen was nowhere close to being level and had a very interesting dip in the one corner. I leveled the area with some two-by-fours so that the freezer would behave properly. The skunk evidently decided that in the corner underneath the freezer was the place to spend the winter. I thought otherwise.

I lured the skunk outside with some cat food and locked the door. That night the skunk ate a hole in the wooden door and returned to its lair under the freezer. More cat food got it out, and then I screwed a steel plate over the lower portion of the door. The next morning it was clearly evident that the skunk had gone around to the back of the summer kitchen, burrowed under the wall, created a hole in the floor, and was back under the freezer. So I got the skunk out again and, with some paving stones I had lying around, I covered the entire floor with three inches of concrete slabs. But the skunk hung around. I could smell it. It wanted back in.

This called for drastic action. I borrowed a live trap from the neighbor and set out cat food closer and closer to the trap, which I placed each night on the milk house stoop. Meanwhile, I got a 45gallon drum, filled it with water and attached the trap to a rope and pulley system, placing the pulley directly above the drum. I drilled two holes in the driving shed wall facing the milk house which was about 50 feet away. One hole was for the rope, and the other for my eye. The skunk took the bait and was caught in the trap. **Important note**: *ensure wind direction is favorable before attempting*.

Now skunks, as you are all aware, are smelly. And as such they need to have a bath. So before the actual cleansing process, I put a CD of Mendelssohn into the player of the pickup truck and cranked out the *War March of the Priests*. I poured a good drink and hoisted a jar to the well-being of my skunk as I pulled on the rope, raised the live trap up over the barrel, and lowered the skunk into the water. I had taken the precaution of lashing a brick to the downward side of the trap so that gravity would do its job properly and also to reduce the likelihood of missing the barrel on account of skunk turbulence. Engineering at its finest. It worked, shakily, but it worked. I gave the skunk a bath for maybe half an hour or so, and I was right. It no longer smelled. He then joined his cousins in the coon burial establishment behind the barn.

Ah… the joys of good country living!

The author's siblings. From the left: Anne, Gordon, Esther, Fred, Lorraine, Ruth, and Kenny. Consider the enlightened and mature visage of the author.

CHAPTER

Mea Culpa

I am a sinner. I was taught this already as a small boy both at home and at church. I was conceived in sinful lust, I was born in sin, and I am a sinner by nature and by practice. Well, I'd say that about covers all the bases, probably the short-stop and the outfield too. I did bad things and these were called sins so in the eyes of both God and His servants, such as my father and the elders of the church, I was and doubtless still am a sinner.

When I was a boy we went to church in Hawkesville, a small village located on the banks of the Conestoga River about eight miles to the south and west of Elmira. It was not a large affair, with perhaps 20 families in attendance. This church was the result of mom and dad, together with a bunch of their henchbuddies, having left the Old Order Mennonite church around 1939. In the 1930's some people from England known as the Plymouth Brethren came along, preached their version of the gospels, made converts, and then set up Brethren Assemblies. These were autonomous units of faith which we would now call fundamentalist community churches. These Brethren Assemblies were loosely connected by faith and tradition but did not respond to any central Synod such as the hell-bound Catholics did to Rome and the Pope (that blasphemous apostate) or the evil Anglicans who cow-towed to the Archbishop of Canterbury, or any of the other *denominations* who were dictated to from some kind of central authority.

The Bretheren Assemblies believed that every man was responsible directly to God his Maker, and that anybody getting in the way of direct communication with God needed to see the error of his ways and get saved and join the Bretheren who were, after all, God's Chosen People. We were *not* a slice of the religious cake: We *were* the Cake, the Real Deal. We were not down there with the heathen Lutherans and

Baptists and Presbyterians and such, and certainly were heavenly mountains above the Catholics and idolatrous Buddhists and Muhamadans and other similar heathen who were, without question, on the broad road that leads to perdition.

We did not go to church. We the people, the saved, the saints, *were* the church. We all gathered together in an assembly hall or meeting house and worshiped according to the leading of the Spirit. The first service on Sunday morning was known as worship service and technically was without form. Everybody trooped in and sat down and worshiped in awesome silence, until such time as the Spirit would lead one of the brethren to get up to do something like request that we all sing hymn number such-and-such from the book. Or perhaps he would say a prayer or give a testimony, a word of encouragement or a recounting of some such enterprise that had occurred in a spiritual manner to that individual that week. Notice I say *he*, because the women with covered heads were, one and all, silent except that they could join in the singing.

Sometimes the Spirit appeared to be away someplace else, or had perhaps gone to the cottage fishing with the Apostles or was attending the golf services. Often the silences could last for quite a while. When it came to the singing of the hymns there was no piano or organ, and the singing was led by Brother Ezra Frey, a very good singer who probably possessed perfect pitch. He loved to sing and did so at work as a carpenter as well. He sang hymns and mostly worked with younger men. One time one of his co-workers asked him to sing some rock and roll. So Ezra sang *Rock of Ages Cleft for Me* and *Rolled Away, Rolled Away, Rolled Away, All the burdens of my heart rolled away!* Pretty sure that was the last time a request of that nature was conveyed.

At any rate, Ezra led the church singing and it went well, that is, so long as he was there. And while he was mostly there, sometimes he was on holiday or visiting elsewhere. Then it didn't go so well. Whoever else was leading the singing at that particular time often started the song in the wrong key, either too high or too low. If the hymn was afflicted with the latter there was a lot of Gravel Gertie growling going on, and if the former was in place we were treated to much yowling and screeching in the upper register. And I, doubtless blasphemously, though this was pretty cool.

Depending on who stood up to give out a prayer you could pretty much tell verbatim what was going to happen. One brother would fall asleep and start to snore whereupon his wife would jab an elbow into his ribs. He would immediately jump up and, in a sing-song voice accompanied by much bobbing and weaving of the head (maybe he was trading invisible jabs with the devil), pray a sermon encompassing pretty much the entire Bible. He'd start with the creation in Genesis, recount Adam and Eve and the chomping of the apple, Moses and the bull-rushes, David whacking the head off Goliath, then on through the major and minor prophets, Jonah and the whale, the life and death and resurrection of Jesus, the coming of the Holy Spirit, the acts of the Apostles, the second coming, the great tribulation, the four horsemen of the apocalypse, and end up with divine warnings about the whore of Babylon, the last judgement, and the lake of fire. Then he would sit down and go right back to sleep again.

Another brother, who was a farmer and doubtless a very fine gentleman indeed, was afflicted with sinusitis. On the farm it was no problem to hork and spit pretty much at will (perhaps Will was one of the hired hands) except at the dinner table. In church, however, it was another matter. He was delightfully hard of hearing and so doubtless considered the horking matter to be silent, which for him it was, but for few others. So when the horking was done, he had this problem of how to dispose with the accumulation within, and we were treated to some pretty interesting bobbing up and down of his prominent adam's apple as he swallowed in a manner also anything but silent.

It was also interesting to observe who had fallen asleep. One time, I asked father whether the spirit couldn't have led these people to stay awake, and I was informed in no uncertain terms that it was highly unlikely that these Brethren in the Lord were actually sleeping. Rather, they were deep in meditation with their eyes closed. So that was the end of that discussion. I have never yet, however, observed anybody in serious meditation who is also snoring. They never did it for long at one shot because a dose of elbow by the spousal Sistern would render the brother's head back up and eyes once more open. At least temporarily.

There was another brother who was really hairy. His eyebrows traveled bushily across the bridge of his nose with great gouts of foliage emanating from his nose and even his ears, and he was also afflicted with serious boogers and ear wax. He would do this trick where he inserted a massive pinky finger into one of those orifices and go digging, and in so doing made his hand oscillate back and forth at high rates of blurred speed. And he could do this with either hand! An ambidextrous booger-digger! On the farm he could dispense with the gob of wax, or whatever was now rejoicing in residence on the end of his little finger, by simply wiping it on his overalls. But in church it was different. He would just sit there and look at it until his wife caught on and went *hmmmppphh* in disgust and rooted in her purse for a hanky.

I had to sit sandwiched between mom and dad because I was a Bad Boy and prone to giggling. Let's face it, these services were about as exciting as a confessional for geriatric nuns, and any diversion was more than welcome. For example, the horking was a great cause for mirth, as was imitating the bobble-headed brother who preached the whole Bible in a sing-song voice. Of superlative humor was, of course, farting. When one of the brethren let forth serious audio manifestations of gastro-intestinal fortitude, how could a small boy *not* snigger? So dad would pinch me. He pinched my inside upper leg betwixt finger and thumb and held the pinch and it hurt like hell! And I dasn't yell out in pain because that would fetch a dose of The Stick later on at home. I had to hold my howling because, after all, this was a place of silent meditation and, of course, love and forgiveness.

We had a weekly contest. My older brothers kept track of the number of horkings and after the service we all went outside where I pulled down my pants and we counted the bruises on my leg. If there were more leg marks than horkage I won. Not sure what if any material matter might possibly have changed hands as we had no coin. And even if I won, it was a Pyrrhic victory at best.

The other church services included people on the platform leading the singing, giving out prayers, or perhaps some special music like a duet or a trio or some such to the accompaniment of the piano. These introductions were followed by a sermon. Most of these sermons were pretty dry affairs. We did not have a professional pastor but rather had lay ministers. One member of the congregation might be employed in the sermon that Sunday, or perhaps a brother from one of the other surrounding assemblies would do the honors. The Scriptures would be opened and passages read and expostulated upon at mind-numbing length. When the speaker's throat dried up, the sermon was finished with an interminable prayer. Add to that the closing hymn, and we could finally escape. I learned to sit for long periods of time on hard pews and I can also quote you very major portions of the King James version of the Holy Book. It was mostly a very desiccated affair. I often wondered how it was that seemingly otherwise rational humans would take the good time and trouble to stretch a five-minute group of thoughts into about three quarters of an hour. So far as I know they

were not paid on piece-work. Then, many years later it hit me: They were softening us up for eternity – the sermons seemed to take forever.

On Sunday mornings, however, after the worship service, the children got to go downstairs to Sunday school. This was a little better, but mostly a younger version more or less cloned on what was going on upstairs. We sang songs and there was often an object lesson or some kind of an illustration to pick up on a Bible theme. For example the giver of the lesson might bring a couple of chunks of two by four and then nail them together in the shape of a cross. Then, to make sure that we understood Christ's suffering, take a sharp tool and rough up the wood surfaces, thus hammering home (oops) the fact that the cross on which Jesus died was not a smooth cushy comfortable place. After some such as above, we would disperse to our separate Sunday school classes and be subjected to more teaching in the Christian faith. Again, pretty dull stuff. Christ and the apostles went fishing and boating, didn't they? Why couldn't they teach us stuff like that?

One time, between the worship service and Sunday school, I went out into the cemetery behind the church. After sitting for an hour and a half, I needed to run around a bit and let off some steam before I got my ass parked on another chair and went through that all over again in a different guise. As it happened I came upon and captured a fairly large garter snake and went into Sunday school with this serpent secreted under my jacket. I thought it would be pretty cool to use this snake is an object lesson. After all, we were taught that in the Garden of Eden, Eve was seduced into taking a chomp out of the apple by some critter which then was accosted by God and turned into a snake. The Scriptures say that God declared that *There shall be enmity between the snake and the woman.*

Presently I discovered that this was true. A snake by its very nature is slippery, and even though I tried to keep it under my jacket, it got away, slithered all over the place, and I couldn't catch it again. We all were treated to the spectacle of one of the Sunday school teachers, a Mrs. Martin, now standing on top of a desk and screaming her head off. Men came down from the church service above to see what the ruckus was all about, and there was no small effort applied into the capture of this devil serpent that had invaded the Sunday Sanctum. Eventually it was also determined whence the snake had come. I was in seriously deep doo-doo and when I got home the dreaded Stick came out and my ass shone brightly thereafter much like a rosy-red

Canadian onion. I was not content that this was justice because, after all, I was trying to illustrate a time-honored Biblical principle, and this multi-whackage is what I got for it. It appeared that there was an overriding Biblical principle at work here, because our father had it straight from God Almighty that it was his obligation to whack small boys who brought manifestations of the devil into church. But not, it seemed, to give much exercise to the principle, or practice, of forgiveness.

In church I learned that I was a sinner and I needed to be saved. So, at some point when I was maybe seven years old, after a sermon that said Jesus is coming back anytime now (perhaps even any minute), and if I wasn't saved I was going to go to hell. This, according to Scripture, after having been bashed around by seven years of tribulations like plagues and pestilence and famine and flood and fire, all brought onto us courtesy of the Four Horsemen of the Apocalypse and their henchbuddies. So I got scared and got saved. *Scared into the Kingdom,* is how they put it.

That was all fine and dandy. I was now saved and didn't have to worry about going to hell anymore. The Bible says, *By grace are ye saved through faith and it is not of yourself, it is the gift of God, not of works, lest any man should boast.* However, the powers that be were also very big on pointing to other verses in Scriptures such as, *By their fruits shall ye know them,* and, if you were busy producing rotten mangos then you were sinning and thus probably you were not saved at all and were still going to hell. I was pretty convinced that I was not leading a Perfect Christian Life and so felt guilty about many things. For example, comic books were forbidden. They were tools of the devil along with playing cards, Coke, potato chips, and many other enjoyable matters which were fingered as being sinful along with radio (except for the CBC news with Allan McFee at noon) and TV. Don't forget books by Zane Grey and *Mad Magazine.*

Also I was guilty of the sin of lust. As an early teen I was starting to take an interest in what might possibly be going on under girls' dresses. Then I liberated a *Playboy* (October 1965) from the local corner store. I dared not buy it because the store owner knew my dad and might have ratted, so I slipped it under my jacket and left the money on the counter beside the cash register when he wasn't looking. The pictures inside augmented my already active and normal attraction for matters anatomical of the fairer sex. This was surely sinful and I felt guilty about it, but not guilty enough to tell my parents and make confession. So I was a guilty sinner, especially because, if the truth were told, I very much enjoyed this type of sin, which made me doubly guilty and thus officially headed for hell.

So what about hell? What is it like there? Well, we were taught that there is a fair jag of heat and humidity, but without the beach and the tan and a cold beer. There was also miscellaneous other unpleasantness but, in short, it was described as a place to which you did not want to go. Therefore, get your ass saved.

Heaven, however, is a rather trickier subject. What does one do in heaven? The first thing that we were taught was that in heaven there is no such thing as time. At the end of all things and when all the judgments and the tribulations and all that sort of thing are done, the Scriptures tell us that, and I quote, *The heavens shall be rolled up as a scroll, and time shall be no more.* So take that, Stephen Hawking and Roger Penrose and Lee Smolin (all of whose books I find endlessly fascinating: these guys are so smart I am pretty sure they never learned to tie their shoes) and all you other high-powered physicists out there. I have the answer to the end of the universe. The scale factor is a negative number! The expansion of the universe is going to slow down and stop and then everything is going to contract into the Big Crunch. Dark Matter and Dark Energy is really God, and He will collect up His DM and DE and take them back Home. There, guys. I just saved you a pile of time and money. Relax. Go fishing.

But back to what we do in heaven. It was taught that we are going to praise God for all eternity. Well, how can that be if there is no time? Any act, such as praising, meeting for tea, or having converse with Moses and the Apostles, or golfing, would appear to take up some time. After all, how can there be any organized converse if it is not done in an orderly manner? And if there is order to the manner, then it would appear that there need to be consecutive events. And consecutive events are pretty tough to do if you have trashed time. Besides, how long can you go on praising and singing and such before you get tired of it. Oops! I forgot. There is no time so how long does not apply.

When I was a boy we were made to believe that heaven was a really groovy place and that if you are a Good Boy and Saved you could go there. In heaven, by definition, you could do and have whatever was most pleasing to you.

In my case that meant that heaven is full of black licorice. Not red and not orange nor certainly not that putrid green stuff. It had to be black. And it took all manner of forms, such as ropes and twizzlers, flat stock and pinwheels, nibs and allsorts, and pretty much any other form of licorice that you could imagine so long as it was black.

Cigars and pipes were not included, as the Scriptures tell us to *avoid even the very appearance of evil*. And, therefore, as smoking is another tool of the devil, there would be no manifestations of such truck in licorice heaven.

So, presuming that I get to heaven in the first place, it will be incumbent upon St. Peter et al to make sure that I have an infinite amount of black licorice. To do this they will have arranged a room which is infinite in size in length and width and depth. Big Pete will give me a bicycle and say, *Okay boy, fourth door on the left. Go and enjoy your heart's desire, which is as much black licorice as you can possibly now enjoy.* So hop me on a bike and off I will go.

I think that someplace in scripture – this be the semi-holy scribing you understand – *The eating of black licorice worketh up a powerful thirst*, on account of all that sugar and so forth. So in heaven it shall be what happens down here on earth, at least in this particular department. Enter A&W root beer. On very rare occasions I was treated to root beer and, in my mind at least, root beer was nectar of the gods. Coke was of the devil, but root beer, well maybe not so much. Root beer was seriously plenty tasty, yet somewhat less demonic.

Therefore heaven is black licorice and root beer. It seems reasonable to me: bike around heaven and help myself to black licorice washed down by A&W root beer. We shall see. A boy could do a lot worse. Maybe have to listen to politicians or clergy, but it doesn't seem to me that many of those will get to heaven in the first place. But meanwhile it remains a somewhat open question as to the eternal status of people like me, a boy who was taught in no uncertain terms that he is just another sinner…

CHAPTER

Books

Looking back on it, one of the great mysteries of our household was the fact that we were allowed to read books, all kinds of books. The summer when I was 16 I read the entire unabridged *War and Peace*. We did not have television and the radio was reserved for the one o'clock news with Allan McFee on CBC. Any other entertainments were pretty much self-contrived out-of-doors games. We played road hockey by the hour, employing miscellaneous boots, bricks or boards found in the garage and basement for goal posts, and for the projectile we normally had a hairless tennis ball that had been procured in the bushes behind the tennis courts over by John Mahood School. These courts were hard by the bush, so we hid in the undergrowth and made like vultures on any errant ball bouncing over the side screens. Pounce on the prize and zip off. Larceny at its very finest.

There was very little vehicular traffic on William Street in Elmira and so when a car came we would simply clear off to one side and let it go by. We had no money to procure hockey sticks, so we laid wait in the arena until somebody broke a stick and flung the shards into the stands. These were highly prized and pounced upon, and we took them home and patched them back together again with the crudest of tools and a few odd nails and screws.

When it rained we played in the garage or the basement. There was a four by eight piece of plywood down there which served as a ping pong table, and that was lots of fun indeed. Not sure where the bats or the balls came from. The garage would inevitably turn into a hockey match. In the north end of the garage was a window which, to my pretty certain knowledge, in my childhood was broken at least 15 times. A vast assortment of projectiles found its way through that glass: tennis balls, hockey pucks, boots, shoes, arrows, bricks, and any number of other such items that, under the tender administrations of young boys, could be persuaded to take flight. The penalty for turning that solid piece of glass into shrapnel was that the perpetrator of the crime had to dry the supper dishes for one month. This may not sound like all that serious a punishment but there were nine people in the family and, especially in summer if everybody else was allowed to go out and play immediately after supper and the convict had to stay back and dry dishes, it was retribution of a fairly stern and inconvenient nature. Nevertheless, that was the law of the house. I know of this personally. A fair few times.

All of the above was pretty much carried out during daylight hours. But what about after dark? Nearly inexplicably we were allowed to read, and to read all manner of books as long as they came from the library downtown. Most of the books in the house were of a very religious nature. There was, of course, the Holy Bible together with a few other tomes of spiritual commentary and enlightenment. One of these was entitled *Great Men of the Faith*. It obviously belonged to our father which art in heaven and was the stimulating (at least to dad) biographies of a fair few of his predeceased henchbuddies. In it there were also photographs of these men (they were all men) and most of them had a lot of facial hair. Full beards, serious mutton chop sideburns, hair coming out pretty much everywhere including their noses and ears – eyebrows to make an eagle blush. In my day it was incumbent upon all of the current brethren to be clean shaven. I asked father about the facial hair of these dead dudes and was informed, *That was then and this is now*, and thus ended the conversation. The underlying threat of course was that if I wished to continue the discussion, the rebuttal would be carried out via the business portion of The Stick.

I loved books then and I love books now. The first non-Bible book that I remember was *If I Ran the Circus* by Dr. Zeus

> *In all the whole world the most wonderful spot*
>
> *Is behind Sneelock's store in the big vacant lot*
>
> *It's just the right spot for my wonderful plans*
>
> Said young Morris McGurk, *If I clean up the cans...*

How this volume got into and stayed in our house I do not know. But it certainly had a lasting impression on my idea of, first of all, *a story* and secondly, *how it should be presented.* There were also stories a-plenty in the Bible, and to this day I am fascinated by their presentation. In Sunday school pretty much every lesson would revolve around a Biblical story of some sort. Right off the get-go we had Adam and Eve in the Garden and the snake, and Noah and the ark, and all manner of great stories. But Dr. Zeus stayed with me in that particular book. I could pretty much quote its entirety before I was in kindergarten and still can, to the general dismay of anyone who gets me started. The sound of the words, the beat and cadence of the rhythm, the juxtaposition and melding of the sounds, and the pictures of those words in print is astonishing. Surely he was the ultimate master of the craft.

So we were allowed to read. But it was incumbent upon us to go to bed every night at eight o'clock, even in summer when the sun was still pretty high in the sky and it was very warm. The exception was Friday evenings when we could go to bed at 8:30, still not a very satisfying circumstance for energetic boys wishing to be outside at play. There was still a great deal of light coming in through the west window of our bedroom, so we read books.

Some of the most memorable books of my youth were written by an English author named Enid Blyton. The Adventure Series consisted of perhaps seven or eight books describing the antics of some English youths during their summer holidays. They would become entangled in all sorts of, well, *adventures – The Island of Adventure, The Castle of Adventure* (scared the living crappeola out of me, that one), *The Circus of Adventure,* and so on. I would recommend them to anybody to this day.

The problem occurred when the sun went down and it got dark. Anybody who is a reader will understand that when you get caught up in a page turner (not *this* book, you understand – *a real book!*) then a method of continued reading must of necessity be procured. Once in a while there was enough money to buy batteries for the household flashlight, but that didn't work because there were three of us boys and only one flashlight. I rummaged around in the town dump until I found a broken lamp. I extricated the working guts from same, liberated a light bulb from the cupboard in the kitchen, and used this for reading after dark.

The next hurdle to overcome was that we were supposed to be in a dark room sleeping

and the light from the lamp would shine out under the bedroom door. One of our sisters would spy this and holler down the stairs, *Mom, dad, the boys have their light on*, whereupon it would be necessary, in the cause of family discipline, for mother to holler up the stairs, *Boys put out that light*. So we would take the mat from our bedroom floor, roll it up and stuff it into the crack under the door. That would work until mother and father went to bed and could see that there was a light coming out of our boys' bedroom window which was directly above theirs. Not good.

So there was no help for it but to try to hide the light under the covers. A naked light bulb is a very hot nasty matter. Just under my left thumb, to this day, I can still feel the burn from a 100-Watt bulb whose contact raised a burnt blister the size of a looney. Pretty hard to explain that the next morning at breakfast. And then there was the time when we decided that candles might be the answer... How the house did not burn down is probably a tribute to the overtime exertions of the parental guardian angels. Pretty good chance that our own g. angels had given up on us and gone fishing a long time before that.

But read we did. I discovered that there were incredible adventures to be had between the covers of a book. There were, however a few limitations to the allowance of our reading. For example, Zane Grey was forbidden. Mother's flat out rule was that Zane Grey is *wild and woolly*, and not to be brought into the house. I can understand the wild part, what with rustling cattle and shoot'em ups and so forth, but the *woolly* was never explained. Precious few sheep baa-ing about in the Wild West World of Zane Grey. *Verboten*.

The natural outcome of this censorship was that we read every Zane Grey novel that there might possibly be available to us. *Betty Zane, Riders of the Purple Sage*: Great Stuff. Steely-eyed hard riding on lathered horses. Men of few words with six-shooters. Let the Colt .45 do the talking. In matters of dispute, Let the Big Dog Bark. We could not just sort of pussy-foot past mother in the kitchen with these books. A good way of fetching out The Stick. Instead we had to tie them up with string and hoist them up the outside wall of the house to our open bedroom window and then hide them under the mattress until such time as we returned them to the public library.

The other anathema was *Mad Magazine*. This periodical was sinful and evil and idolatrous and rebellious, and rebellion is of course right up there with the sin of witchcraft. *Mad Magazine* made fun of everybody and everything and sent up a lot of items which I did not understand, such as television shows and movies. But there was a lot of seriously funny stuff, and I suspect it colored my outlook on matters of this nature in no small measure. Alfred E. Neuman forever.

Once in a while, when I was a teenager, mother and father would go off to Pennsylvania to visit relatives. After all, this is from where our forbears came 200+ years ago. They also visited other PA folk of their acquaintance from time to time, and came back with three items of note. One of these was Hershey Chocolate Kisses. Another one was candy corn. Last but not least were tales of signs by the road put there by Burma-Shave. This company was in the business of making stuff that you slather on your face before the application of a razor. There were billboards which they situated approximately a quarter mile apart by the side of the road, each little phrase a separate sign. An example:

> *She missed the turn*
> *Car was whizzin'*
> *Fault was her'n,*
> *Funeral his'n*
> Burma-Shave

Another of them was

> *Angels that guard you*
> *When you drive*
> *Usually retire*
> *At 65*
> Burma-Shave

So *Mad Magazine* took it upon themselves to make fun of this:

> *Empty beer cans by the road*
> *Are ugly, many say*

> *But at night, reflecting bright*
> *They safely guide the way*
> Burma-Shave

I dared not show this to my father which art in heaven for fear of a trip to the closet and The Stick. But I thought it was pretty cool. And still do!

The bottom line is that to this day I find wonderful adventures between the covers of a book. Not *this* book, silly! A *Real Book!* Try *War and Peace.*

School Daze. Graduating class of grade 8, Riverside Public School, Elmira, 1966. Author second to back row on left.

𝕌𝕟𝕔𝕝𝕖 𝔸𝕓𝕣𝕒𝕞

I am indebted to my crazy Uncle Abram for my life-long love affair with hot hamburger sandwiches. A thick slab (or better yet, two!) of hamburger nestled on bread, slathered in gravy in the middle of the plate, mashed potatoes with lots of gravy on one side, veggies on the other flank upon which hopefully the gravy has spilled, and you're good to go. Did I mention about the gravy? Comfort food at its finest. At least for me, it doesn't get much better than that. And all that started with a visit to uncle Abram.

My father which art in heaven had a brother Abram who was crazy. Now I don't just mean he was rather eccentric and did things like BBQ spaghetti, he was seriously nutso-batso. So much so, in fact, that the Government of Canada sent some people around to offer him new digs. As it turned out his new home was the Penetanguishene Institute for the Criminally Insane. They did this because he had a penchant for taking pot-shots at passersby with the .22 and torching barns. Also other matters which involved unseemly congress with the incorrect sort of very young people. The above antics were not recommended in most socially acceptable how-to-do-it manuals, so they locked him up, rowed the key out into the middle of Georgian Bay, and threw it overboard.

I loved uncle Abram. He was the ticket for our annual road trip. Right after church on a Sunday in summer we would all jump into the smoking jalopy and head for Penetanguishene. Mother would have packed a lunch for the road so we got to eat sandwiches – yum. It was often hot and dry, and many of the roads in those days were still gravel. Also the old '58 Meteor was blessed with a holey but not righteous floor, and we boys had discovered to our great enjoyment that if we bounced up and down on the cloth seats we could fill the car with dust. This fetched us considerable amount of bony-handed whackage from mother in the front seat. But every so often there was just no help for it. Whacking or no, it was worth it.

After about three hours we would get to Penetanguishene and were taken through steel doors with bars in them and ushered into a room which was perhaps about the size of a school classroom. This was seriously cool. Once we were ensconced in the visiting room, dear uncle Abram would be ushered in. He was not a man of great stature and was a somewhat rotund, soft fleshy man with a handshake much like the greeting of a dead fish. We boys didn't care, this was a road trip and any amount of adventure could be had.

The room had a window out the back, which, while barred, opened onto a courtyard where there were often games played by the inmates, including high jump. Most of the participants would, in the normal manner, take a run at the bar and seek to leap over it on the fly and land in the pit of sawdust below. There was one chap, however, who walked up to the bar and sniffed at it like a dog. He proceeded to take one step back and fling himself over the bar, landing again on his feet. Then he stood there and laughed his head off like a hyena. Such were the entertainments of Uncle Abram's place.

My sisters were petrified of him. They were by now in their teens and had some notion as to why he was there. Uncle Abram was no doubt as horny as the rest of us Brubachers and wasn't getting any, uh, *congress* there, and he ogled my sisters. Also he was cockeyed! He could conjure up a two-for-one sale on double-barreled ogling! You really could not tell who he was looking at or ogling at any particular time. That really didn't bother me, but my sisters were terrified of him and the place and the whole nine yards.

One time, I opened a side door and ventured into the kitchen where there were very large pots of stuff on the stove and also men buttering home-made bread. There were large bowls of softened butter in front of them and they took spatulas to butter the bread with one swipe. I thought this was pretty cool because at home we buttered bread with great care and precision, and here these guys were doing swipe, swipe, swipe – one shot for each slab.

Evidently a headcount had been taken and I was AWOL. I was happily informing the butterers concerning the error of their buttering ways, so one of them had given me a spatula and asked for a demo. I was performing heroic acts of instruction in precision butter spreading when armed guards burst through the door and extracted me from the room with very little ceremony indeed. Evidently I had been enjoying the company of people who were put there because they enjoyed, uh, *communion* with small boys such as myself, a matter which was frowned on by society and the courts. I thought my extrication somewhat inopportune because I was having a whole lot more fun with these guys and doing something very much more useful than being with boring uncle Abram who was busy ogling my sisters, so why not teach them how to spread some butter! At any rate, it was impressed upon me *in no uncertain terms* that I shall not do that again.

The one and only time that I recall being in a restaurant before I flew the coop at 18 occurred on one such trip. For whatever reason, we were not fed our evening meal at uncle Abram's digs that time, and so suppertime found us in downtown Penetanguishene. As dad was in the wheelchair we all went into the only restaurant with no stairs. There were nine of us, so tables had to be pushed together. A couple of large cards with writing on them were brought forth and given to mother and father only. None of the rest of us would have had any clue what to do with one anyway, but it soon dawned on me that there was actual *choice* of meal! You could pick and order your own supper! Amazing!! Pretty sure that father dear father blanched at the numbers on the menu, but what could he do. It was suppertime and the family had to be fed.

Pretty soon a young lady came along with a pencil and pad in her hand and inquired of father whether he would like something from the bar. Father colored up like a thermometer. They had offered him the Demon Drink, as if to say that he looked like an alcoholic! Father and mother then pondered the question of *whether it was legal to get up and leave a restaurant, after you had sat down there, and they pushed tables together, and you had menus in your hand, and get up and go out without buying anything. Was it lawful?!* They didn't know. And so they decided that discretion was the better portion of wisdom and that we would stay and have supper.

While this was happening, I had watched food go by. One particular offering looked and smelled like heaven. It was generous portion of hamburger imprisoned between two, count them, *Two Layers Of White Bread With the Crusts Cut Off*, with wonderful mashed potatoes to one side. The mashed were shaped like a spud volcano with a hole in the centre filled with gravy, which had also been generously slathered over the sandwich. Green peas beside. Never seen or smelled anything like it before. So I vigorously lobbied for one of those, and the Lord is Merciful and Gracious and I got one. No meal before tasted better, and few since. The lady who brought me this ambrosia asked me if I wanted ketchup and, while I had no idea what that was, I was bent and bound that nobody was going to screw up this repast by the application of any foreign muck so, no thanks very much indeed. I guarded that plate with my left forearm and dug in. It tasted even better than it smelled. I filched a piece of bread from yonder basket and mopped up my gravy until only a dog could have licked it cleaner.

And when they ask me before they truck me off to the gibbet for my iniquities, which are copious in quantity and grievous in nature, what I want for my gallows' meal, I shall without hesitation say that it be a hot hamburger sandwich smothered in gravy with the mashed potatoes. It was a foretaste to heaven, and when I get there I think it should be just fine to arrive at the pearly gates with mashed potatoes and gravy on my breath.

And oh yes. Eating green peas is tough with a fork and probably of negative caloric intake. It's all fine with a spoon but if you ask for a spoon with mashed you look like the village idiot. Eating with a spoon in one hand and a fork in the other is also somewhat frowned upon. So I have graduated to coleslaw or corn.

Many years later uncle Abram shuffled off the mortal coil and there around his coffin stood his brothers and several nephews, many of whom were now Men of the Cloth. But not all men cut from the same cloth. They were impaled upon the double-barrelled nasty sharp pointy horns of a thorny dilemma. They had worked through the problem of who was going to deliver the eulogy and that logically fell to the oldest Brother of the Cloth, since Uncle Abram never officially joined any church.

The nasty dilemma was, while he was certainly a brother in the flesh, or what was left of his flesh, was he for sure a Brother in the Lord? Successive waves of family cloth had tried to dress him up in salvation but with evidently rather limited success. Now this was hardly surprising to me as it was clearly evident that uncle Abram rejoiced in an IQ roughly that of the temperature of a cool room, and so the concept of salvation by grace *It is the gift of God and not of yourself, not of works lest any man should boast*

was by no means in his case a sure thing. But they had to get up and say something.

They were not at all sure that he was *Saved*. Oh for sure, when prompted, he had repeated the words of confession, but those cock-eyed orbs wandered and his stomach rumbled – he was always ready for his next meal, as witness his frame. So there was the problem. They were not at all sure that he had been Saved, but to stand up and publicly consign him to the flames of hell they would have done with little rejoicing. So what to do? It was like a hung jury.

Finally they got it right. They dunked him in the Blood. In our particular brand of Christian paranoia it was understood that not everybody could come to a decision on getting Saved, especially if that person were very young. If an infant was gunned down by a bus, then it appeared logical to embrace the concept of Christ Jesus having died and shed His blood for the forgiveness of all people's sins, and if you are incapable of grasping that concept for whatever reason, then you were *covered by the blood*.

So that's what they decided to do. They figuratively dipped uncle Abram in the blood of Christ, muttered suitable words of admonition to the rest of us, especially in the matter of our own shortcomings and needing to be Saved, et cetera, and we took his mortal remains out to the cemetery.

Uncle Abram was a pretty tall man – from side to side – and together with a solid oak coffin his leftovers were a very weighty matter. I know this because I was a pall bearer. I was chosen for this task not due to my piety, but because they knew the poundage and I was plenty strong in those days. Even though they backed the hearse in as close as they could to the grave site the six of us struggled with the burden. To complicate the matter it was November and a cold wet wind was keening through the trees and laying down sleet.

We nearly all went down into that hole together. If it hadn't been for the experienced eyes of the undertakers who saw a mishap-in-the-making and jumped to grab handles, I am pretty sure that we coffin bearers shod with slippery leather soled shoes would all have gone down into that grave. It was a near thing.

With much thanks we safely ensconced his coffin on the cross straps. I was sweating hat-less in that sleet as we croaked and screeched *Shall we Gather by the River*. But I could tell that the Clothites present were not at all sure that uncle Abram was going to join them, the Saved, on the other side of the river. *By grace are ye saved through faith. Not of your own good works, lest any man should boast.* But best not to end up like uncle Abram either.

I mouthed the words and paid politeness to the benediction. But I had driven far and missed lunch, and hoped that my neighboring pall-bearers couldn't hear my stomach complaining. After the interment we all were to troop down into the church basement and partake of Funeral Fare, cold cuts and cheddar cheese with pickles and white bread scantily buttered, and all washed down with weak coffee into which you could put the sugar and milk (not cream – that would be extravagant).

My mind's eye now framed visions of hot hamburger sandwiches. White bread with no crusts imprisoning succulent flesh, volcanic mashed all slathered with rich brown mushroom and onion gravy. With coleslaw AND corn on the side. There was an old-fashioned diner just over the way, and my path would first lead there to celebrate the life of one of God's less fortunate creations, at least by our standards. I would thus join our dearly departed Uncle Abram, at least in what measure I could for now, in his favorite activity: the pleasures of the plate.

CHAPTER

𝔙𝔞𝔪𝔭𝔦𝔯𝔢

I played a lot of baseball in my time. Most of the time not all that well, I suspect, but good enough to play with some of the better teams in my area. This brand of baseball was also called *fastball* or, as it is today in the Excited States of America, *softball*. I was a pitcher. The biggest differences between the two games are that in baseball the field is much larger, the ball smaller, and the pitch is thrown overhand. In fastball the diamond is 1/3 smaller, the ball 1/3 larger, and the pitch comes in underhand or *wind-mill*.

I played with and against other pitchers who were very good indeed. I cut my teeth on the game in our local church league, then moved on to the Kitchener-Waterloo Super V's, the Waterloo CHYMers, and then to various teams in the North Waterloo Fastball League. It was, in its day, the second longest running league in the country and superseded only by the Beaches League out of Toronto. One year in our league we had three pitchers who could throw the ball more than 100 mph. Such a pitch comes in very quickly, especially at a distance of 48 feet 6 inches, as opposed to 60 feet in baseball, where almost *nobody ever* throws that fast. I don't suppose I ever threw a ball more than 90 mph, but the batters were very good and they certainly knew the difference. Therefore I had to try to be a little bit cleverer in my approach and deliver my pitches more precisely and with spins which, for that particular batter, were more difficult to hit.

There was a lot of fastball played under some very rigorous conditions. Midsummer's games on a Sunday afternoon or during a weekend tournament were especially hot and sweaty. These games however made for very good post-game beer. Generally, the first beer was pretty much inhaled, the second tasted great, while the third still went down very smoothly indeed. There is nothing like a cold beer or three when one has been sweating in the sun.

Looking back on it, I was not a natural pitcher. Those who are born to the manner are generally long lean tall drinks of water and built out of whip-cord. These men can generate tremendous arm and hand speed due to the length of their limbs. I am built more like a pale chunky excuse for the enterprise and had to rely on hard work and trying to fool the batters into thinking that I was a whole lot better pitcher than reality should have portrayed the matter. However I played a lot of ball. I suspect that this was more a circumstance of the scarcity of pitchers than of any superlative prowess which I might have brought to the team. But it was excellent exercise, good camaraderie, great fun, and a superlative platform for the inhalation of cold amber fluids.

Due to the nature of my lack of natural talent and, by exceeding my natural capabilities in a violent manner over extended periods of time, I would *throw my arm out*. Something would get unglued in my shoulder or elbow or wrist and then I would have to quit for a good while until I healed. But I loved the game and so took up officiating.

I think I was a much better man in blue decorated with miscellaneous paraphernalia of defence against getting the crap kicked out of me by tip flies and pitches that went merrily through the catcher, accoutrement such as a really good facemask and a lot of padding including shin guards, a chest protector, shoulder armour, and special shoes which had instep guards and reinforced toes. And DO NOT forget that most important item of all, the one which allows procreation even after a spheroid enters that particular area of the male of the species at high velocity. OWWWW!!! I also learned to duck and weave and hide behind the catcher as much as possible, because the hind catch was as much a piece of my equipment as anything that I strapped on. I hated those wee little guys that crouched down about the size and shape of a frog. Precious little of these chaps behind which to hide.

The good baseball official is seen all the time and heard from as little as possible. For example, to what useful purpose, when there is an obvious foul ball slammed over the side fence, does the umpire make huge gestures and holler at the top of the voice, **Foul Ball!**, when it was clearly evident to everybody in the ballpark that it was indeed a foul ball and had gone over the side fence. Similarly if the batter took a cut at an incoming pitch and missed it by a mile, why is there much arm motion from the official and hollering loud enough to be heard in the next county, **SteeeeRiiiike!!** Stupid. A simple arm motion will do to let the players and fans know that the event has been observed and recorded, no loud noises, and the game can continue. Thus it became evident that a good umpire *manages* the game as quietly as possible. Get it right, and keep quiet except when it counts. In time I became the Umpire-in-Chief.

But all was not always rosy. There were normally two umpires in the game but in the dog days of summer there were a lot of people on holidays, both players and officials. It was the job of the umpire-in-chief to assign his colleagues to the games, but there were times when there were not enough to go around and the game needed to proceed anyway.

One such game occurred on a Friday night in midsummer and there were a lot of people away. I was the only person available to officiate that game, a matter which did not bother me a whole lot because a good official, unless he is very unlucky or inattentive, can see what all is happening and make the calls accordingly. This particular game was in the dog days of holiday season in Baden, Ontario, and a lot of the regulars were not there. Most notably absent was the regular catcher for Baden. They had substituted another player who, it soon became clearly evident, had little or no experience in the fine arts of that position. They put the mask on him, strapped on his pads, and he with little comfort set out to catch the pitches. I took up my usual position behind him.

It did not go well. The pitcher that evening was one Donny Ray who was one of those long lean fellows and did indeed throw pitches that came in at speeds in excess of 100 mph. We knew this because from time to time somebody would bring a radar gun and clock them. It must also be noted that the balls did not come in straight. Even at those speeds there was a lot of curving going on. So there I was trying to hide behind this non-catcher who proceeded to completely miss many of the incoming pitches. This is not recommended in most umpire self-preservation manuals. I was going to get killed! Getting hit by one of those incoming fast-balls was pretty much the same as taking an unprotected haymaker from Mike Tyson, and literally knocked you back off your feet. After the third shot came in untouched I went out and stood behind the pitcher and officiated the game from there.

Another time, I was the lone umpire in St. Jacobs. It was a tight game going into the later innings and there was a runner on third base. The batter was a right-hander and the catcher called for an inside rise ball. This pitcher could also throw with great velocity and the ball came in with backspin and indeed rose dramatically, perhaps going up 2 feet in the last 12 or so. So here is the incoming pitch and its rising and going to cross over the inside portion of the plate. The batter is crowding the plate and so there is no way he's going to get the fat part of the bat on that ball if he's going to hit it at all. Now one of the things that a good umpire steels himself to do is not blink. Even if that ball is coming right straight on his face he has to have faith in the catcher that the ball is going to be caught. However, in a circumstance of this nature, that was not necessarily going to be the case. Indeed there was every degree of probability that this was going to be a tip foul and that the ball was going to just clear the catcher's glove and pretty much get me smack on the button and very nearly take my head off. Yet I dared not blink.

If I blinked or shut my eyes at all, in the split instant that the bat was coming around, there could be contact with the bat. If and when this happened there could well be a screamer shot down the third base line. Normally this would not necessarily be a problem because you had another official with whom to consult as to whether this was a fair or foul ball, but as I was alone there would be no such luxury. Therefore I dared not blink.

One fine night in Linwood I was again the sole official and the score was tied at zero in the later innings. There was a line drive hit which screamed out over top of the pitcher's head into centerfield and the batter was held to a single. However, the pitcher had flung up his glove hand in an effort to catch this line drive over his head and the glove left his hand. I thought I might have heard the *tick* of the ball touching his glove as it passed. Again, I could not ask anybody neutral there present. The batting team said, *no way*, and the defending team said, *yes way*. So what to do?

It was important to get it right if at all possible. If the ball had not made contact with the pitcher's glove then the play stands as is, the batter gets a single, and play continues. If, however, there was a ticking on the fly-by, then by rule the batter is awarded an automatic triple. No small matter of difference indeed.

I was pretty sure that I had heard it tick and awarded the triple, much to the delight of the batting team and the yowling consternation of those in the field, at least for the moment. I was, however, well respected for my judgments. It works like this, not only in baseball but in pretty much every aspect of life: get all of the obvious stuff right all the time, and when there is a matter open to close question for interpretation, people will give you the benefit of the doubt. And so it was this time. Happenstance provided that the runner did not score from third base, even though there was nobody yet out. The game was settled without question or controversy in a later inning.

After the game there was parking lot beer. Pickup trucks and cars pulled up and everybody sat on the bumpers the tailgates and had a beer. So along about into the second beer (a civilized period of time) the question was put to the pitcher who had thrown up his glove. Was there a ticking or not? He admitted that there had indeed been contact.

I remember the time when I had to quit playing on the field of battle and went back to officiating again after I had screwed up my arm. I was asked to join the battle, once more dressed in blue, so I rounded up all my paraphernalia; mask, shin pads, ball counter, chest protector, belt, uniform, safety shoes and so forth, and laid them all out on the table while I polished my shoes. My daughter Genevieve, who was rejoicing in her sixth or seventh summer at the time, came into the kitchen and looked at all the stuff on the table. *Daddy*, said she, *Did you used to be a vampire?*

CHAPTER

MennoTech
(Insomniac Therapy, Part III)

Until about 100 years ago, Mennonites and technology really didn't run into each other very much. Mennonites were pretty much like everybody else in those departments. Very few people had electricity or cars and, aside from steam engines, tractors were only starting to rear their noisy heads. Some Mennonites broke away from the horse and buggy crowd and got cars and electricity and tractors, others had black cars and were known as the Markham Mennonites. Some got colored cars and heathen clothing and were pretty much indistinguishable from everybody else, having the Mennonite name only, and were known as Conference Mennonites.

But there was tension within the faith over technology, particularly tractors. Some said that tractors were worldly and should not be allowed. All farming was to be done with horses or by hand, with perhaps a gasoline engine on the barn hill to run the threshing machine or grind the grain. No electricity, no tractors, and no cars.

Then, slowly, technology started to find cracks in the fences that they had tried to put up around their way of life. By the time I came along in the 1950s, even the Old Order Mennonites had tractors. Then some of them started to get electricity, but for use in the barn only. This was followed by the introduction of telephones but again, only for use in the barn. When I was a boy very few Mennonites did anything other than farming. There were as yet no industries, such as woodworking or the manufacture of other commodities, on the homestead. Radio and television and all other electronic devices were forbidden.

The custom of Mennonites was, and to some extent still is, that when a son got married he got a farm. This works out very well until you run out of land. So about 200 years ago the Mennonites ran out of land in Pennsylvania and migrated to Waterloo County. The first wave came to the area around Kitchener with names like Eby, Bricker, Schneider, and Erb. The second wave, approximately 20 years later, sported names like Martin, Bauman, Frey, and Brubacher. This second group bought 60,000 acres of Crown Land for the princely sum of roughly 30 cents per acre, parceled it off into 100 acre properties, got out the axes and saws and commenced to clear the land. The first property I ever owned was in Hawkesville, a small hamlet to the southwest of Elmira. The title deed read Part Lot 14B of the John Hawke survey, this same man responsible for parceling out the land in those days, and after whom the town is named. Hawkesville was once larger than Kitchener and sported several hotels, a dam, and gristmill and was a bustling metropolis. The reason that Kitchener (then Berlin) became larger than Hawkesville was because the railroad later went through Kitchener.

Then, along with the introduction of manufacturing facilities on the farm, it was realized that telephones had now become a matter of business survival. Soon after that the telephone was also allowed in the farmhouse. When the word came down from the Powers That Be to allow phones, Bell Canada was booked solid in rural installations for eight or nine months. I first became aware of it when an Old Order Mennonite lady came into the shoe shop with her husband's boots. He had some type of impediment that made him walk quite crookedly and there was question as to what exactly the man wanted done. To my great surprise, the lady said that he thought there might be some discussion and here is the telephone number. I pointed out where the telephone was on the wall over there, and it soon became clearly evident that she had never dialed a telephone in her life. I took her to be about 40 years old. So I had to dial the number and give her the receiver, whereupon I had to gently take it and reverse the matter so she was speaking into the business end, not the hearing end.

Radios, of course, were strictly prohibited. However some of the black car driving Mennonite teenage boys often had a portable transistor radio secreted somewhere around the vehicle, which was exhumed and enjoyed when the parents were not in attendance. One fine Sunday morning I was attending the golf services at our local club just outside of Elmira. We were waiting on the sixth tee and I heard music from

down the way. I thought maybe Craig Schwindt next door had opened a window, but the music got louder. Country and Western music getting louder and louder coming up the road, and sure enough, it was an Old Order Mennonite young man with a boom box blaring from under the buggy. He had his head back and he was singing away! Later that week I was in the hardware store, which also doubled as the local electronics shop, and John Pettie, the owner, told me about a young Mennonite lad who had come in with a mud-covered boom box the day before and wanted his money back. Claimed it didn't work right. In reality he had received a visitation from one of the deacons in the church, who had informed him that either he or the boom box would have to go. So the boom box went. At least for the time being.

Then came the day when I observed a horse and buggy Mennonite come driving up the road working on his BlackBerry. I wasn't quite sure whether to laugh or cry. But that has now become a fact of life for at least one flavor of horse and buggy Mennonite. These people are known as the David Martin group or Newborns. They have no electricity coming in from the road but they have a diesel generator where they make their own. They reach back into a verse of Scripture, *Be ye in the world but not of it*, so if they don't have electrical lines coming in from the road they are evidently in the world but they are not connected to it. However, the fuel truck comes in the lane to feed that diesel generator, which in turn feeds their industries which run on 550 Volt, 3-phase, electrical power and from which they communicate worldwide on the web and sell globally. But there is no electricity in the house, with the lights, heat, refrigeration, and even clothes dryers all running on propane.

They are not allowed to own or drive cars, but they can hire me or you to drive them anywhere, including now on holidays. A few months ago I was going into a Chinese buffet restaurant and a van load of David Martin Mennonites pulled into the parking lot. Out came a family of six, husband, wife, and four children, aged from roughly 18 down to six. They were followed by their heathen driver. As it happened, I was put into the same room with them and, perhaps for the first time in my life, saw them in public without their hats on. You never *ever* see Mennonites of this flavor in public without hats. It was hilarious! The lady and girls took off their bonnets and were bareheaded. The man and boys doffed their hats and sported what for all the world looked like very broad Mohawks. I was really tempted to take a picture of them eating but, I suppose that out of old habit and respect for their wishes that they not be photographed (something to do with Biblical *graven images*), I refrained. It is also possible that they may have known me from my professional capacity, but I suppose I just plain did not want to offend them. However, upon reviewing the matter, I was not invading their home at all. They were loose in public heathen spaces, and so should have been amenable to the customs of *our* house.

So technology in various forms and guises has invaded the Mennonite scene. On one hand some have Internet access and smart-phones, with doubtless much converse in worldly matters of entertainment. On the other hand most don't have a radio or television or electricity in the house. Recently I was passing through a nearby town and there was the buggy tied to a tree and the two teenagers sitting at a little table by the side of the road selling maple syrup. They were both intently working on their smart phones. Go figure.

Urias Brubacher Brubacher
1919 – 2000

CHAPTER 🐊🐊🐊🐊🐊

Wḩat a Crock! or Wḩat? A Croc?!

As a purveyor of foot comfort, at least in theory and hopefully in practice, it has been incumbent upon me to procure and distribute the very finest and most comfortable footwear to those in need. My father which art in heaven had a very serious thing about leather shoes. If a shoe was not made out of leather, it was anathema.

I can very well remember when shoes were pretty much made out of leather and nothing but leather. There might have been a cloth lining in the front of the shoe, but aside from that, various kinds of leather were pretty much it. For example, a work boot was made out of the hide of a full-grown cow while the lining of that same boot would have come from a bovine beast which was perhaps only halfgrown.

Men's dress shoes, at least the better variety, were made from calfskin on both the outside and the inside lining. When any mammal is born there is X amount of tensile strength per square unit of that hide. As the animal grows, the hide stretches so that the belly of a cow, now very much distended and stretched and weakened by age and weight, was certainly used for leather, but not for any purpose that demanded a high level of strength and flexibility. The area of the skin at the top of the back, on the other hand, was not nearly as stretched out and so was used in the areas of shoes or coats that required a high degree of wearability.

Back in the 1940s and 1950s, most of the every-day and Sunday shoes for women were made out of the skins of goats and lined with pigskin. A very common shoe for a lady was made from kid leather and had a Cuban heel, universally of a chunky shape and one and a half inches high, for daily wear. For their Sunday shoes very often the toe was a little bit pointed, and the heel was more in the shape of an hourglass and was thus known as a *Louis heel*.

One of the kings Louis, the fourteenth by that name, was a man of diminutive stature and caused his shoes to be made with high heels so that everybody did not look down on him. His shoemaker obliged, but did so in a manner that was not pretty enough for this king – it did the trick but was too chunky. So the designers got together and made the heel in the shape of an hourglass, and any heel to this day of that shape is known as a *Louis heel*.

This king also had small feet so he caused the toes of his shoes to be extended, thus giving increased balance and symmetry to the matter of his heels, and he was in less danger of falling flat on his face on account of his high heels. Having your king doing faceplants in front of everybody is not recommended in *The book of How to Make Royal Shoes*. (see chapter 17, verses 11 through 18, *How to make shoes so as not to flatten the king's Nose*). It was incumbent upon everybody to follow the example of the king in their fashions, and so it also became incumbent upon (I just love the phrase *incumbent upon*) all and sundry to wear high heels and extended toes. This kind of got out of hand. The toes became so long that people started to trip and fall and get flattened noses by mashing their collective proboscis on the floor and other hard flat objects. Not the king, you understand. He had holderupper people. To fix this they, the rest of his entourage, started to fasten ribbons to the fronts of their toes which many a time extended an extra foot (!) or more beyond the norm. They then fastened the ribbons around the calves of their legs in a crisscross manner and thusly the fashion of cross-garters was born.

Achtung! *There will be a short quiz on matters of similar historical redundancy at the end of the book. Failure to successfully complete the test will result in the contestant having to read the book all over again!*

One fine time I made another sojourn to South Florida to lend a hand to my buddy Howard in a technical problem in the proper shaping of shoes for a certain kind of medical problem. It was around the first part of autumn but South Florida was still plenty hot, especially in the daytime. Just for the sheer joy of it I rented a fire-engine red Ford Mustang convertible. This car was seriously cool. Cool, not in the sense of thermal units, but rather of prestige and, especially with the top down, it turned a lot of heads. It also had serious power and went like hell. But still nowhere near as fast

as the vette.

It was still hot enough in the environs of Fort Lauderdale that during the day I had to keep the top up and drive around with the air-conditioning on. A cool ride not so cool. I tooled up to Howard's place of business and he could see the car from his office window. He came out to look at this lovely red vehicle and, with a straight face, informed me that in South Florida only gay people drive red convertibles and where is my rainbow flag? It took me several seconds to realize that the nearby clanging sound was him jerking my chain. It was a fun car.

By the time the sun was pretty much down it had cooled off enough outside so that I could drive with the top down. Lots of fun indeed and still lots warm out to drive with no jacket.

I came upon a shopping mall which rejoiced in the title *Sawgrass Mills*. It was huge. I think it took approximately 20 minutes just to drive around the thing. Amazing. I am always on the lookout for polo shirts with breast pockets, and increasingly they appear to be hard to come by for reasons I don't understand. Into such pocket I like to put a pen or a shoehorn, perhaps my glasses, a business card or any other such item which needs a temporary home. I parked the Mustang hard by one of the men's clothing stores in this shopping mall and went inside.

There, to my everlasting mirth and delight, was a stand of fur-lined Crocs. Just imagine! South Florida, summer barely passed, and here they have Crocs which were lined with fur. Not, you understand, the real skin of an animal, but a furry type of substance nevertheless. I did not know whether to laugh or cry or pee my pants but all the same I bought two pairs of these critters. Friend Howard and I had pretty much the same size of feet and so I took one set around to his house and offered them to him as a gift. I had known that Howard was, and still is, very particular about his clothing and the shoes upon his feet. The very concept of him wearing Crocs did not compute, and he did not even allow them into the house. I had to leave them on the stoop until I left again later that evening. I took these and the other pair that I had bought for myself home to Canada, threw them into a corner on the shoe shelf near the mudroom door, and there they stayed for several years undisturbed.

As of this writing I live on an old farm a couple of hours north of Toronto near Creemore of beer fame. The old house and barn and driving shed sit on 100 acres pretty much seriously out in the middle of nowhere. Most of the time, I can see nor hear little of other human activity. The house was built in stages starting approximately 150 years ago, as was the driving shed, which was used to park such farm implements as needed to stay out of the weather. When I moved there I started to clean that shed out and turned it into a workshop where I can do things like woodworking or other such similar enterprises as are required around the farm or upkeep of the house.

The floor was originally dirt and all manner of other crapiolla which had insinuated itself into the substrate over a very long period of time. I excavated and substituted this with gravel, and the next year I poured a cement floor. In winter this concrete floor is very frigid. The cold comes up through the concrete and when I worked out there, even in my warmest boots, I was getting cold feet. I went back into the house, took off my boots, warmed my feet by the fire, and cast about for something warmer than my supposedly arctic temperature boots to wear on that cold shop concrete floor.

There in the corner were my fur-lined Crocs. I thought to myself, *What have I got to lose?* and gave them a go. They are without doubt the warmest footwear for that purpose that I have ever encountered. It was necessary to grab a pair of orthotics from one of my sets of running shoes and stick them in. Mission accomplished. Fur-lined Crocs with orthotics inside are my cold weather slippers to this day.

And oh yes: if you were near me now, that subterranean rumbling you might hear may well be father responding to my assertion that the most comfortable shoes which I employ are made from exactly zero real skins of four-legged beasts. Him rolling around in his grave.

CHAPTER

𝔗𝔯𝔲𝔠𝔨𝔰

The most useful and applicable equation in all of history is *not* the one made famous by Albert Einstein at all. The most universally applied equation is

$$B_s = T_s$$

which gives us

The size of the Boy = The size of his Truck

I am pretty sure Einstein never drove a truck. In point of fact he never even drove a car. I have it on some pretty good (but not perfect) authority that Einstein (aka Big Bert) liked to tool around in pickup trucks. He had a large bathtub placed in the back and got one of his buddies to drive him around. He did some of his best thinking while scrubbing himself and blithely enjoying the scenery sliding by on the back roads.

One fine day he was scrubbing and theorizing about his relatives, specifically about his Uncle Egbert, who was much enamored with being in charge of the proceedings of square dances. Now Einstein was one of those folk who was so smart I am pretty sure that, perhaps on a good day, he could have managed to tie his own shoes. This is how you tell really *really* smart people from the rest of us – they never figured out how to tie shoes. When they were supposed to do this as kids they were already bogged down in becoming Theoretical Physicists and formulating equations and such, so bits like this passed them by. Einstein was one of these. He could and did, however, make very clever equations about nearly anything, including Uncle Egbert.

Einstein's Uncle Egbert had a passion for square dancing and was very good at it. So much so, in fact, that he mastered the art of the "caller", or the person who calls out the instruction as to what form and configuration those on the floor are to accomplish as the dance progresses.

So here we have our erstwhile scrubber enjoying a lovely summers' day out in the pickup tub, and suddenly he has a BM (not *that*, ye of scatological bent – a Brilliant Moment). *Eureka*, he ejaculated, borrowing an expression from another chap so smart – you know - and one who froths forth all Greek to me, *By Jove I've got it!*

And so he had indeed. He had formulated an equation to explain the why's and wherefore's of his relative Uncle Egbert. It goes like this:

Egbert is equal to the task of Master of Ceremonies of the SquareDance

thus

$$E = MC^2$$

This in no small measure proved extremely helpful in future dealings with his family, and came to be known as The Theory of Relativity. But I digress. To Trucks.

My first truck was a toy fire truck when I was busy rejoicing in my ninth Christmas. It was (what else!) fire engine red and was a pumper truck. It had a spring-loaded cylinder in the back which was much like a syringe. You put the attached hose into a sink full of water, pulled on the back of the cylinder and sucked the cavity full. Upon release of the sprung mechanism the contents of the cavity were pumped out of the hose. This was very effective in the matter of the aqueous application down the necks of my older sisters, with predictable screechage and yowlage, together with much whackage upon the body of the perpetrator. But worth every drop of H_2O. Pretty sure my parents repented of the matter with alacrity. Every Christmas both the Eaton's and Simpson's catalogues came around. My younger sister Lorraine and I sat on the couch, side by each, and played a game called *choosing*. One of these catalogues was spread across our knees and we took turns wishing for the impossible. But after much lobbying I got my fire truck. Lightning strikes someplace. Somebody wins the lottery. I got a fire truck.

The first item of coherent projection of a small boy (other than peeing straight up while his diapers are changed) is to point at a truck. Then he learns to say *Vroom* while pointing at trucks. Graduation occurs where he says **Vroom *Vroooom*** while

pointing at trucks and saying the word **Truck**. Many have wondered at why small boys cry when there appears nothing much the matter. This is due to the subconscious frustration of the male of the species even at such a tender age in that nobody has as of yet instructed them in the art of articulating the word **Beer.**

Boys grow into young men and as they do so their appreciation for T&B (trucks and beer) is augmented in many satisfactory ways. They learn to congregate in discrete packs where they are preyed upon by The Fairer Sex, who seek an amalgamation often known as *Marriage*. This can well be a highly commendable circumstance, but the amalgamationee, subject to the restrictions of the amalgamationor, very many times (no matter how fair the sex was/is) jumps into a pickup truck in search of beer as a further expression fulfillment. Also doesn't scripture teach us, *Good sex worketh up a powerful thirst!?*

There are those who escape the snare. Some totally (bachelors), some sooner (the poor), and some later (the vast majority). The later variety usually belong to a very expensive club. Half off, eh! Yes. The Fairer Sex always get their half. *At least* half. Then the guys join the ranks of the poor.

My older brothers Gordon and Fred drove trucks. Lots and lots of trucks. They drove for Hoffman Feed Mills in Heidelberg which was owned by Amos Hoffman, elder in our church, and where we boys went to holiday in summer. Then they went on to do some trucking for Rothsay Concentrates, a company which took leftover animal parts and turned them into things which end up in animal food. To do this you have to hydrolyze, or render by boiling under high heat and pressure, whatever it is that's coming in. When all the do-dads and thingamabobs which are scurrying around in this stuff has been thoroughly eradicated, these substances, which shall go nameless just in case the reader is contemplating a meal any time soon, goes into the food chain. The resulting stuff coming out the other end of the process is called meat meal, bone meal, feather meal and other substances which are mixed into said animal food, and eventually re-enter the general food system in harmonious fashion. Needless to say, the raw goods involved here are anything but savory.

The process of hydrolyzation and rendered cooking is also one given over to serious, ah, olfactory result. Shall we just say that downwind knowledge about the matter was often appreciated (in the negative sense) miles away. When they brought truckloads of the raw goop to the plant, they backed up to a pit and dumped in the contents. A big auger then took the contents of the truck to its appropriate holding tanks, or many times directly to the processing portions of the plant. One particular time they had put in a larger pit and a new auger that could probably have handled an entire whole cow. This was a pretty serious piece of equipment and did the job very well.

The trucks came and went all hours of the day and night, and as it was a very big place, there were not always people in attendance to monitor every portion of the plant. And then the unthinkable happened. In the wee hours of the morning they found a truck backed up to the pit, its box still elevated over the pit and empty. The area had been slippery, and the driver of the truck was nowhere to be found. This, naturally, caused no small amount of consternation amongst the hallowed ranks. Alarms sounded. People came. There was no help for it but to fear the worst. It was necessary to go through the meat meal which had already been hydrolyzed and gone through the cookers. And sure enough; they found the buckle of the belt of the driver of the truck.

The grieving widow was looked after financially. A lot of safety measures were put in place. Nobody could henceforth go into that area, now guarded, alone. It was obviously too late for this go-around, but the matter was put into such order that it was extremely unlikely to repeat itself.

But the insurance company which had issued a massive payout didn't just take the matter at face value. They were suspicious and set a watch on our grieving widow. After a period of time it was determined that she was taking a lot of trips to California, a place she had never much habituated before. So they followed her and, sure enough, they found her rejoicing with her husband. He had made a miraculous comeback from the realm of the dearly hydrolyzed departed and was among the living in Monterey.

One fine night I went on a run with brother Freddy who was driving a feather packer for Rothsay. A feather packer looks like a big garbage truck. I suppose it looks like that because it *is* a garbage truck. We went to Campbell Soups in Listowel and picked up a load of feathers. At this plant vegies and birds came in one end and cans of soup out the other. In betwixt and between many unsavory but necessary projects occurred, including the removal and disposal of chicken feathers. A lot of feathers. They were soaking wet and were then put in a large overhead bin. Freddie backed his truck up under the bin, opened up the hatch, and down dropped these stinking wet feathers. And they were very heavy.

On this particular instance, he was way overloaded and was stopped by a pair of erstwhile fellows from the Ministry of Transportation (Ontario). They could see that this truck was in a serious burdensome situation. The springs were practically flat. So they asked Freddy, *What you got on there?* Freddy told them with a straight face, *It's just feathers.* They laughed and laughed! *Good one! That be the best ever!* Freddy told them to go up and check. They climbed up the side of the truck, opened the hatch, and sure enough. It was feathers! So they let him go.

Brothers Gordon and Freddie bought their own truck. It was a beauty, and rejoiced in the title *Iron Lion*. Never mind that it was mostly fibreglass and aluminum, at least the frame was steel. A 1971 Kenworth cab-over, brand spanking new; a beautiful machine. They hauled transport trailers for a company called Fruit Belt Trucking out of St. Catherines, Ontario. One time Freddy was sent to Halifax and picked up a load of herring fish in oil in wooden casks. It was hot summer. The wooden floor of the trailer box had to absorb any of the spillage that occurred from leaking barrels. By the time Freddy got to Chicago and they unloaded his cargo, the whole place reeked of fish. Then Freddy was instructed to bring back a load of strawberries to Toronto. You can imagine the sale value of the strawberries not being exactly what they should be if they smelled like they had been cured in fish oil, so Freddy phoned dispatch in St. Catherines. He explained the problem and they said, *Well, what about the coffee? Huh?*, Says Freddy. *Yeah. Did you use the coffee? Go and get a dozen cans of coffee and sprinkle them all over the floor of the truck. Wait a couple hours and it will be all fixed up.*

Freddy thought they were jerking his chain. The trailer really stank badly under the hot summer sun. What was coffee going to do? But dispatch insisted, so Freddy got coffee, sprinkled it on the floor, took a power nap, and then washed the whole thing out with a pressure washer. And by golly it worked! I guess this is why when you smuggle a lot of drugs, at least in the olden days, you filled your suitcase with coffee so that the sniffer dogs couldn't smell the drugs. But then, of course, they taught the dogs to smell coffee and then that ploy didn't work anymore. In this case, however, it did, and the strawberries arrived at the Toronto Food Terminal minus the smell of fish.

That truck was a beauty and mostly went up and down the eastern seaboard of

Canada and the Excited States of 'Merica. One fine December they took a refrigerated truck full of Christmas trees to Miami. There had been a great whack of snow in Quebec, whence came the trees, and some of this snow survived the trip intact. When they off-loaded the trees in Miami there were a bunch of little boys running around gleefully having a snowball fight – boys who never had seen snow in their entire lives.

Unfortunately that truck was not destined to live to a ripe old age. They were driving down Highway 15 beside Susquehanna River towards Harrisburg in Pennsylvania and it was late at night in December when a drunk pulled out in front of them. The crash caused the steering mechanism on their truck to jam and the Iron Lion went through the guard rails made of heavy steel cables. This cleaned off all the axles as it went over and through them and then they tobogganed down through a grove of trees into the Susquehanna River. It was early winter and there was ice floating around. Freddie doesn't remember much of it, but they pulled him unconscious out of the water several hundred yards downstream. The impact and the jostling about had ripped all his clothes off, so out he came naked as a jaybird. A real still-alive miracle out of that freezing river. Another miracle was that there was no lasting damage to brother Freddie. Eventually, when they pulled what remained of that truck from the river, it was nothing but a heap of junk piled about three or four feet on the road. That was the end of the Iron Lion. Too bad. She were a real beauty.

I've driven a fair few trucks in my lifetime as well. When I came back from my travels, one of my jobs was driving a 10-ton truck for a local farmer. He had a lot of land and a lot of cattle, together with a continuously large collection of that which emanates from the north ends of said south-bound beasts. To attend to this situation, he got a contract with a sawmill to take away the sawdust and also the debarkage. The bark of hardwood trees is very hard on saw blades, so they had these two huge rollers which looked like massive medieval weapons of warfare with large nasty steel spikes sticking out of them. They rolled the logs between these spiked cylinders, which ripped off all the bark before they went into the saw. The blade of that saw was 5/16 of an inch thick (or about 7 1/2 mm) and six feet in diameter. If the mill was busy they made a lot of sawdust and debarkage, and the farmer I worked for needed a lot of this material for bedding the cattle.

Halfway between Kitchener and Guelph, hard buy Breslau, is a place called Hopewell Creek. Near there was an establishment owned by Seagram's, a large company who were distillers of whiskey. Canadian whiskey is mostly made out of corn. Some is made out of rye, but mostly it's corn. When they are done with the distillation process, there is a huge quantity of mushy crud left over. This mash is called corn distillates. Whatever starches and so forth needed to turn corn into alcohol have by this time largely been removed. However, there are residual nutrients in it, and instead of hauling it away to the dump, some wizard in the offices of Seagram's decided that they should feed it to cattle. Animals of the bovine persuasion like this stuff, and so they thought, alright, fine. Let us build barns and feed cattle. So they did. On a chunk of adjacent property to their whiskey storage and aging facility at Hopewell Creek they erected four barns, each 600 feet long. Normally cattle need bedding like straw or shavings or similar, but this costs money. The wizards decided to circumvent this problem by sloping the concrete stalls so that the effluent which comes out of the north end of all those south-bound cattle beasties would run away into lagoons they prepared hard by the bush just over there.

All went exactly to plan except for one minor detail: what they didn't calculate in their equation was that when cattle are fed mostly these corn distillates, it passes through them at a very high rate of speed. Also in significantly greater quantities than anticipated. If cattle are fed normal stuff like hay, corn, and chopped grain you have one sort of requirement later on. If they enjoy a pretty much steady diet of corn distillates, the matter increases exponentially.

Pretty soon all this schitteolla filled the lagoons to capacity and then overflowed their banks and out into the bush beyond. Under the summer sun it not only smelled to high heaven but it also smelled to either Kitchener or Guelph, each of them miles away, depending on the direction of the breeze. So the health department came in and shut them down. The place sat empty for a considerable period of time, until the farmer for whom I worked rented the premises to fatten cattle – about 1200 of them. Of course, that many cattle need a lot of bedding instead of just letting the crud run away. That's where I came on the scene. I would bring 10-ton truckloads of sawdust and debarkage to this establishment, and the manure was soaked up.

Along about this time brother Freddie and cousin Wally were framing a house for my high school history teacher, one Robert Huschka (R.I.P.). It was summer and Freddy and Wally where creating the rafters for the roof of the house. In those days you didn't buy them, you had to get a skill-saw and cut them by hand. Then you nailed them together and wrestled them up into position. You made a pattern rafter first. Then you placed lumber and traced each piece off the pattern and went to cutting, with the lumber sitting on sawhorses. By the time they were nearly done there was quite a pile of sawdust, at least by the standards of a hand operated power saw, underneath the sawhorses. It was quite impressive, and might have been – oh I don't know – something on the order of what might have filled three or four basketballs. This is a lot of sawdust.

It was a hot day in late Spring and I swung by the building site with some cold beverages, for which they were suitably thankful. We were sitting in the shade of a tree drinking our pop hard by my truck full of this debarkage and sawdust from the mill, soon to head off to do the cattle bedding. We thought it would be a good idea to augment the pile of sawdust from their rafter work, so I backed up the truck to the sawhorses, opened one of the back doors, and maybe an extra half a cubic yard of my sawdust fell out in the environs of their own pile. It looked pretty cool. Soon after, Mr. Huschka came to observe the progress, the teaching day now done. He inspected the proceedings and was very, very impressed by the amount of work that must've occurred to have that pile of sawdust sitting there. This, of course, clearly in violation of anything that stood to any sort of logic, because what comes of the skill saws is a fine powder compared to what came off of that huge sawmill blade. Thus it was reinforced upon all and sundry that our dear friend Robert Huschka, though an amazing fellow in many fine respects and an excellent and thoughtful teacher was, in matters practical, a complete disaster. The account of this episode made the rounds and was cause for much mirth among his family and friends.

Various trucks came and went when I was working for the farmer. One time, and again it was a summer's day, I delivered a load of sawdust up country. Whatever my employer did not use, I sold to other people who also used it as bedding. I was driving on a tar-and-chip country road which was slick under the summer sun. Trucks going over it had sucked up tar and so it formed a very, very slippery tarry surface on top. It had rained and now the sun was out hot and steamy. I had already delivered the load and was coming towards a stop sign with the truck box empty. There was a sheen of water on top of this tar, and I didn't pick up on this in time. I went to brake and nothing happened. Quite probably I was going faster than I should have, at least for the conditions. Once more the brakes were applied and there was precious little in the line of deceleration occurring. It was as slick as greased schitteolla. So now I'm coming up to my stop sign and crossing in front of me is car driven by an adult lady with maybe four or five kids as passengers.

You know how they say that in a life-threatening crisis everything slows down into discrete slices of time? Well, I found out that this is true. I could see very clearly that unless evasive action occurred, or a miracle, that there was going to be a collision, and with probably catastrophic results. I'm no hero. I don't recall thinking about it at all. It's just one of those things. A hand took the steering wheel of the truck and turned it to the right and into the ditch and that's all that I remember of that. I'm pretty sure that the lady and the kids in the car never had a single clue how close they came to a visit from the Angel of Death. I suffered a bunch of scrapes and bruises and they picked a lot of glass out of from my ears. Also a generous helping of lacerations. I felt like I had spent half an hour in a clothes dryer on bennies. The truck was a piece of rubble.

That was more than 40 years ago. I have driven miscellaneous trucks since then. Right now I drive a pickup made by Chevy. It is silver and is an Ado. A Silver Ado. I like it. It has gizmos on it and computerized stuff of all kinds, such as a backup camera and automatic slip resistant things which will go on without being told. It purportedly stabilizes me and will discreetly apply pressure to the brakes of any wheel which apparently tells the computer that things are going astray. It does stuff I have no clue about and probably never will because, at last count, I am no longer 12 years old. But it's a nice truck. I like it. Hardly a day goes by when I don't throw something into the box in the back and haul around things to do with the farm, or whatever needs to be ferried about for family and friends. I have a truck and trailer, and all is well.

In The Olden Days, we used to pile a case of beer into my truck and drive around country roads partaking of said beer and just hanging out with others of similar ilk. We don't do that anymore. Drinking beer while driving trucks is no longer politically correct, and, if truth be known, probably never was a good idea, even when the traffic was very thin. It was nothing in the bad old days (or were those the good old days?) to partake of liquids after a hot night baseball game, a cooler of beers in the back of a pick-up, imbibe a couple of beers with the boys and then another one or two on the way home. We don't do that anymore. It seemed very civilized at the time, but they frown on it now, so we don't.

But once in a while it's nice to get in the truck and take a beer or two and go to a place of meditation. Watch the wildlife go by. Once in a while I espy an indigenous species which is highly inspirational, but hazardous with which to attempt dealings. Especially at my advanced years. A passing beautiful young woman requires appreciation. When a man gets old and he observes such a one, the old war horse smells the battle, strains against his tethers, and waits for *Cry havoc, and let loose the Dogs of War!* But then reality, like the fog, creeps in on little cat feet. What if the dog chasing the bus actually caught the bus? What the hell would he do with it? Whirling tires have a nasty habit of removing teeth.

So I just sit in Chevy and enjoy the beer and the wildlife. Have another sip of beer. Yes, I know. I'm not supposed to sip beer in my truck. But once in a while I do. Boys do that. Boys and their trucks and their beer, and meditating on the ones that got away.

So let us consider the ultimate truck. What would be the most awesome truck ever?

Let us also lay to one side minor impediments such as the rules of the road, the size of highways, the encroachments of buildings, the depressing confines of overpasses, restrictions of bridges and other such matters which have hitherto prevented the creation of the Ultimate Truck. If all these monkey-wrenches flung into the gears of truckery were removed, and the Ultimate Truck were to be brought into fruition, how would such a truck creation grace our landscape?

The answer, of course, is big. Very Big.

I have seen The Vision of Truck. I myself am nothing, merely the scribe to the Prophet of the religion Truckery. Bow down, oh ye heathen truckless masses who drive bootless electric cars, miserable excuses for overgrown sewing machines. Offer WorthShip to the god Truck, for Truck is great, and shall be more Great, and Mighty, and even now sends his children godlings Ram 1500, Sierra 3500, and Super Duty Platinum to reward the Faithful! Also the gods Mack and Peterbuilt and Kenworth. Ye shall harken unto these gods or they shall slay ye all of the tiny cars. Drive aside, all ye of hybrid putt-putts! The gods of Truck shall take up the lion's share of the roads and shall squash the tiny tin (not Tim) of the land. Let there be Truck!

So if a man had no limits placed upon his Truck, it would be about the size of Manhattan. It would dwarf the entire American aircraft carrier fleet, burn the equivalent energy of several A-bombs per second, sink into the solid bedrock nearly to the axles, create enough noise to be heard on the other side of the continent, have the hauling power to pull Iceland, need a helicopter to lift the driver to the control room, and make tracks visible from the moon with the naked eye.

Now That Be Truck!

Let $T_m = Truck$

$$T_m = \int_0^\infty \sin\alpha \pm \sin\beta \; x2 \sin\frac{1}{6}(\alpha \pm \beta)\cos\frac{1}{2}(\alpha \mp \beta) + 3\pi 500r^2 + \delta_y^{45pt} - \sqrt[7]{56\sqrt{25a - 300gxt}} \; kgGVW$$

$Since \begin{bmatrix} 30 & 45 & 781 \\ 35 & 23 & 232 \\ 56 & 69 & 29 \end{bmatrix} * f(x) = dfa_4 + \sum_{n-1}^\infty \left(4\cos\frac{n\pi x}{L} + box_n \sin\frac{n\pi x}{L}\right) and \; \frac{-23\pm\sqrt{b15^2 - 4*23c}}{30} = 7.8^{23} BHP$

$and \; if \; H = 780, W = 367, L = 1378, then \; \oiint_0^\infty \cos\alpha H + \cos\beta W + \tan\theta L = 2\cos\frac{1}{2}(\alpha H + \beta W) = m = 1.234^{34}$

$because \; E = mc^2, \; E_m = 1.234^{19} * 2.99729 * 10^{10} = 2.6507 * 10^{19}$ megatons of TNT $\therefore MPG \cong 4.3^{-12}$

$thus \; acceleration \; (A) = \sum_4^3 16 + \forall \frac{dy}{dx} \; x \; \lim_{n\to\infty}\left(1 + \frac{1}{n}\right)^n - \sqrt[3]{1.34629} + 1103°C \; x \; e^{-i\omega t} + \iiint .847 + 1.65$

$or \stackrel{def}{=} x \; +\max_{0\le x\le 1} xe^{-x^2}\sqrt{\infty x\infty} \; - \; x = \csc^{-1} 3.14528 + AXe^{-i\omega t} \; and \; y = \frac{-b\pm\sqrt{b^2 - 4ac}}{2a} \; so \; V_{17}^5 \; x6.52947$

$gives \; T_m \; or$

TRUCK!

CHAPTER 🎯🎯 🎯🎯🎯

𝔇𝔢𝔳𝔬𝔱𝔦𝔬𝔫𝔰

It was incumbent upon my father which art in heaven to spiritually furnish the torturous road to my salvation and that, naturally, of my siblings, with repetitious readings of the Scriptures, prayer power, and M&M's (multitudinous meditations).

This commenced daily with the morning reading of the Bible and prayer before breakfast. Every morning at eight o'clock, irrespective of any other activity or climatic disaster, or any such circumstance which may in a normal household have occurred to disrupt routine, we read the Bible and prayed. There was no deviation from this routine. Ever. Not that there is anything inherently wrong with these activities. If everybody did a little more of this and a little less yowling at each other, I suspect the world would be a better place.

At eight o'clock sharp we, all nine of us, gathered around the table, each of us with our own Bible open in front of us. The King James Version of the Scriptures was read aloud, verse by verse. We went around the table in a counter-clockwise fashion and each one of us had to read from the Holy Scriptures, one verse at a time. These readings sort of followed a chronology of the unfolding of events in the holy land of ancient Biblical times. We were very big on going into the details of stuff like Moses and the bulrushes, Joshua and his whole pack of henchbuddies marching around the walls of Jericho and blowing trumpets until those walls fell down, David and Goliath and firing rocks through G's forehead (*It simply had never entered my head before...*) and many other scenes of God-fearing heroism.

Portions of Scripture were either omitted or glossed over with great alacrity, however, because there was stuff in there considered to be too gruesome and/or racy for us kids. Thereby our father w.a.i.h. spared himself the indignity of having to expostulate on some of the less savory matters contained therein.

Stuff like in Genesis, for example, which dealt with certain Jewish folks going and trashing the neighboring tribe on account of one of those heathen dudes had kidnapped a daughter of one of the children of Israel and forced her into marriage. The warrior men of the Jews were pretty ferocious, yet offered the men of the tribe who did the kidnapping a way out of a battle if they submitted to circumcision. The choice between adult circumcision and a battle in which you are liable to come out extremely dead is an evil dilemma. In this particular case the kidnapping guys submitted to having their foreskins cut off. Yes, y'all got it right: this be the pointy end of their peckers. Yikes! Then it goes on to tell us that, *While they were yet sore* (meaning the guys who were missing bits of their peckers) and were not in prime fighting form, the Jews came back and slaughtered them all anyway. We mostly jumped right over that one.

I only discovered this later while I was in church and paging through the Bible during a particularly boring sermon. There were lots of those. I acquainted myself with some of the less savory portions of the King James Version of the Holy Scriptures while some yahoo up there in the pulpit droned on and on and on…

There was also the chapter in Genesis where a man's married brother had died and this man was instructed by God to marry the widow and *Go in unto her. Going in unto her* was their way of saying that the guy had to marry her and drag her off to bed while proceeding to prepare his equipment in such a manner that he could implant his fluids into the widow's appropriate receptor location. Evidently he did not consider this to be a good idea, not sure why. We are not told, but maybe he just plain did not have the hots for this gal. In any case it is recorded, and I quote, *He spilled it on the ground.* I don't think we need to have an illustration or video here, but at any rate it greatly angered the Almighty God who smote him. And when God *smote you* then that was usually the last chapter in your earthly experience and *you stayed smitten.* End of lesson – adios, stage left. The real fun juicy chapters in Genesis of this nature never graced our breakfast table.

At family devotions in the mornings, not only did we do this scriptural counter-clockwise round table of saintly dissertation, but upon its cessation or, as I later

thought on it, *It's mercy killing for the day*, there was read by our father which art in heaven a page from a tear-off daily calendar rejoicing in the title *Choice Gleanings*. Every day a Gleaning of Choice commenced with a verse from the Holy Scriptures followed by some wise commentary by a person who pretty much thought hand-in-glove with father and his henchbuddies. The elders in our church and, presumably all of their Heavenly Henchbuddies, peered down on this family aggregation, all the while nodding with approval. At the bottom of the page was a verse of poetry which may have been devised surrounding some salient point in the verbiage above, or perhaps stolen from a hymn.

When all of the above solemn mumbo-jumbo was complete it was time for prayer. Each of us in turn was obliged to offer some serious prayerful commentary or supplication before the Almighty. We might seek God's intercession in the matter of somebody who was sick or perhaps a missionary out in deepest darkest Africa who is in danger of either getting perforated with spears or getting munched on by crocodiles or beset by tsetse flies in the course of the acquisition of malaria or some such. I never remembered that we prayed for ourselves because it was considered evident, or at least outwardly so, that we had all been saved by grace through faith and were on our way to heaven and so we did not need any extra help than what we already had. We prayed again in turns counter-clockwise around the table, one of our number offering the obligatory dissertation daily.

I dreaded this. When my turn came, looking back on it, I suspect that I had the intellectual capacity to have memorized the words and phrases which were required to bring us all before the Throne of Grace. The problem was that I was a Bad Boy and it was already then recognized that there was a high degree of probability that I was headed straight for hell. But I was still young with benefit of the doubt to be afforded me in that the final hell-bound chapter was yet to be written. So I, a sinner, was obligated to pray.

Many years later I wrote this song:

JUST ANOTHER SINNER

When I was a boy my daddy said son,
You think that you are having fun,
But look ye here it makes me sad
To see that you are turning out bad.

Your hand is in your mother's purse,
Now you should pray this Bible verse,
So Good Book words I tried with feeling
and but that prayer did not pass the ceiling.

'Cause I'm
Just another sinner,
Just another sinner,
Just another sinner on the way to his grave.

I'm just another sinner,
Just another sinner,
Just another sinner on the way to his grave.

So I went out into the world,
Did evil till my toes were curled.
Women and whiskey, powders too,
Smoke that weed 'til the room turned blue.

Wake up inside a garbage dump,
My head sprouting a goose egg bump.
Life's a horse radish sandwich! It sure is bitter,
Some days I believed I'm better off a quitter.

'Cause I's
Just another sinner,
Just another sinner,
Just another sinner going cold to his grave.

I'm just another sinner,
A lost and lonely sinner,
A lost damned sinner on the way to his grave.

My dad was right! I turned out bad,
Good thing he's dead – he'd sure be sad.

Life's a be-atch, it will not do,
To keep on thus – it sucketh poo.
So I thought I would set things right,
And I became a Menn-O-Nite.

No more shall I head for the cliff,
Feel better now, yet even if

I'm still another sinner,
Just another sinner,
A lost and lonely sinner
Going cold to his grave.

Just another sinner,
Now a Mennonite sinner,
A black-hatted sinner on the way to his grave.

Lord have mercy,
Tender love and mercy,
Mercy on us sinners headed cold to the grave.

Love shine on the sinner, all us sinners,
Each and e'vry sinner on the way to the grave,
I'm just another sinner on the way to my grave.

The Scriptures teach us that *By grace are ye saved through faith - it is not by works of your own. It is the gift of God, lest any man should boast.* But turn over the pages about an eighth of an inch beyond and a different text reads *By their works shall ye know them.* In other words, even if you supposedly accept God's salvation by faith through the finished work of Jesus Christ on the cross, you had better live a good life otherwise you might not be saved at all. *By their works shall ye know them.* And being considered a Bad Boy on account of I greatly enjoyed *Mad Magazine* and candy and hockey games, not to mention potato chips and Coke (that dark devil drink), that it was clearly evident I went to church merely to obey the tenets of the household. It doubtless appeared highly probable to father and his h-buddies that I was a bad apple. The black sheep – maybe even a goat. The Scriptures teach that at the last judgment the sheep munching on all that spiritually-scented ambrosia are going to get a one-way up-ticket, and the goats are going the other way, down that elevator over there, the one with the smell of fire and brimstone coming out of that big clattering elevator shaft every time the doors open. The up-elevator to heaven will be relatively small; the downward shoot to perdition a very large enclosure, with all the goats chewing on candied thistles washed down with the demon drink. All herding in and down.

Sarah Bauman Bowman
1921 – 2008

CHAPTER
DR

I have been to the Dominican Republic a fair few times. It is the eastern portion of the island in the Caribbean, originally Hispaniola, which it shares with Haiti. The people of the Dominican Republic have pretty much nothing. The people of Haiti have less than nothing. What they do share, however, is lots of sunshine and sand beaches, and it is much beloved as a vacation and or retirement destination by peoples from colder climes including Canada, but more thickly inhabited by Germans.

I was introduced to the joys of DR by Dave Delandrea, a medical doctor who lives and practices his trade in North Bay, Ontario. I'm not exactly sure how he came to learn about my skills as a shoemaker, but I think it might well have been indirectly through mutual acquaintances, all of whom are loosely connected via the brethren assemblies, the church to which I belonged. If memory serves, Dave's father was a minister in this church and preached in front of our congregation from time to time.

At any rate the good Dr. Dave came to me in the early days of my career and wanted a pair of special shoes made. There did not appear to be anything wrong with his feet and, as my business was primarily in medical necessity, it seemed a little bit strange. Then it came out. Dave wanted elevator shoes.

Dave and his wife Carol, an Irish beauty rejoicing in red hair, green eyes, and long legs, was taller than him by a wee smidgen. These people were socialites. Dave was heavily involved in the Ontario Medical Association in some capacity or other, and he and Carol greatly enjoyed going to high-profile social events in Toronto. Nothing wrong with that, but the problem was that when they made their grand entrance to the charity ball or joined the rest of them on the dance floor, if Carol wore any sort of shoes with heels at all, she was clearly taller than he was.

So I was commissioned to make a pair of shoes for Dave which had disguised in them extra heel height of maybe three or four inches. The toes of the shoes looked normal, and one would have had to hoist up the legs of his trousers to determine that there was anything different about his shoes, in this case black dress shoes, than anybody else's. So I made him elevator shoes. They worked, and the striking couple could attend their favorite fashionable events without Dave having to borrow a step ladder to gaze into Carol's ravishing green eyes.

Let me explain that Dave is a seriously good guy. Carol is too, but of course not a guy. Great people, and considerably more acquainted with the finer things in life than with which I and my family had hitherto known. They sort of took us under their wing and from time to time we would go to North Bay and stay with them in their very gracious and spacious home on the edge of the cliff overlooking the town. They had things in there unheard of, such as a guest suite with a hairdryer and extra toothbrushes and toothpaste in the drawer in the bathroom. They themselves were always very accommodating and gracious hosts. Dave and I would often go golfing and we were very evenly matched. Both of us were quite competitive, yet in a very good-natured manner, and we got along very well. Sometimes when one of our golf balls would settle onto a chunk of real estate which appeared to be designed specifically to make us pissed off, he would say, *Just consider it a matter of unlimited opportunity*. Not a bad philosophy – plenty of life's adversities should well be taken in that light.

Along about that time I was introduced to the DR. Both Dave and his brother, Jon, owned property in a gated community called Costambar right on the ocean just outside of Puerto Plata. They both owned condominiums on the ground floor of an eight-plex, four up and four down. The views were wonderful out across the lovely sand beach and the ocean, with its coral reef maybe 50 yards out into the water. The reef was completely submerged during high tide but poked its top out at low tide. We often went snorkeling out there and it was very beautiful, with all the colored fish and the lobsters and much other sea life which I had never spied before. We had to be very careful not to cut ourselves on the coral.

The property was surrounded by the type of fence which would only keep the honest people out. Even though this was supposed to be a guarded and gated community the perimeters were very porous and the security lax. To this end, at the driveway with its gate entering onto this property, there was a security guard who had his own little hut. I am not exactly sure what the business arrangements were but each of the owners of this eight-plex theoretically clubbed together to pay for a guard 24-7. I soon came to realize that whatever it was in theory, in actual practice it was much the same concept as the centerline on Airport Road – *a loose guideline for discussion purposes.* Many times the guard was not there. This, in and of itself, was not necessarily a felonious matter, as the guard may have been commissioned by one of the condo owners to go and do something such as buy rum at the little store up the hill, or zip over to the golf course with a piece of bent re-rod to shake down half a bag of lemons or limes, these to assist in the garnish of Cuba Libres. Lots of times, however, the day guard had been moonlighting someplace else and had found a convenient place to sleep during the day. The majority of the guard's duties were performed at night, when he would be seen at all hours securing the perimeter with a flashlight. The people of DR are extremely poor and the principal form of national sport is liberating anything not nailed down, especially stuff owned by foreigners.

The supply of electricity was also very problematic. Power was created using an oil-fired generating system over by the harbor. Depending upon the economic circumstances of the moment, there may or may not have been funds available to purchase oil, so electricity was rationed. The power might go off for three or four hours or even for a whole day and nobody knew for sure when it would come back on again. This was not all that big a deal for the most part except that the overhead ceiling fans would not work and there was no air-conditioning. And as it could get pretty warm there, even in winter, this could result in some sweaty nights. Also the water pumping system depended upon electricity and, even though the water was heated with a solar panel, when we went to take a shower it was generally done with great speed because we never knew when the water would quit.

We pretty much always flew with Air Canada. They had a direct flight that went down and back nearly every day. Once in a while Dave's wife Carol came along, but mostly it was an event for the boys. One particular time there were four of us, Dave and brother Jon, friend Jack, who was an accountant in Kitchener, and crazy George. I never did quite figure out what George actually did for a living but I think it had something to do with real estate. At any rate, while we all liked to party, George

enjoyed his partying in liquid form considerably above and beyond the call of normal partying duty.

Once this started already on the flight down. The drinks were free with the flight and George was very fond of vodka. The drinks cart did not pass our seats with nearly the frequency that pleased George. We had aisle seats right across from each other and, as the drink cart settled in to serve very close to us, he looked at me and cocked his head and I looked at him and nodded my head. He then performed some form of diversionary tactic to capture the attention of the flight attendant to his side, whereupon I liberated a whole litre of vodka from the tray under the cart and hid it behind my back. Sleight of hand at its very finest, and probably only able to be so slickly managed by those who had already received considerable inspiration and courage via the auspices of that same drink cart.

By the time we hit the tarmac at Puerto Plata International Airport George was comatose. We dragged him off the plane and propped him up against a large suitcase while we hunted for the rest of our luggage. In those days the terminal consisted of a couple of tin shacks, and the luggage was simply thrown out of the aircraft onto the side of the runway. Everybody figured out what belonged to whom and then took it through customs, such as it was. Depending on who was minding the gates that particular evening the entry fee was fixed at a certain number of American dollars. Also it was incumbent upon every person to pay an exit tax of about $10 US. Dave, however, was a VIP due to his charitable medical connections, so he got swift passage through the formalities together with his traveling companions, which in this case included a seriously slumbering crazy George. No questions asked.

Then the adventure of the taxi. Brother Jon's Spanish was pretty good because he had been studying with a private tutor for about one hour every day for more than a year. During that hour he would simply disappear off the face of the earth and his wife figured that he must have a mistress stashed someplace. The proof of the truth however was in his ability to speak the lingo, and so Jon did the necessary negotiations with the drivers of the taxis. A bargain was struck and the taxi driver was commissioned to ferry the four of us to Costambar in a vehicle which looked like it was held together with duct tape and binder twine, and was also in size woefully inadequate to the task. Not to be deterred, the first item of business was to deal with crazy drunken George. No problem. We slabbed him out on the roof of the taxi, a set of golf clubs under his head for a pillow, the other bags of clubs on either side and under his knees. Several other suitcases were then piled around and the whole mess strapped down to the bars of the roof rack. The trunk was crammed with luggage, we all piled into the taxi, with the rest of the luggage thrown in on top of us, and off we went.

The road was full of potholes and the driver had to weave his way around them. It was not a very fast process but soon the lights of the town started to appear. On instruction from Jon, we pulled into the place where there was a house and what appeared to be a large open BBQ oven in the front yard. Jon got out and banged on the front door. All was dark inside, as it was now about 10 o'clock at night. But Jon kept hammering and after a while the light came on and a face peered out of the window. John was hollering something in Spanish and brandishing a bunch of American dollar bills in his hand. Presently the door opened and, after more conversation, there appeared six whole barbecued chickens for which money was exchanged. Nothing so fancy as packaging, and the birds were soon being devoured as we bumped and wove our way down the holey (but not righteous) road.

Then there was another stop at a shack whose lights proclaimed the words COLD BEER. So we soon were washing down our pollo naturale with lovely cold beer. Along about this time crazy George sort of regained consciousness and started hollering and banging on the roof of the car to which he was trussed. So there was no help for it but to stop again and have Jon pour a beer down his throat to slake the terrible thirst which was now consuming him. George wanted free of his bonds, strangely enough, but Jon just patted him on the shoulder and said we were almost there.

And we were almost there. After passing through the gates of Costambar we were soon unloading our stuff and our George who, logically enough, was not exactly a happy camper. He was pointed in the direction of his lodgings and his bed and passed from our knowledge until the next morning. But the chicken was good, the beer was good, and the night was lovely. Soft sea breezes washed warmly up from the ocean and it was time for a beach walk.

Every time I set foot on the sands of Costambar I take search within myself as to why I most of the time perch where I do. Snow, cold, sleet, slush, frozen crappiola of all sorts. It is no wonder that the peoples of these islands, who, by our standards at least, have nothing, are very happy people. It is as though nature says, *Ahhh… Here you are again. Back home. Enjoy!* And so we do, and then inexplicably go back to the sleet and the crap and the snow and all of the crud which requires shovelling.

Later the next morning, after groceries have been procured from the Super Mercado up near the top of the hill, we relax on one of the front porches overlooking the beach. The time is first beer, which roughly translates into 11 a.m. This is a very civilized portion of the day to crack open one's first beer. Walking up the beach come the inevitable urchins peddling their wares. Most often for sale or rent are their sisters, all of whom are guaranteed to be virgins, yet all extremely skilled in the arts of carnal pleasure. Their offers are politely declined. Then these same boys offer to catch lobsters, for our culinary enjoyment, on the coral reef just offshore. This meets a more positive response whereupon they disappear and soon come back with running shoes, eyewear suitable for a swimming pool, and a coat hanger.

For the next hour or so we are treated to the site of these young boys searching the coral reef and coming up with lobsters. The unraveled coat hanger is employed like a fish stringer, with the pointy end piercing the tales of the lobsters while the hooked end keeps them from sliding off. When there are a dozen or so good-sized lobsters impaled upon the wire, the boys come up to the porch and the negotiations with Jon began. I am not exactly sure of the numbers, but I think that the opening asking price was about $15 and the final sale price was about half that.

So there we are, the proud possessor's of roughly a dozen lobsters at least one pound each, and this is going to be a very spectacular supper indeed. From somewhere comes a huge pot, firewood collected, the pot suspended full of lobsters above the beach fire and taken back into one of the condos. The remainder of the chickens from the previous night are also brought forth, and there is a chicken and lobster-fest garnished with lemons and limes from the trees just over there. All washed down with El Presidente beer. I am not sure how food gets a whole lot better than that.

Besides relaxing on the beach and drinking beer, the chief pass-time was golf. There were two notables from which to choose; the full course across town at the Jack Tar Village Resort, or the nine-hole cow pasture just up the way from the condo.

The term *club-house* was loosely applied to the tin shack at the start of the pasture where the caddies lurked, and where also the head honcho took our greens fees and ceremoniously deposited them into an old shoe-box.

It was incumbent upon the four of us to hire five caddies. The fifth caddie's sole responsibility was to fetch beer. There are few finer circumstances in life than to go golfing under the hot tropical sun with a caddie to carry your clubs while you walk the golf course with a cold beer wrapped in newspaper in your hand. It is the responsibility of your caddie to figure out into which portion of the cow pasture or the hedges or the brambles and the briars your ball has settled, thereupon to rearrange the location of said ball so that it could be struck without impediment of minor details such as trees and so forth. When you get to the ball you exchange your beer for the golf club which the caddie gives you, strike the ball, don't worry about where the ball goes, exchange the golf club for your beer, and soldier on. This is how the game of golf should be played. There are few matters finer in life than walking around on God's green earth under the broiling sun and seeing a young man come running up the fairway with four fresh cold beers in his hands.

The perimeter of this golf course was naturally located so that there was a thick hedge separating it from the properties of the local residents. There were a lot of chickens which darted through the hedges out onto the golf course to see what sort of foodstuffs and seeds might be available. One time we teed off at the edge of the course with our caddies in tow. I happened to hit a drive known as a West Texas Bug Fokker, that is, a mighty blow much more on the top of the ball, as opposed to the middle target area which would allow the spheroid to behave in a proper manner. It was a low screamer and, as fate would have it, struck one of these chickens squarely amidships. It was like a bullet into a feather pillow, and when the feathers had all settled, it was clearly evident that there was lying on the ground a dearly departed hen.

There was an immediate huddled conference of the caddies. They apparently elected a spokesman who approached me and invoked a large amount of Spanish in my direction. This was interpreted by brother Jon, who informed me that the local custom was that, now, *The mortal remains of this bird belonged to me*, and clearly by inference, *What was I going to do with it?*

By now it is clearly evident to the reader that I have done very few intelligent things in my not-so-illustrious career as a human being, but in this case I did the clever thing. I informed their spokesperson that I now gave it to them all collectively. With a great deal of Muchos Grassias(es) one of their number picked up the carcass and disappeared through the hedge. It was a cause for rejoicing in somebody's pot that evening and thereafter I was treated with considerably more respect than hitherto I had enjoyed.

Another of the wonderful experiences that I enjoyed with my fellows in Costambar was brunch. We would all troop up to a place that overlooked the nine-hole golf course nearby and go into a restaurant called La Paloma. The restaurant proper was about eight or 10 tables perched upon the open top floor roof of a house. It had a covering and archways surrounding, in short, pretty much an open air establishment. This was no problem as the weather was almost always very fine.

We generally sat at a table overlooking the golf course. It was always fascinating to observe that the people who were trimming the rough, and I use this term *rough* extremely loosely because the whole matter would've been termed the rough on most golf courses, but in this case the portion of the course which is rougher than the other rough. They did this by hand with sort of long serrated knives affixed at pretty much a right angle on the end of a stick. These scythes were possessed of edges on both sides and so the rhythmic back and forth and back and forth cut the grass. These people came from Haiti across the dividing line. The folks from Dominican Republic had pretty much nothing. Yet they imported people from Haiti to do their dirty work for them because they Haitians had less than nothing.

After a while, sometimes a very considerable while, a waitress would appear with a pad and pencil in her hand. We each had menus but they were in Spanish and so I had no idea what was being offered. I took my cue from the others there present, and we all ordered breakfasts. There were requests for eggs easy-over with ham, eggs sunny-side up with bacon and toast, poached eggs with white toast and breakfast sausages, omelettes, and any or all of the items on the menu. This was accompanied at least in theory by a selection of juices and coffee, so we waited. And we generally waited some more. After a while I learned that it really did not matter what I had ordered, or what any of my fellows had ordered, it all came the same thing. White bread toast and butter with scrambled eggs and bacon accompanied by orange juice and black coffee. And it was all fine and tasted great, but I think the blessed memory of the matter was in the ritual through which we went every time.

Some days we went over to the larger, formal golf course at the Jack Tar Village. It was soon determined how many times we were going to golf during that particular week and then a caddie was assigned to each of us for the duration. These were professional caddies. That's all they did. They pretty soon figured out what kind of a golf game you possessed and we learned to trust them when we got up to our ball and they handed us a club. This is indeed a very fine way to golf. Each day we would tip our caddie I think about five US dollars, which was pretty serious coin in the time period, roughly 1995, and much appreciated.

Another fine watering hole was a few hundred yards up the beach and rejoiced in the title Roberto's Beach Bar. Roberto was of smooth face and indeterminate age, probably someplace in his mid50's, and presided over an establishment right close to the water that was in the shape of an L. There was a bar on the two sides opening to the ocean, which could be shuttered at night. In behind of the L were the miscellaneous refrigerators, ice makers, storage of booze, and the residence of a huge parrot, which greatly enjoyed in accompanying conversations going on at the bar. From my observation Roberto could speak at least six languages and utilize them not only in the conversation with the patrons of the bar, but in the instruction of the two urchins who prepared the barbecue chicken on the floor just behind the bar and also the hamburgers which were cooked on the charcoal fire in the back. Most of the bar was for patrons, except for the last stool on his left, which was graced by his 16-year-old wife who spent her days polishing her fingernails and looking bored.

It was a great pastime to go over to Roberto's Beach Bar and sit on the stool diametrically opposite to his wife. From this vantage point it was possible to observe all the antics of the animals in his little private zoo. A fascinating study indeed. The parrot wanted in on the conversations and as the decibel level of the patrons increased, so did the decibel level of the comments of the bird. After a while it was clearly evident that the parrot could out-shout all of the bar people together and it became impossible to hear anything besides the bird. At this juncture Roberto would holler curses in six languages back at the bird and pelt it with a storm of chicken bones through the door right at the parrot, yelling something which included *el cannibal*. The bird then took refuge as best it could in the back lowest portion of its cage and would shut up for a while. This, at least, until Roberto turned his attentions elsewhere and the level of the conversations came up once again.

On one particular mid afternoon I was habituating said barstool, and a lady rejoicing in her mid40s perched along side of me. It was clearly evident that she was fresh off the plane from Germany, an observation due not only to her manner of speech but also the fact that she was about as colored as the underbelly of a beached whale. We struck up a conversation, such as it was due to the fact that my German was extremely problematic and her English was anything but precise. But, as is the custom in circumstances of that nature, where one does not have a German word, one just tosses in the English, and vice versa. These exchanges are generally ably greased with the application of alcoholic lube.

She asked what I was drinking and I informed her that it was a Cuba Libre. *Great,* said she, *I would like one of those.* What she did not understand was that the Cuba Libre was composed of rum and Coke with a twist of lime. In the normal state of affairs it would've been a small amount of rum and a much larger amount of Coke. But because in DR rum was much cheaper than Coke, the bartenders were under strict instruction to give as much rum as possible with little Coke. The lady beside me enjoyed her Cuba Libre with significantly more alacrity than what should have occurred under the circumstances and ordered another. The young lady behind the bar provided her with just exactly that, except that this time she was pouring, and the dregs of the rum bottle were fast approaching. She looked around to make sure that the customer was not observing the methodology of the process, and dumped the rest of the contents of the bottle into her glass. Then came the splash of Coke and the twist of lime, and the drink again went down way faster then was wisdom. So I watched this and waited and, sure enough, about five minutes later I caught her as she collapsed off the barstool.

This was not a circumstance without precedent. She was made comfortable in the shade of a palm tree until the shuttle came. Her wristband proclaimed that she was a guest at the Bayside Beach Hotel about a half a km up the hill. In those days there was a small train, consisting of a little steam engine and the narrow track railway, which connected this hotel to the rest of Costambar, including proximity to Roberto's establishment on the beach. The train wound its way through the neighborhood and was a very convenient method of going from place to place, not only between the hotel and the beach, but also various points within the gated community itself. It went from about 10 o'clock in the morning until roughly midnight or so, and it was not unusual to grab a picnic basket or an aggregation of jars charged with fluids and snacks of choice and to while away an hour or two simply rejoicing in the wonderful late afternoon or evening of the beach area of the Dominican Republic riding this little train.

This was also a beach where clothing was optional. The German tourists especially were prone to flinging off most of their vestments, slathering themselves up with oil, and sunning on the beach. While it was clearly evident that the vast majority of the ladies who lounged around topless should have remained somewhat clad, once in a while there was a specimen which, shall we say, was *highly inspirational*. One such lady, who was probably about 30 or so, would appear every afternoon on the beach with her boyfriend and proceed to do the flinging away of the clothing and the application of the oiling act . She was very well stuck together and everything she did appeared to be accomplished with much energy. It is said that some women are built for comfort and others are built for speed. This one was a high RPM model, possessed of fluid drive. She also rejoiced in mirrored protuberances just below her shoulders the tips of which were very perky indeed. We named her Fluida Nipplosis. Along about four o'clock every afternoon, she would sit on her boyfriend's lap facing him and they would *commune*. Evidently this communion was of such a nature that soon thereafter they would gather up their things and jump on the little train going back up to the hotel. We could understand it. Sitting out in the sun in that heat can make a person rather tired. They probably had to go back to their quarters to take a nap.

One of the most fascinating and enjoyable circumstances involved with my trips to the Dominican Republic revolves around our out-trips to the hospitals and other circumstances of charitable donation that my buddy Dave had accumulated over the years. I remember that he was of the habit of filling suitcases with medical supplies such as syringes, rubber gloves, medications, bandages, and other accoutrements that we take for granted here. We went to a hospital ward and there was somebody, gravely ill, lying on a steel cot with a piece of mattress padding. The mattress was provided by the relative sitting in the steel chair overlooking the bed. The medicine cupboard was bare. *Literally bare*. Nothing in it. The patient on the steel cot had no medications whatever and may well have been lucky if a doctor poked his nose in once or twice a week. Hard for us to imagine.

I myself packed large suitcases full of children's running shoes that I procured from the local shoe stores. Runners that were out of style, which I could buy very cheap or persuade the proprietors to donate to the cause. The climate in Dominican Republic was such that I didn't need to take along a lot of clothing, so shoes it was. We would go out into the poorer sections of the countryside, called the Barrios, and I wish I had a video of the response of poverty-stricken parents to the reception of shoes for their kids. Again we take matters of this nature for granted. But in DR, it was a rule that if you are going to send your children to school they had to be in shoes. Parents of children with tears of joy running down their cheeks because the Gringos took the time and trouble to facilitate the matter of their children going to school. What price that?

Then of course we rich Touristos played golf. We always paid the golf club whatever fee it was required and then privately tipped our caddies five dollars or so per round. I was given to believe that this was a significant amount of money to their general welfare, but I had no idea exactly what that meant. Then one time I found out firsthand. We were coming to the end of our week and after the golf on the Friday we were invited to a celebration at the home of my caddy. After navigating a lot of narrow streets, we came to his place of abode. It was about half the size of a one-car garage, divided by a curtain into front (living) and back (sleeping). Four kids. Thence inside the front, to sit around a table, at which were two chairs and two up-ended orange crates. A small basket of oranges was on the table and we were invited to partake. While we did so, it was eventually made clear to me the cause for the celebration. Over the last two or three years, the caddy had saved up my tips and now they were celebrating a wonderful luxury. Instead of mud, their floor was now concrete.

The author waxing, "Trust me, it's a great car! Belonged to my Mother and she didn't drive…"

CHAPTER 🐜🐜🐜🐜🐜

𝔗𝔯𝔦𝔨𝔢𝔰 𝔞𝔫𝔡 𝔅𝔦𝔨𝔢𝔰

As a small boy I rode a tricycle. There was a sidewalk out the front of our place which ran clear around the block, except for the west side of the Lichty property next door to us. The rest of the block one could circumnavigate on sidewalk, which of course we did. It wasn't all that long after we had moved to that house in Elmira that Union Gas came through and laid pipes into the turf between the sidewalk and the road. I was about five and this was seriously cool.

To dig the trench, they employed a dragline device known as a Ditch Witch; the name of this machine was written on the side of it. Right away it was clearly evident this was a tool of the devil and operated by the devil's servants. After all, the very name proclaimed the fact. We were not allowed to speak this name because it gave off reference to heathen idolatry and devilry and, of course, witchcraft. It was not at all clear whether this machine's ultimate destination was hell or not, but nevertheless this loud snorting beast chewed out the earth to a depth of perhaps two feet or so, into which the pipe was laid. The pipes were made out of some kind of steel or similar metal and had to be welded together. This was done by men who were not always clean-shaven and who spoke words which we did not learn in Sunday school. Strong, hard men who doubtless needed to be saved (and shaved).

I knew this right away because they smoked cigarettes. These were Demon Sticks, palpably designed to give these men a foretaste of their fate after death, because no Christian person who was saved would puff on any sort of tobacco and here they were with fire at the ready to consume them. I knew this because we were taught this in church and by my father which art in heaven, and he and his henchbuddies would never tell me anything that wasn't 100% true. They lit their cigarettes off the burning

tips of their oxyacetylene welding torches and did not employ matches. I thought this also was very extremely cool but I dared not say so.

It was fascinating to watch these men weld together and install these pipes. The mound of earth churned up by the Ditch Witch pretty much lapped onto the environs of the sidewalk. There was no help for it but to try to ride my tricycle up onto this continuous mound of earth and stones, kind of like a three-wheeled earth-boarder enjoying a semi half-pipe.

After a while, my tricycle tipped over and fell sideways onto the concrete walkway, breaking off one of its arms in the process. So there I was, a small grimy boy tearfully grasping the body of the trike in one hand and its severed arm in the other. Lacramentation abounded, not so much because I had come to any major personal or painful grief on account of the tipping over, but because I was pretty sure I was likely to catch The Stick when father came home and found out about it.

One of the hell-bound smoking sinners right next to this non-blessed event said, *Come on over here kid and bring the trike with you.* I was sort of afraid to do this, but I had been taught to obey my elders and took the shards of my three-wheeler with me. The cigarette smoking sinner deftly proceeded to braise the arm of my trike back onto its original position. I expressed great gratitude and admiration in the matter of this Blessed Event, and he said to me, *Kid it was nothing. I can mend anything except the break of day.*

It was a matter of no small rejoicing when I was able to graduate to a bicycle. This was a hand-me-down of a hand-me-down of a hand-me-down of my two older brothers who got it from one of our oldest cousins, Demas. It was a CCM 26-inch wheeled bike which rejoiced in having a total of one speed. No matter. It was a good solid bike and I drove that bike from approximately grade six to the end of high school. A lot of the time I drove it with no hands on the handlebars, even around corners.

I know I drove pretty fast because one time, along about when the police got radar, I was stopped going down the hill into Elmira and the officer told me that I was speeding. Thus I was going in excess of 30 mph in an unsprung vehicle using no hands. Gives me the willies to think about it now. Pretty sure the cop had a pretty good laugh over it after he let me go. Nothing on the books that says you can charge anything but a motor vehicle with such an offence. It was a good bike.

I found out later that cousin Demas had won this bike in a cereal box competition. It was required of the contestants to send in a short description of *Why I like Cheerios*. Demas won third prize, which was this bicycle. I have no idea what the first and second prizes were. But Demas wrote in, *I like Cheerios because they do not go snap crackle and pop. They just lie there and sog.*

I have rode (ridden on?) a fair few bikes since then, some of them pretty fancy and some very expensive. The mountain bikes, with all their spring-loaded forks and shock absorbers and about 800 gears, I can thank for my trashed shoulders. I discovered, to my to-this-day pain, that a biker is well advised to stay on the path and not take the short-cut over the cliff. Then there were the serious road bikes, which I am pretty sure are palpably designed to keep the physicians who deal in festering crotch rot in lucrative business. And I have a very nice hybrid bike out there in the shed largely collecting dust because the roads these days are packed with speeding and texting morons.

So I think a comfortable tricycle may well be the answer. Wide comfortable seat. No need to clip in my cleats. No worries about falling over if I want to stop – I'll just slow down and put down my feet! Enjoy the scenery. Unlike a bike, it is legal to drive a trike on the sidewalk. Best avoid the spoor of any lurking Ditch Witch. There may not be any immediate hell-bound heathen to bail me out.

CHAPTER ❧❧ ❧❧❧❧

Grampa Bowman

My grandson Isaac, six as of this writing, is the thinnest veneer of civilization badly pasted over a two-legged atom bomb. I tell you, *that* one walks in the spitting image of his great-great-grandfather, Daniel M. Bowman, my grampa on my mother's side. He was quite a fellow, too. The words, *We can't do this*, were not in his vocabulary. He *did* things. He was a genius inventor, engineer, and builder, and he built pretty much anything you could name, including bridges.

They were putting in a new bridge across the Conestoga River at Wallenstein and they ran into the quicksand and it swallowed them up, figuratively and pretty much literally too. They were stymied. It stymied all those wonderful engineers from Toronto, or wherever they came from, and they called in grampa. Grampa came and he took the job. He went upstream and dammed up the river, diverted the river around the jobsite, dried up that quicksand and excavated it, then drove steel pylons into the living rock, boxed them in, and poured the concrete abutments for that bridge. That bridge and successive bridges have been built on my grandfather's, Daniel M Bowman's, abutments to this day.

When they built the planing mill in Elmira, down by the river where Home Hardware now stands, they put in a new dust and shavings collection system, and it was a thing of beauty except for one minor problem – it didn't work. So they fussed and fretted and tried this and I don't know what-all, and finally somebody said, *How be we call in D.M. Bowman.* Who? *Daniel Bowman.* Who's he? Well, that was a little bit more difficult to answer. He's a guy who, um, well, just knows how to figure things out. So what did they have to lose?

So they sent word for my grampa, and presently he came. He wasn't nothing much to look at. He was five foot and maybe a shoebox on top, and that was about all. A dusty little man who had come in a buggy, an Old Order Mennonite in black boots, black pants, black coat and a black felt hat. Grampa unlimbered his panic kit of tools and went to work. He poked and prodded and adjusted and did who knows what-all for quite a while. The engineers and contractors viewed him askance down their aquiline noses, surreptitiously sniggering at this Old Order Mennonite with his bag of funny-looking goodies. Eventually grampa said, *Turn her on boys!* So they started it up, and he flung his black felt hat down under the intake and it sucked that hat through the whole system, through the cyclone and out into the bin beyond. That was my grampa.

He was a man in a hurry. Things to do, places to go. He liked to get there in a hurry. To do this, he bought used racehorses. You could tell grampa was coming from quite a ways away because of the cloud of dust. One such horse was Mabel. Mabel loved to run and mostly grampa let her run. That was all fine and dandy if there was a construction site to get to or a bridge construction to visit, but going to church was another matter. The unspoken, unwritten rule among the Old Order people was that nobody passed anybody else on the way to church. Well, Mabel had been bred and trained to pass any other four-footed beast on the road with a conveyance attached, and by the time they got to church, grampa's arms and Mabel's mouth were both plenty sore. So there was no help for it but for grampa to get up earlier on the Sunday morning and take Mabel for a run. And when Mabel didn't want to run anymore, out came the whip and he ran Mabel until she was froth tired. Grampa would tie her up to the hitching post by the house while he went in to take his breakfast while she cooled down. Then he came out and hosed her down. Then they all piled into the buggy – and now Mabel stayed in line.

Grampa built most of the town of Floradale, just outside of my home town Elmira. He built the gristmill and the cooperage and the sawmill and who knows what all kinds of mills. To get power, he dammed up the Canagagigue River and diverted the water through the mill race to the big mill wheel built against the side of that edifice. It was a steel, over-the-top wheel, with the buckets handriveted to the spokes. Cold peen riveting, with one hammer held to the head, the shaft through the hole in the bucket and the cross-member, and another round-headed hammer peening those rivets. Nuts and bolts would just have shaken loose. The noise of hammering in that concrete crypt would have put a rock band to shame.

So while grampa and a couple of his sons were down in the hole doing the riveting, other of the sons came and shouted down the hole, *Dad, Dad, come quick! Mother's dying!* Let it here be observed that the milk of human kindness did not run richly in grampa's veins. He suffered fools with little gladness and the rest of humanity with very little more. He considered his wife to be a hypochondriac – she bore him nine children, but hypo nonetheless. *Dad, Dad, come quick! Mother's dying!* There was a pause in the peening and then grampa's voice came up through the hole, *Well, go on home and tell her to try it then.* The peening continued. I don't know if grandma died that day, but she might have.

So, when it became clearly evident that none of grampa's sons were going to grow up and turn out just like him, many people were very thankful. *Thanks be,* said they, *that mold is broken.* But it wasn't broken. Somebody had just hid it, probably on the far side of one of the moons of Jupiter or someplace such. But then I came along, and people were concerned. Many said that I walked in grampa's image but with a few of the pricklies filed off and minus, of course, the genius. And when I had no sons – I had two beautiful daughters who turned out normal like their mother – many people got down on their knees and thanked the Good Lord Almighty in His Infinite Grace and Wisdom that I had no sons, because the little buggers might turn out like me. Hah!

But, there goes that boy, my grandson! That mold was not broken. I tell you, *that* one is a force with which to be reckoned! I fervently hope they invent Cold Fusion before whatever it is that powers that boy goes off!

You are invited to visit
www.mennonitecobbler.com
for information on the stage play
by the same name.

CHAPTER 🐛 🐛 🐛

Mennonite Order of Service
(Insomniac Therapy, Part IV)

The officials of the Old Order Church are the Bishop (one per congregation), the deacons (four or five), and the ministers or preachers (generally two or so). These, all together, make up the church council or governing body of that particular congregation. The council appoints a new bishop or deacon, while a new minister is selected by lot (see below). All the above sit on a raised platform at the front (one step up only) facing the congregation. There is a lectern at the middle front of the platform to hold the preacher's Bible.

The Old Order Mennonite Service of Worship always starts with the singing of two hymns in German. One of the preachers or deacons will give out the number in the hymnal, which, interestingly enough, has words only and no music. Then a *forsinger*, or song leader, starts the singing. He does this without the benefit of a pitch pipe or tuning fork or anything else, except his own memory of the starting note, and has memorized a selection of choices of music which are supposed to go with that particular hymn. While most of the time this works quite well, once in a while matters go astray. For example, one time in the Elmira church, the singing was started with a tune that did not match the text in the hymnal at all, and everything ground down to a screeching halt. A different tune was attempted with a similar result. The third go around was equally unsuccessful, whereupon an awkward silence ensued. The minister then gave out a different hymn number, and this one went off without a hitch.

Whoever gives out the song number then makes some comments on the contents of the song and delivers a mini sermon on the message and its merits that have just been sung.

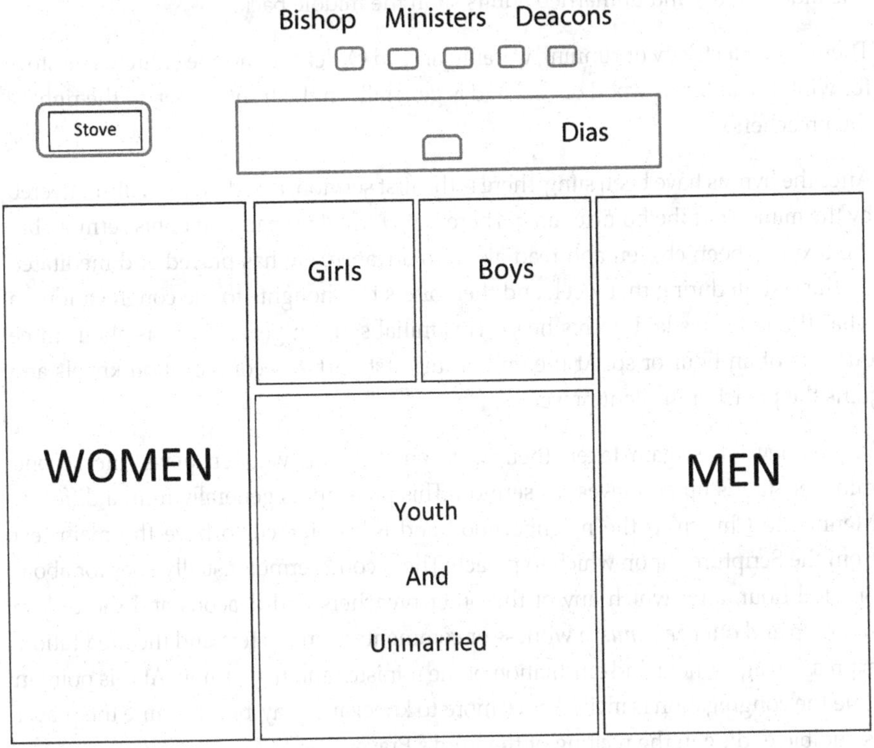

Bishop   Ministers   Deacons

☐   ☐   ☐   ☐   ☐

Stove

☐   Dias

Girls   Boys

WOMEN

Youth

And

Unmarried

MEN

The members of the congregation are divided into their respective age and gender. As you will see from the accompanying diagram, the men sit to the left of the preachers and the deacons and the bishop on the platform, while the women sit to their right-hand side. Children also have their respective positions, with the boys in front and to the left of the minister and the girls also at front and sitting on the right-hand side. The older youths and unmarried adults sit in the middle back.

There is no electricity or running water in an Old Order Mennonite church. The stove for winter heat burns wood or coal and is generally in the front corner, to the right of the preachers.

After the hymns have been sung, there is the first sermon, and this is usually delivered by the minister of the home church. There is no formal preparation of his sermon, but the text has been chosen and read aloud in advance. He has prayed and meditated on the text all during that week and then offers his thoughts to the congregation on what the Lord has laid on his heart. This initial sermon generally runs about three quarters of an hour or so. At the end of this first part, the congregation kneels and joins the preacher in silent prayer.

When they have again taken their seats on the hard wooden pews, the second minister stands up and gives his sermon. This preacher is generally from a different Mennonite Church in the neighborhood and is considered to have the main text from the Scriptures upon which to preach. The second sermon usually goes for about one full hour, after which any of the other preachers and deacons and the bishop stand up and offer *zeichnus*, a witness or commentary on the text and the meditation, expressing agreement and affirmation of the minister and his sermon. At this point in time the congregation is invited once more to kneel and pray, but this time the prayer is audible ending in the reciting of the Lord's Prayer.

The congregation then sings the closing hymn, after which the visiting minister gets up and pronounces the benediction and any other such announcements as need to go forth, such as points of instruction on daily life. One such might be that the women's' stockings are getting too sheer and their hair is showing through, therefore lose the silk and lace and make with the heavy opaque woolen hosiery. Or that it has been observed that some of the brethren were driving their tractors to town, which is forbidden, and they had better shape up and harness their horses or they will receive a visitation from one of the deacons. Perhaps a boom-box or two has been heard from under the buggy of several young men driving home from a barn get-together late on a Sunday night and to adios stage left the heathen noise-makers. The congregation is then dismissed, having largely sat on seriously hard wooden pews for a very long time, and also having enjoyed the scintillating comments of the ministerial staff, together with the entertaining edification of the a cappella hymns and, of course, the cogent comments from the ministers and deacons and bishop who have offered appropriate *zeichnus* in the affirmation and agreement of that which has been provided by the preachers.

There are, of course, special services such as the ordination of a preacher. If one is needed, there is a box with a slot in the top beside the door, and men (only) can write the name of whom they figure might be a suitable candidate for the position on a piece of paper and slip it into the box. The deacons and existing preachers then privately interview each one whose name has been placed in the box to find out whether they will stand for ordination. If there is doubt or hesitation, then such a brother is free to go. At the end of the normal service on the Sunday in question, the ministerial candidates will be sitting front and center. There is a table provided and hymn books are placed on the table, one for each candidate. One by one they go up and take a hymn book and sit down again. Then after a suitable offering of prayer by the bishop, the hymn books are opened all at the same time, and the brother who has the book in which has been placed a piece of paper is the new preacher – for life.

Funerals are mostly conducted on a weekday and, while the order of service is much the same, they will beforehand have buried and covered the deceased in the cemetery out the back. The life and deeds of the dearly departed are not discussed in the sermons, but rather admonition is given to the living as to their responsibilities to live a good life, so that when they pass on, the Lord God Almighty will welcome their souls into heaven.

Twice a year after the normal service is complete, all of those baptized into the church and who are of good standing will take communion. They go forward to receive the bread and the wine, at which point also, the deacons perform the ceremony of the washing of their feet. This is to indicate that their leaders are also their servants and that all are equal in the eyes of the Lord and of the Church.

However, there is strict discipline which is enforced in the daily activities and the theological pronouncements of the brethren. If one of the brothers voices Biblical opinions contrary to current theology, or screws up by driving his tractor to town, he will get a visitation from one of the deacons. If, after suitable inquiry to the delinquent matters at hand, the perpetrator of the crime is not suitably repentant, the deacon has the power to excommunicate said brother and his family on the spot. Welcome to the world of the Mennonite Hit Man. Any excommunication will be publicly announced at the next church service and, if the crime is suitably heinous, and if the brother is unsuitably unrepentant, said brother and his family can also be shunned. Nobody in the Church is to have anything to do with him or any of his family, ever at all, or until such a brother publicly repents. No small matter in a community of faith of that nature. And don't forget, besides the faith, the love and joy and compassion. And forgiveness.

It will be noted that all matters of church policy and governance are created by the council – pretty much all old men – and done behind closed doors. One of the deacons or preachers will announce new rules after the sermons on Sunday morning.

See also the complete Mennonite credo, Appendix III

Dordrecht Confession of Faith (Mennonite, 1632)

CHAPTER

Grampa Brubacher

Everything tastes better fresh from the garden or straight off the farm. Whether it's lettuce or spinach or tomatoes or beets or beans or anything else from a country garden, or critters having rejoiced in the freedom of having four legs or two legs and two wings or fins or what have you, it always tastes best fresh and if you know whence it came.

We lived at the edge of Elmira, a block from the farm where Grampa Brubacher hung his hat. He and his second wife (#1 long deceased) lived in the doddy house of Cleason Martin, an Old Order Mennonite farmer. Grampa Brubacher was not at all well and never went out. My father, who was in a wheelchair on account of the polio, was of necessity carried up a flight of six or eight steep concrete steps to get into the doddy house and visit his dad. They spoke to each other in a language unintelligible and, doubtless, on matters inexplicable. We boys would go along ostensibly to pay our respects to our grampa but, as soon as we decently could, gleefully escaped to play on the farm and in the barnyard.

The farm boys were big and strong and they greatly enjoyed baiting us. *Now you boys are city boys*, they would say, *and you are fast. We think that you fast city boys could put your hand in the water of this horse trough and get it out again quick enough so that your hand don't get wet.* So, of course, we had to try because these were our hosts. The predictable results caused these big strong farm boys uproarious mirth.

They had a dog named Buster. Buster was about the size of a collie, I suppose, and of dubious parentage. He was tawny in color with very long hair. He also loved to stalk behind the hay rack or the wagon when the sheaves were being pitched for the threshing and jump on and gulp down the mice that were freshly exposed. Buster could consume an astonishing quantity of mice at one sitting, or running, as the case may be. One time, in the middle of summer, it was clearly evident that long-haired Buster suffered in the heat. So the big strong farm boys caught Buster and shaved him with hand clippers from the shoulders back, except for a tuft on the tip of his tail. Buster looked for all the world like a small lion, and when they picked him up and threw him into the horse trough, I'm pretty sure he enjoyed it greatly. He swam around there a little bit and then clambered out and shook himself vigorously in our midst. It felt terrific. Seldom does one feel as alive as a small boy on a hot day with a dog having sprayed him with cool water.

The hay was picked up in the field and went into the barn loose. Horses drew the wagon, which pulled the hay rack picking up the hay from the back and sending it up to a level about as high as the head of the farmer spreading the hay on the wagon. Then the full load was pulled up the barn-hill onto the threshing floor and a big fork on a pulley hoisted the loose hay into the mow.

In time of threshing, the cut grain was bound into bundles called sheaves, and eight or a dozen of these were stood up together to form a stook. Men with pitchforks picked up those sheaves and pitched them onto the wagon heads in first, because the stalks were bulkier. The stalks were always to the outside so that everything gravitated towards the middle and the wagon bumping through the ruts would not spill the load. Then horses pulled the wagon up onto the threshing floor and the sheaves would be put through the threshing machine. It was a huge noisy contraption that separated the grain from the straw and chaff. A hot dusty thirsty business indeed. And all hard, hard work.

We loved going out to that farm. One time, they were cleaning out the calf pens in the middle of winter. When the manure spreader was full, I indicated that I would like to go out into the field too. However, as there was only one metal seat up front for the farmer, there was the problem of where to put me. So the farmer picked me up and plunked me down on that hot steaming pile of calf manure, which I rode like a horse all the way out into the field. Later, dealing with my pants, mother was not amused.

And then there was the time on the Thanksgiving Monday when I would have been

rejoicing in the matter of seven or eight summers we delivered father to visit his dad and soon realized that there was something unusual afoot. We could hear the noise of many running chickens that were not happy. When we escaped to the yard it was clearly evident that they were catching the loose chickens – those that had gotten out of the henhouse and had been running free in the yard and in the barn all summer. We knew that they were loose, because they laid eggs all over the place and we had helped to collect them. It had taken little in the way of rocket science to figure out where the nests were, because the hens were sitting on their eggs and clucking away to beat all. But now they were on the run, and coat hangers had been unraveled to collect these birds. Once caught, they were segregated to a cordoned off portion of the manure yard. Pretty soon the farmer appeared with an axe and a stump into which parallel nails had been driven.

I had never before seen chickens running around minus their heads but I thought it a matter of no small interest. That didn't happen in town. I thought it was pretty cool and ran, tearing off across the orchard over the border fence with this strand of barbed wire on top, and raced down the street and told mom. She looked at me in a kind of peculiar way, gave me a two-dollar bill and said, *Go and ask for some.* So I did, and pretty soon I was the proud possessor of four chickens, two in each hand. Getting them across the orchard and the field was not a problem, but now I was faced with a fence with barbed wire on top. Easy enough to vault in normal times, but these were not normal times. I had seen what chickens could do without their heads attached so I clung to the feet of those birds for dear life.

Somehow, at the expense of the crotch of my pants, I managed to overcome the problem of that fence, and was soon dragging these birds down the block to our house. Little in the matter of Sherlocklike diligence would have been necessary to determine the path of my progress. I suppose the next strong rain got rid of the evidence. At any rate, mother soon had a big tub to the boil and we kids were yanking feathers off scalded birds. There was also stuff inside chickens that I had never seen before. We were adjured in no uncertain terms that we do not touch that green thing. *That is the gizzard with the bile, and if you disturb it in any material fashion the evil demons inside will come out and spoil the meat, so don't you dare touch that thing.* So we touched it not.

That night we ate chicken that had enjoyed all the blessings of a free life in the farmyard. It tasted nothing like the stuff that came from the store. Much more flavorful. It was only much later that I determined that a good deal of the flavor came from the chickens rooting around and eating the stuff that came from the north end of a southbound horse. Chicken and new potatoes and squash straight from the garden. But the crowning glory was the chicken off the farm just over there, one block and one barb-topped fence and one field and one orchard and one barn-yard away.

The author waxing pensive...

CHAPTER ❧ ❧ ❧ ❧❧
𝕸𝖔𝖓𝖊𝖞

According to the wag, *If money is the root of all evil then I would like to be the world's champion gardener*. This is not really what the holy Scriptures say. The Bible teaches us that *LOVE of money is the root of all evil*. This may indeed be the case. Some would make an argument in favor of *Power*, I suppose. But when it boils right down, I am not at all sure there is much difference. The one begets the other.

The official version of money in our household growing up was that there was none. It was very seldom that actual cash money was in the hands of anybody in our house. Our father which art in heaven kept the business money tied up in an elastic band in his pants pocket. From time to time at the shoe store he would make change for the cash register, and then out the wad would come. At the end of the business day all of the bills, except for a token float, would disappear into his pocket.

In the house, mother kept her purse in the bedroom. The only time she ever went to fetch money from her purse would occur when a salesman came to the door. One such was the Fuller Brush Man. Another sold Raleigh's products, one of which was a menthol paste concoction in a circular tin, while another was a sort of amber paste that rejoiced in the title *Antiseptic Healing Salve*. Both of these were used for application of sniffles, chest rub compound, cuts, scrapes and scratches, and miscellaneous other uses as a universal specific.

Another salesperson who came around was one Cranson Brubacher. He drove up the driveway in his buggy and tethered his horse to the doorknob. He was a man of great exuberance and few teeth. I don't know if he actually had any molars back in there, but I never counted more than three teeth, one down and two up, (or was it the other way around?) in his front gums. He spoke with mother in Pennsylvania Dutch

with triple G (great glee and gusto), peddling stuff like fresh pressed apple cider, apple butter, cheese, butter, horse radish, and whatever else he could lay his mitts on, including eggs. He lived in a rundown ramshackle old house on the far side of town, and we knew that he never mowed his grass because there wasn't one square foot of his entire yard free enough of junk to facilitate such a matter. We always loved it when he came because mother always bought his apple cider and we got to drink it pretty much right away. Sometimes it was a hair too ripe, whereupon it kind of frothed and tingled a bit as it went down. Great stuff.

My first recollection of money occurred when I was five years old. I was in kindergarten at the time and went to school half days. One fine morning, when I was going to Riverside Public School in Elmira in the afternoons, mother dressed me up in my Sunday best, made sure my shoes were shined and that the rest of little Kenny was as nearly akin to a newly minted penny in countenance and clothing as possible. She gave me a 10-cent coin piece to hold as we went downtown to the Royal Bank of Canada. This was the first time I had ever seen mother off the property aside from going to church. We got to the bank and climbed up the concrete stairs and went inside. The hardwood floors creaked, and the hardwood walls reeked of tradition and gravitas. We had to wait our turn at the wicket, which rejoiced in brass bars to separate potential thieves and robbers from the sanctuary within. On suitable instruction, I opened my now sweaty fist and deposited that one thin dime on the shelf under the wicket, standing on my tippy toes to get a look at the proceedings. Then I was given a book with my current deposit and savings balance hand written therein. Savings account number 4660. Balance – $.10.

When I was approximately seven years old, I started my first paper route. Part of the duties of the paperboy in those days was to go around every Friday or Saturday and collect the money from the recipients of the *Kitchener Waterloo Record,* which I had deposited on their front porches or between their doors six days per week. Some people paid once per month, but most paid weekly. Every Saturday, I had to take the correct amount of money to the post office and buy a money order which was then sent to the offices of the *Record.* What was left over was my wages.

There was however a minor problem with this wages bit – I wasn't supposed to get any of it. The word from above was that all monies acquired in the household went into the general coffers, and that I would get an allowance in the princely sum of ten cents per week. I must confess, however, that with regards to the paper route proceeds, there was from time to time a bit of *shrinkage*. I was never called into question on the matter, but I greatly feared that if an audit had occurred I might be in trouble. I'm not sure if this was grand larceny on a boyish scale or whether I was merely helping myself to the due rewards from my working deeds. There are generally different ways to view a matter. For example, have I spent a career in being the gift of the Almighty in the alleviation of the human condition or have I been a parasite on human suffering? You decide.

My father grew up in the time of the great depression, in the dirty 30's, on the farm just east of Elmira. He came from a very large family and they were dirt poor. I don't mean poor in the sense they got a sermon from their parents to cut down on their data usage on their smart phones, I mean that they could not put food on the table for all of those hungry mouths and several of his siblings had to go and live with relatives. They were the caretakers of the Balsam Grove School next door, cleaning and scrubbing and getting the stove going on cold winter mornings, mowing the grass and cleaning out the latrines, and generally keeping the place in order. For this they received the annual stipend of $100 and without that money I am pretty sure that grandfather would've lost the farm. They were that poor.

Father never shook this. Don't get me wrong, it's not that we went hungry and lurked about in rags. Not at all. There was just very little in the line of extras. Father told us that at Christmas time when he was a boy there was keen anticipation in the matter that they might each receive a real orange and a single chocolate. That was the highlight of the season. Just imagine. Father was a very frugal man so far as his own person was concerned, but I know for certain that he donated a lot of money to charities and other circumstances which deserved help.

Over the decades I suppose that a lot of money has come and gone in my own personal experience. I have driven new cars and old. I have lived in nice houses and those in which very few modern females would consider dwelling. I don't take much stock in expensive clothing and houses and extravagant automobiles, though I suppose if it came right down to it I could probably go out and get some of those. But I look back to little Kenny and his brothers, scrounging along the ditches of Snyder Avenue in Elmira in search of pop bottles thrown out of passing cars. If the stellar alignment was fortuitous, with enough time and effort we might exhume three such from the weeds.

Thus armed, we could go down to the end of the street to Gord's Garage where our haul would be valued at the grand total of six cents – two cents apiece. In those days there was a lemon-lime drink called Flip. If you bought the Flip and took it away from the premises it cost seven cents. If you drank it there in the garage and left the bottle behind, it set you back the princely sum of five cents. Now, especially as we did not get pop at all at home and as it was railed upon as being right up there almost with that devil drink beer, the consumption on a hot day of my portion of a five-cent Flip was a matter of great rejoicing. As I was the smallest boy, I suppose I would've been hard-pressed to exact my one third, but that didn't matter. We were drinking cold pop on a sweltering day in the middle of summer.

But the above meant we had one cent left over. Two blocks over was the grocery store of my dad's cousin, one Isaac Brubacher. One single cent was enough to purchase three black-balls, or jaw breakers as we termed them, one for each of us. We could then happily head back home.

Life is good. Life is Sweet. It doesn't get much better than that. Maybe it's been all downhill ever since.

CHAPTER

Cousins

Every summer, cousin Donnie came to play. He stayed with his grandparents down the street, in the next block, right across the road from Riverside Public School. Donny was the son of my dad's brother Reuben and was in age about halfway between myself and my older brother Freddie, so it was a good fit. As a by-the-way, Donnie was the grandson of my father's first employer on the first farm east of Floradale near Elmira.

Those were the days. There seemed to be an infinite variety of things to do and places to go and games to play. Games such as *hide and go seek, kick the can, sheep in the fold,* and myriad others tailored to summer sunshine. We went down to the creek and swam in pools formed from dams we made from clods of earth and weeds. We went across the street to the schoolyard and played in the sandbox and on the swings and on the teeter-totters. It was an idyllic time.

One time, in the early afternoon on a lovely hot, steaming summer's day, there boiled up a thunderstorm. The rain came down in large quantities and pretty soon there was a fair deal of water running down each side of the street into the storm sewers. The street was not actually paved but was surfaced with a kind of tar impregnated with stone chips. There was no curb as such and there was a fair deal of sand and gravel lurking between the street proper and the sidewalk.

Growing in this strip of land between the sidewalk and the road right outside the front door of the house where cousin Donnie stayed was a giant maple tree. It had massive roots, some of which were above ground for a while before they disappeared under the street.

It doesn't take very long before small boys and water get together in some form or other. In this case there was no help for it but we had to build a dam to corral a bunch of the storm water that was running down the street. We found a shovel in the garage, and pretty soon had a dam of sand and gravel to impede the progress of this running water. We thought this was pretty cool because then we could puddle in the water.

Larger boys lived on either end of this street. They had bicycles and were roaring up and down in the fashion that such boys do. To their great glee, they came upon our dam and one after the other drove through it until it was pretty much destroyed. They did this with much mirth but, from our perspective, even more consternation.

The waters continued. We decided it was time to take more drastic action. Back to the garage we went to rummage forth a couple of sections of old planks. These we positioned where our former dam had been and proceeded to cover them with sand and gravel. By this time the sun had come out plenty hot and pretty soon had done a credible baking job in the matter of the solidification of our makeshift dam.

Along about this time, the large ruffians on their bicycles came by again. They saw no immediate reason why they should not repeat the destruction of our newly created edifice by applying the wheels of their bicycles to same. This time, however, matters did not go exactly as they planned. The dam held, even under the tender ministrations of those bicycles. It was a source of great satisfaction to us boys to see the riders of the bikes going over the handlebars and doing face-plants in the gravel and road beyond.

Our immediate retreat from the scene of battle was the better portion of continued valor. The big boys were not amused. The bicycles were equally not amused, in that there was significant mayhem and bendage of the wheels and even the front forks of the vehicles in question. We fled to the safety of the front porch of Donnie's grandparents.

I am reminded of some years later, in the dead of winter, when we built the snow-fort at our house between two of the maple trees on the west side of the property. Nothing special; it was a waist-high wall constructed of snow the like from which one would create a snowman. One of the other big strong boys a block away delivered newspapers, and did so on his bicycle every day regardless of snow, sleet, rain, or any other sort of weather. Our newly constructed snow fort came into his cross-hairs as

he peddled up our street towards his house. The snow wall didn't have a chance, and that wall disintegrated under the tender ministrations of his bike.

There was no help for it but to reconstruct the fort, but this time with the aid of some buckets of water to solidify the structure. The weather became colder overnight and it froze solid. Next afternoon our erstwhile paperboy sought to re-create the scenery of the day before. This time the solid frozen wall held, and he ended up inside the fort with a mangled bicycle. We observed this Blessed Event with much rejoicing from the safety of our garage.

I knew that I was not supposed to take pleasure in the misfortunes of other people, and was, even at that tender age, not nearly as devout a Christian as I was taught to have been. Christ would doubtless have turned the other cheek and, without a murmur of complaint, made fort after fort and allowed this heathen Presbyterian boy to wreck them all. But I hugely enjoyed watching him trash his bike on my premeditated handiwork of deliberate destruction, and that was sinful and evil. And, if truth be told, if the same circumstances arose tomorrow I would do it again. And sinfully enjoy it again! As Garrison Keillor (may he live forever) put it, *The Lord knows what's on the heart, so why shouldn't I tell you?*

But back to Donnie and the summer. One fine time, we were playing under the bridge over the Canagagigue Creek at the north end of town. It was in the heat of the season and the waters had abated to a trickle. With very little flow coming under the bridge there were small pools where tadpoles and minnows were trapped. It was lots of fun to catch such critters. And then we hit the gold mine. Somebody had left a couple of half-filled five-gallon pails of driveway or roofing tar down there. It did not take very long before we were dipping dried moss on the end of sticks into this tar and flinging this sticky crud against the abutments of the bridge. Seriously great fun. This took us a fairly long time in the late afternoon until the tar was exhausted. We realized that the sun was westering, and our stomachs informed us that it was time to go home for supper.

It takes very little imagination to envisage the result of small boys flinging tar about their environs. We did indeed manage to make some very interesting designs on the abutment walls under the bridge, but in so doing we managed to get a whole pile of tar upon ourselves, including not only our clothing, but also our faces and hair.

Mother was not amused. I'm not sure what happened to our clothing which was summarily divested from us, but I do have a strong recollection of the application of Johnson's paste wax, which was normally used on the floors. But in this case it was applied to my person with very little ceremony, and even less sympathy for my yowling when scrubbed into my scalp in particular. Thanks be for very short hair at that time.

But the kicker was not the humiliation and pain of being cleaned up with the floor wax. The rule of the house was that if you were late for supper you got no dessert. We were fed a cold supper, but dessert was withheld. Normally this would not have been a problem. Generally speaking dessert was some of mother's canned fruit or some such. Maybe a cookie.

But this time it was watermelon, and that was a big deal. A maybe *a once a year a big deal*! Freddy and I had to eat the rest of our cold supper while watching mother and father and our siblings slurp wonderful, glorious, joyful watermelon.

CHAPTER

𝔅𝔬𝔬𝔷𝔢

Alcohol is either the gift of the Almighty for our enjoyment and pleasure or a demonic fluid sent by the devil himself with the sole intent of ensnaring us in its wiles and facilitating our being dragged down into hell. Take your pick.

The Scriptures teach us that it is fine to have a little wine for the stomach's sake. There also appears to have been therapeutic values to wine, as witness the Good Samaritan dumping some into the wounds of the wayfarer who had gotten savagely mugged by thieves. We must also consider that, when Jesus was attending a wedding and they ran out of wine, he personally took it upon Himself to turn water into wine. I have often wondered what that wine tasted like. After all, if the Creator of the Universe turned his hand to the skills of a vintner, I'll bet that was pretty amazing stuff. In all likelihood the best ever. But we are instructed, *Do not be drunk with wine, wherein is excess, but be filled with the Spirit.* Not spirits plural. Pretty sure by *spirit* the Scriptures did not mean Alberta Premium rye whiskey either. Too bad, that. I have enriched the coffers of that particular establishment for many years, and I think I deserve a case of their finest in exchange for the plug.

The only booze that was officially condoned in our church was communion wine. It was very sweet and I think it was made out of Concorde grapes. Every Sunday morning at the worship service we took communion in the form of pinching off some bread from a loaf that was passed around and then partaking from a communal cup of wine. I think the Guardian Angels in charge of Diseases in the church had to work overtime, on account of the creepies and uglies that must have been rampant on the brim of said vessel. Or perhaps we all survived because of the Invocation of a Blessing on that cup and its contents before we partook. But all other alcohol was Fluid Devil in a Bottle.

Mennonites used to drink. After all, they came from Europe in a day and age when the drinking of straight water was a very hazardous matter. By the time the hydrogen dioxide got from the springs in the mountains and appeared in the rivers and lakes, it had passed by a lot of dwellings which dumped their refuse out the door, and much crud found its way into the water. People understood the hazards and mostly drank fresh milk or beer or wine. It wasn't until the coffee-houses of Amsterdam appeared in the 1600's that people didn't have to wash down their oatmeal porridge with beer. The Mennonites brought their customs to America with them and it wasn't until about 100 years or so ago that the practice started to be phased out. There is a report that, along about this time, one of the bishops had declared, *Booze is now out!*, and a bunch of MennoMen at a barn-raising walked off the job to protest the lack of beer on the site. So, as of this writing, horse and buggy Mennonites, and most other flavors of Mennonites as well, officially don't drink.

When I was a boy, however, there was an Old Order Mennonite farmer in our community who was as near a thing to an alcoholic as you can get. It was clearly evident that he was continually into the sauce, but nobody could figure out where he kept his stash. In retrospect it was easy to figure it out. One fine day the pump that ran the system for milking the cows overheated and caught on fire. The extinguisher canister was quickly employed in the dousing of the flames, but with serious negative effect. Rye whiskey is not a recommended fluid with which to put out a fire, and it cost him his barn. He had been considered somewhat eccentric in taking his fire extinguisher to town to have it tested on an extremely routine and repetitive basis. One must applaud ingenuity – to a point.

Our house was tea-total. The demon drink did not darken the door to our domicile. It was a Sunday noon in summer, and we were all sitting around the table tucking into our roast beef dinner, when there was an unexpected knock on the door. There stood a stranger who wanted something to drink. Our tea-total father indicated that we would be happy to oblige, and he could have choice of cool water from the tap, or mother could put a pot to the boil, so that he could enjoy a nice cup of tea or coffee or Postum, or even mix up a pitcher of Kool-Aid. *No*, said our stranger, *Something to drink*. But dad told him that the above list was all we had and off he went. It was only many years later that I realized, and to my eternal mirth, that somebody had fingered my ultra-religioso tea-total father for being the local bootlegger!

Then there was the time when one of my older sisters, who was going to the University of Waterloo, brought home for Christmas dinner a man who was very black. It was not a date per se, at least not so far as I know, but rather I am pretty sure that it was done in Christian charity as this gentleman was very far from his homeland. In accordance with the general custom of his temporarily adopted country, he brought a gift. But not just any gift; it was a bottle of port. So here we have mom and dad impaled upon the nasty sharp pointy horns of a terrible dilemma. Are they going to break the avowed custom of the house and serve booze, or shall they possibly offend their guest by refusing the gift. I am not privy to that conversation, but I am pretty sure that the aura surrounding it was turbulently murky.

The result was a compromise. Mother mixed up a pitcher of grape Kool-Aid and poured us each a glass which was not quite full. Then into each of our cups she put two teaspoons of port. I am pretty sure that the gentleman in question to this very day recounts the story to the great hilarity of his home folks. As do I.

But the really fun bit about booze in our household revolved around a digestive aid medicine type of drink which dad took with meals. It came out of a little brown bottle and had the name *Maltlevol* on its label. He would take two or three tablespoons full of this reddish-brown fluid at the beginning and end of his meals. He explained that it was his stomach medicine and that it was not for children. I remember one time I absconded with this bottle and sampled a slug. It kind of burnt on the way down my throat and tasted of cherries that certainly did not grow on any local tree. Again, many years later, I determined that the contents of this bottle were in no small measure pure alcohol. Good for the stomach indeed. Very Biblical. *A little wine for the stomach's sake…*

CHAPTER ❧ ❧ ❧ ❧
𝕿𝖍𝖊 𝕾𝖙𝖎𝖈𝖐

My father which art in heaven, or so we are led to believe (still no post-card, *weather fine, greens fast, did another iron-man warm-up today*, no sky-writing or h-mail, nothing yet. Could take a while - heaven might be quite a ways off), also believed in the adage, *Spare the rod and spoil the child*. He also warmed to a portion of the King James Version of the Holy Scriptures which tells us, *The blueness of a wound cleanses the heart*. So, from time to time as it seemed wisdom to father, I received correction regarding my sinful activities via the tender administrations of the business end of The Stick. AKA, *Getting The Stick*.

The Stick was just exactly that. It was a piece of lumber perhaps one inch by two inches and roughly 30 inches in length. Nothing smooth about this. It was an instrument of punishment and serious pain. May well be that it was roughly the same texture as the Cross. Roughly rough.

Now I suppose that I deserved corporeal punishment, at least in-so-far as the rules of the house were concerned. House rules declared that we shall disobey nothing of father's edicts. These included a lot of things by which our heathen neighbors were not constrained. Stuff like watching television, listening to the radio, the reading of comic books, going to hockey games, dancing at school noon-time sock hops or Saturday night dances proper, potato chips and pop (especially Coke, *that very nearly Demon Drink*), *Mad Magazine*, and pretty much everything else in sight contrary to the teachings of father and his henchbuddies, the church elders. That list was plenty long.

I suppose I was pretty adept at contravention of the house rules, or at least I did it a lot. For example I very much liked to watch television. But, as we had no such

idolatrous device at home, and since we were forbidden to go into any house of our neighbors and acquaintances, watching TV was very much problematic. Thus we missed stuff like Elvis and The Beatles, Red Skelton, The Three Stooges, and all their ilk. We knew the Beatles existed because some of the girls in my grade eight class wrote names such as John and Paul and Ringo on their pencil cases. It was also clearly evident that John and Paul were not the revered saints of New Testament Scripture, and Elvis the Pelvis with his heathen rock 'n roll and repetitive gyrations of the body, which were of a lewd and lascivious nature, well, all of the above were clearly spawn of hell and were sent up to earth by the devil himself to ensnare the unsuspecting and thus drag us all down into hell to be with the devil and his angels in fire and brimstone with weeping and wailing and gnashing of teeth forever and ever. Don't forget the *Amen*. I knew this because these great truths were expostulated upon at vast length from the pulpit in our church and, after all, would these people lie? Of course not. Not on your life. They got it straight from God.

Once in a while, I did manage to sneak into the house of Paul Kroeller, who lived beside the house where cousin Donnie stayed for several weeks in the summer. There, in the middle of the afternoon, I watched TV shows that had shoot-'em-ups and thievery and other such terrible matters that were routinely railed upon by those who gave the sermons at our church. This of course would have been very seriously frowned upon by our parents. I am not even sure if they ever discovered the brief sojourns of Freddy and myself in front of the screen of a television, as there is little doubt in my mind that had this terrible evil been brought to light we would have received no small correction via The Stick.

The reception of The Stick was not merely a few haphazard whacks about the seats of our pants and then go stand in the corner and have a timeout. From time to time, for one of the lesser offenses, mother would give me some hand whacking and let it go at that. If, however, the offense was of a more extreme nature, (like if I got caught with a comic book), then it was, *Wait till your father gets home*! And so I would have to wait on tenterhooks in terrible anticipation of paternal retribution yet to come.

Father would make me lie down on his bed and partly closed the door so that the yelling would be partly muffled, and yet the message would still filter through the rest of the house in no uncertain terms. I would lie face down on the bed and out would come The Stick and father would go at it. And while he never, as far as I know, drew blood, it sure felt as though he did. It was not just a few whacks. It went on and on and was a matter for very little rejoicing indeed. In later years I often wondered whether he received similar treatment when he was growing up. Probably not. I think he was probably a pretty good (read *boring*) boy. I, on the other hand, was a Bad Boy and was doubtless in need of a taste of my probable afterlife.

I am certain to this day that he did this in Clear Christian Conscience, all the while basking in the glory of his Lord and Master Jesus Christ, who agreed with father on so many important matters of great spiritual and correctional pitch and moment.

The night of his funeral, I shovelled off the back patio and cleaned out the charcoal BBQ. It was February and cold. I had liberated that stick from the hall closet and, with a smallish knife, slowly shredded that stick into the pot. It took quite a long time. Maybe one strand per blow. My bare hands were as white cold as my ass had been red hot.

The mound of tinder caught immediately from the match and then flared for a tick or two. I did not warm my hands over that flame, but watched that stick reduce to ember and ash. With dry eyes.

CHAPTER

𝕷𝕷𝕯

A very common matter in the modifications of shoes occurs when a person, either through injury like a broken leg or some kind of surgery, ends up with one leg shorter than the other. Or maybe it is scoliosis of the back or hip fixation. There are many causes for a Leg Length Discrepancy, or LLD.

One of the most common causes of an LLD is the replacement of hips, particularly in the elderly. These days they are getting very good at it and so the residual problems are not nearly as numerous or consequential as in the Olden Days. Back then it was very common that a surgical procedure on a femur or a hip would result in one leg being considerably longer than the other. It was then incumbent upon the shoemaker to add material, either inside the shoe or on the bottoms, to provide additional elevation.

One such matter occurred in my Elmira shop. A fairly elderly lady came in escorted by her daughter. About six months previous, mother had received a new hip, and it was clearly evident that there was a significant difference in the lengths of her legs. She brought in a prescription from her physiotherapist, which indicated that I was supposed to put a full two inches of extra material on the bottom of one of her shoes. Now two inches is a lot, so we did what we always did, which was to get samples of material to approximate the finished build-up and have the lady stand on them. She needed help in standing up, and it was indeed determined that the physiotherapist had pretty much gotten it right.

The lady had brought in a pair of shoes which were relatively easy to deal with, by which I mean that the outsoles and heels were of a material to which it was easy to glue more soling. In the bad old days all we could do was hammer more leather layers onto the hard leather soles and heels, thus turning the elevated shoe pretty much into a brick with laces. It's all we had. I do, however, remember one enterprising fellow who had suffered from polio and had one leg about six inches shorter than the other. He had gone to a welding shop and they constructed for him a stainless steel trestle, much like an old railway bridge. There was a steel plate with holes on the top, where it was then screwed to the shoe, and a piece of rubber tire screwed onto the bottom plate which hit the road. Every so often he would get a new shoe and we were commissioned to do the switch. He had only the one trestle and could not walk without it, so we had to affect the exchange while he sat there in a chair.

But this time the lady had shoes that were relatively easy with which to deal, so we sent her home with the daughter in her old shoes telling them to come back in a couple of days. We then affixed the elevation and put the modified shoes on this dear lady when she returned again with her daughter.

It did not go well. We got her shoes on and, quite the opposite to stable expectation, had we not caught her under her armpits, she would have fallen over. It was clearly evident that we had put the elevation on the wrong shoe, and she was now *four* inches shorter instead of *two! Just a minute Madame, have a seat here while we adjust this for you.* We then took the shoes into the back and, as quickly as we could, performed the matter properly.

So what did I learn from this? Well, I learned that whenever somebody brought in a pair of shoes to have one of them built up, we always sent the mate home with them so that there could be no repeat of this mistaken circumstance.

But the LLD situation which sticks out in my mind the most occurred fairly late in the afternoon one very cold and snowy day. It was common for the Old Order Mennonites to come to town and park their horses in the farmers' shed about a block and a half down the street. This was a shelter purpose-built for this reason, and the horses could stay out of the harsh elements while their masters did other business in the town. On a winter's day such as this the horses would be covered with a blanket and given water and hay. There was a room in one corner of the shed where the keepers of the establishment and their cronies would sit on ratty old chairs around a potbellied stove and chew the fat. I had cause to stick my nose in there a few times and it would get plenty ripe.

However, on this particular occasion, the door to my shop opened, and in came Elam

Brubacher, an Old Order Mennonite whose farm was just down the hill from where we lived in the northwest edge of Elmira. He was quite a small fellow and rejoiced in the title Half Pint due to his diminutive stature. He also had arthritis and an LLD and did not walk with the ease most other folk enjoyed. As a boy I knew him quite well on account of my brother Freddie and I and cousin Donnie played in the small creek that ran through his property and across the lane to the river beyond. It chanced upon a time that Elam put up a new concrete silo beside his barn. This silo was deliciously white and devoid of any artistic feature whatever, a matter which we boys took it upon ourselves to rectify. We did this in the form of picking a great wad of bright orange mountain ash berries and making our way around the back of Elam's manure yard as close to the new silo as we could get without being seen. It was then clearly necessary, at least in our own minds, to decorate this silo appropriately. We did this by firing large volleys of mountain ash berries at this brand-new concrete silo. The results were decoratively spectacular, in a runny sort of manner. Unfortunately, while we were congratulating ourselves on our great artistic bent, Elam's shaggy mongrel dog chanced upon us and started yelling up a serious ruckus. This caught the attention of Elam who was in the barn. He came steaming out as fast as he could on that gimpy leg of his and recognized us. He not only hollered bloody blue blazes at us but also, at the first opportunity, ratted on us to our father. I remember a rather shiny ass over that little episode.

At any rate, many years later came Elam through the shop door rather late in the afternoon on a cold nasty day. And he was with the horse. He had the horse's reins in his hand because there was no place to tie the animal up outside my shop door. This was by design rather than happenstance because of all the decorative aspects on my parking lot which would inevitably make their way out of the east end of the now west-facing tethered horse. Elam then started to explain his shoe wishes to my first and only employee at that time, one Joseph Henry. Joe was a man of much experience in the shoe repair trades and had come to Elmira upon retiring from his abode in Newcastle upon Tyne in northern England after his son had emigrated here to work for Rogers TV.

Now let it be clearly understood that Elam and Joe may as well have come from different planets. Elam was an Old Order Mennonite who thought in German and did much speaking in German, even though he thought he was speaking English. Joe considered himself to be an Englishman who spoke English, but was from an area

of England where he was known as a Geordie, and the noises that come out of the mouth of a Geordie are nearly incomprehensible even to most of his neighboring Englishmen. Communicating with an Old Order Mennonite was a very difficult matter indeed, and there were many times that I had to intervene and translate. Joseph, fine English gentleman, greatly enjoyed dealing with the customers and making the outgoing repaired shoes look as near to brand spanking new as possible. I liked the ripping apart and reconstructing of the shoes, but had little patience for the *Let's make it look pretty* time. We were a good team.

The video in my head plays Elam trying to explain to Joe about what is supposed to happen to his shoe. As I said, Elam walked with difficulty because he was arthritic and had a bad hip. I am not sure whether he had had his hip replaced by the time of this conversation, but for quite a few years he had needed a buildup of about three quarters of an inch on one of his shoes. Now Elam and his shekels were not readily parted, and in the matter of his shoe buildup he was impaled upon the nasty sharp pointy horns of a terrible dilemma. If he took his shoe to one of the local retired farmers who did a bit of repair in the driving shed for something to do, he would certainly end up with the elevation, but it was never properly balanced. Also the materials would be hard and heavy, thus turning his shoe into the proverbial brick with laces. His hip cried foul, yet his pocketbook was happy. If, however, he came to me and got the job done right, his hip was far more hip-hop happy, but his purse cried foul. So for many years the pendulum swung back and forth, and on this particular cold late afternoon it had swung in my direction.

So there was Elam standing at the counter with the reins of the horse in his hand and the door only partly shut behind him. The space between the door to the great outdoors and the service counter was only about three feet. It was a steel single door with about six glass panes in the upper half. While Elam was seeking to explain the order of proceedings to Joe in louder and shriller tones, as if a more vociferous approach would get through to the Geordie's understanding, the horse wanted in. The reins prevented the door from latching, and the horse could determine that there was light and heat inside. The horse had probably been out in the cold for most of the day and decided it was time to make a surreptitious entrance. Slowly the door opened as the horse's head came in until its nose was right on top of Elam's shoulder. Elam finally figured out that it was not only his own breath that he was smelling, and turned around and informed the horse in no uncertain terms in German as to what it was now to do, all the while whacking the horse's head with a couple of feet of the reins sticking out from his hand. The horse jerkily backed up and resumed its position just outside. Joe, of course, had seen some pretty strange things in his shoe repair shop in his lifetime, but nothing remotely akin to this. He had a rather perplexed expression on his face as I recall. I was in the back, ducking down behind the sewing machine trying not to kill myself laughing out loud. I wish I had a video of the glass panes of the door framing the horse's head spouting great gouts of steamy breath as it rendered the window increasingly opaque.

The author waxing, "Hey Baby! How be we go back to my digs and check out my wax collection!"

CHAPTER ✖✖✖✖✖✖
𝕾𝖙𝖔𝖈𝖐𝖍𝖔𝖑𝖒

June 8, 1990, early in the morning saw me on a jet plane from Copenhagen to Stockholm. We had just attended my brother Freddie's wedding the Saturday before in Copenhagen. Brother Freddie had met a lady from this town some considerable months before and, one thing and another, started to spend a fair amount of time there. So, in the natural course of events, the nuptials were announced and several handfuls of Freddie's relations and friends ended up in Denmark.

It was certainly unlike any wedding we had ever attended. The few days leading up to and following the wedding ceremony proper were filled with parties and general celebration, much of which involved the ingestion of miscellaneous alcoholic beverages. I certainly had no objection to any and all of the above, and I am pretty sure that, for a span of about 10 days, I drew very few completely sober breaths. So the following Friday morning it was no small amount of relief to escape the parties and go to Stockholm on an item of business.

For several years I had been both curious and concerned that custom shoemaking, which was my trade, should get into the real world. By that I mean we should quit doing everything by hand and repeating ourselves to within millimetric precision of what we did last week or last month for a previous customer. Shoemaking, like many other matters, follows patterns of response to the demand. Therefore we should learn to produce a *matching exercise* with corrections, as opposed to a repetitious *creation exercise* for every customer who comes in the door. After all, when you need new tires for your car and go to the tire shop, they do not go out the back and plant a rubber tree in your name. No. They reach for tires matching your needs.

One of the biggest problems that the shoemaker faces is the accuracy of the incoming information. For example, I am supposed to be a master at the craft of measuring feet, having done this for the better part of 40 years. The problem is that human hands get involved. If you come into my clinic and I get out the measuring tape and all the printing mechanisms and measure your feet, we will get one result. Then let us go off for lunch. After lunch we come back and I plunk you back in the measuring chair and do the process all over again. Then we look at the two sets of information side-by-side. Upon examination there indeed may well be question as to whether the before-lunch and the after-lunch measurements belong to the same person. Why is this? The answer is that human hands are involved, and human hands are extremely subjective in producing any sort of findings.

So what was needed was an independent arbiter of the incoming information. Let us produce a machine that can scan your foot and give out extremely accurate information, and repeatedly so. No longer does this depend upon how tight the measuring tape is pulled around the malleable foot and sock of the person requiring the custom shoe.

Prior to my attending Freddy's wedding, I was given information about a company in Sweden which had developed such a toy for measuring feet. I contacted the company and it was agreed that they would entertain me on the Friday after the wedding. I left early in the morning and got to the Stockholm airport at about 10 o'clock, after which I took a taxi to their company on the outskirts of Stockholm. I was treated royally, and they proudly demonstrated their foot digitizer. There were four laser-video digitization cameras which took the 3-D information of my feet, whereupon it was sent into a computer program which turned the XYZ data into an image on the computer screen. You could take the image of my foot and rotate it around any direction and measure it from any angle. This was seriously cool and represented a major advancement in how to measure feet. The entire digitization process took about seven seconds and then another minute or so to crunch all the numbers so that we could observe the completed image on the computer screen.

The problem with the entire enterprise was that there was no other computer program developed at the time to actually do anything with the image except measure it. What was necessary was to invent a program which would take the image and transform it into a solid model on which a shoe could be made for that particular foot. The theory was that then this solid model image could be used to make the shoes themselves. The minor problem was that none of the above had yet been invented. Nevertheless,

I was very impressed with the progress to date, and I was assured that other people in Europe were very close to solving the remainder of the problems to put together the entire puzzle.

By the time we got done with all of the above it was about three o'clock in the afternoon. My hosts were very gracious, and I asked that they might call a taxi to take me to my hotel downtown. I had not in advance known how long it was going to take to complete my business there, and so had arranged to spend the night in old Stockholm and take my flight back to Copenhagen the next morning. Normally this would not have been a problem, but after a while I was apologetically informed that there were no taxis available. They could see that I was somewhat astonished by this information and hastened to explain that this was the last day of school for the year, and all the taxis were hired in advance to ferry around the students in the pursuit of their alcoholic celebrations to mark the end of the school year. The parents would hire them from about the time of afternoon we were discussing until the following morning at perhaps eight or nine o'clock, or whenever these students were ready to quit partying. So I was apparently high and dry.

Then one of their associates named Gunnar kindly informed me that if I had no objection to the matter he would ferry me to my hotel downtown. I told him, *Sure, no problem, let's do it!*, not realizing that I was in for the most terrifying ride of my entire life. I waited while Gunnar changed into his riding clothing, which consisted of all black leather. He was a motorcycle freak, a big strong lean young man, and he and his bike went like hell. Thankfully my overnight bag had a shoulder strap, and while I clung to Gunnar for dear life, I am sure that the bag was pretty much straight out the back as he went roaring down the highway and through the streets. It is a good thing that I was plenty strong in those days because otherwise I may well have disappeared off the back into eternity. Eventually he stopped in front of the hotel and I shakily got off and thanked him for his kind consideration in the matter of the delivery. He would accept no money.

I was shown to my room and, with great thanks, crashed onto the bed for a nap before I went out for supper. It was a beautiful evening and I walked through the old cobblestone streets, eventually coming across a suitable place of repast, and enjoyed a wonderful dinner out in the sunshine of a lovely Stockholm evening. I was very tired and the beer was very good. It was not all that much later that I again sought my hotel room, informing the denizens of the front desk that I was to have an early wake-up call and a taxi, thus to take the morning flight back to Copenhagen. *Not a problem Sir. We will look after it. Enjoy the rest of your evening.*

In my hotel room it was now getting on into the evening but the sun was still very much alive and well in the sky. I knew that the sun sets much later in northern climes than it does where I normally live, and so drew the curtains against the light and took in the remainder of a soccer game on TV. It was clearly evident that the young people who had prevented me from calling a taxi were very much in party mode on the street below. In point of fact it was perfectly acceptable for them to drink, and drink some more, and then smash their booze bottles against the stone walls of the buildings, even in the downtown, but only on this one night per year. Pretty soon after the soccer game had completed itself I went to sleep.

I awoke to a sun pie-in-the-sky. It was clearly evident to me that I had overslept and that the hotel staff down at the desk had failed to call me to the battle of the day. Cursing all and sundry Swedes, I rushed through my ablutions, knowing that I was going to be late for my flight, and expensively so, and then called down to the front desk to give them the bloody blue blazes for dereliction of duty.

Sir, It is 3:17 a.m. Not much dark in Stockholm in June.

CHAPTER

Magic

Come. Let us go to a magic place.

It is a lovely warm summer's evening and we are in Neu-Ulm in Germany. We have had a lovely walk beside the Danube River, watching the boats sculling by. The current here is fast, as the river is often only about 50 yards wide. We have treated ourselves to a cool drink on the patio of the hotel overlooking the Danube, out in the gorgeous sunshine decorated with a gentle breeze.

Come, my dear. Let us freshen up and then go across the river to the old town. Pretty soon we are strolling arm in arm across the stone bridge that leads to the town square of Ulm, with the Munster dwarfing us on the east side. The Munster of Ulm is the highest church in the world. One is permitted to climb the circular staircase within, to the very top. I have done this on several occasions and it is well worth the climb. It seems that nearly the whole world is spread out in every direction, and it is a perfect way to take in the beautiful Bavarian countryside and the Danube River winding through it. The church itself is huge – I think people could nearly play football in there. There are few rivals for it in size or Gothic beauty. (Google it)

Dotted around the edge of the square are a fair few restaurants, many of them Italian, and nearly all of those boasting pizza, with a real hardwood-fired kiln therein. We sit at an outside table and partake of this wonderful pizza, fresh from the oven, and wash it down with suitable quantities of Chianti. Families and lovers stroll by or sit on the edge of the fountain in the center of the square. Small children run and shout and play in the manner of small children everywhere, a beautiful, civilized, and relaxing way to spend the dinner hour.

So now it approaches seven o'clock and time to wander over to the Munster. As is the custom of every Saturday night, there is music in the Munster. It is pretty much always a presentation of classical music, mostly from the Great Masters. I have stumbled upon Brahms' *German Requiem* quite by accident on such a Saturday evening, a piece of music, which, when played and sung in that church, with the acoustics of those Gothic surroundings, is magic indeed.

On this particular evening the playbill framed beside the church door indicates that we are to be treated to a cantata by Bach. A small choir from Hamburg, in the north of Germany, is to do the honors a cappella. We go up the stairs and enter through the great central doors, making our way to one of the chapels attached to the side of the church. It is not lavishly decorated; the walls are of dark walnut, with a domed stone ceiling and stone floor. The pews are also hardwood and seat approximately 200 people. Slowly the chapel fills until there are very few places left. There is no conversation – the room is mostly silent. We sit in my favorite location, where the focal point of the acoustics will be best.

At the appointed hour the choir files in, 32 in all. They stand in two ranks of 16 at the front of the chapel and are then joined by the choirmaster. There is no introduction. The choirmaster and choristers bow their heads in silent meditation for maybe half a minute or so. Then the choirmaster reaches into his pocket and pulls out a tuning fork and a small baton. He strikes the tuning fork with the baton and the choir takes their pitches accordingly. The instruments go back into his pocket. Then the hand of the choirmaster goes up, and for the next 45 minutes or so, there is magic. Nothing but the human voice at its very finest. After each movement of the cantata there is more silent meditation, and then the master's hand goes up again and weaves the cloth of that magic; music which fills the chapel and causes the listener to marvel at the Grace and Mercy of the Almighty, to allow us sinners to worship in this manner. It is not given to us humans to even imagine the harmony of the Choirs of the Angels, to which yet we hope to be treated, but an hour in a chapel of this nature may get us close.

The cantata is finished. The choir and its master once more bow their heads in prayerful meditation, while those of us in the pews are also completely silent. After a little while the choirmaster raises his head and walks to one side of the singers. He then puts his hand out to salute the choir, whereupon there is quiet and gentle

applause in appreciation for what has transpired. The choir files out first, followed by the choirmaster and then those of us in the pews. Many do not leave right away, me included. I sit still and absorb the magic, and seek to take such then as I am able.

We slowly take in a full circle of the inside of the church, stopping to admire the many fine works of art and the symbolism and messages for which they stand. The Munster of Ulm was roughly 1200 years in the making, and it shows.

By now the sun has nearly set behind the walls of the buildings facing the square, birds sing evensong and twitter in the trees dotted about. The families have mostly gone home but there are still many folk who linger over drinks in the cafés. We exit the square in the direction of the river and stroll until we find an Italian restaurant which makes real gelato on the premises. Then we sit beside the river at one of the little tables outside and enjoy real handmade Italian ice cream and a lovely dram of cognac. It doesn't get a whole lot better than this.

Tomorrow morning at 11 o'clock, we will be back in the Munster to take in the organ concert. It is easy to understand why the pipe organ is referred to as the King of Instruments. When most of the stops are pulled and the organist unleashes nearly all of the 10,000 pipes which grace the organ loft, it is a matter which always causes the hair on the back of my neck to arise. This is a serious sensual experience, the complete antithesis of what we enjoyed the evening before. I always take my shoes off because, when the tubas in the base pipes are unlimbered, the sound comes up through the stone floor through the soles of my feet, as well as the other normal channels. When the last of the echoes of the sound of that mighty organ have died away, I always just sit there for maybe 10 minutes or so. Magic.

There is, of course, magic everywhere. The best brand of magic is the kind that unexpectedly falls out of the blue sky or is waiting just around the next corner. Magic cannot be manufactured. The world is already full to exploding with it, and it is up to us to recognize it and then take it for our own. From my perspective at least, this occurs mostly when I am sitting still in a quiet place. Perhaps there is a breeze in the trees and the sound of a brook just yonder, or in the chapel of a Gothic church. These are good places to find magic.

CHAPTER 🏇🏇🏇🏇🏇🏇

Music

Growing up, there was always music flying around. I suppose I knew what four-part harmony was by the time I got to kindergarten, because that's what we sang in church. Around the house, my sisters played the piano and there was always somebody singing something. At school we took weekly lessons in the classroom from a music teacher who was brought in for that purpose. Christmas time created a choir in the school and in the church, and during the annual Kiwanis Music Festival there were choirs and solos and duets and I don't know what all. My first memory of anything in song of a formal nature occurred when I was probably about age six. I sang a song called *My Kitty* at the Kiwanis Festival, for which I received first prize, a silver dollar, and a notation on the adjudication papers which stated, *The expression seems to come out of his eyebrows*. Well it doesn't get any better than that, so I suppose it has been pretty much downhill from there. Not that I was done with music, but I don't suppose I ever achieved any similar level of excellence since then.

If I ever possessed any sort of hereditary musicianship, it most certainly did not emanate from our father which art in heaven. Dad could not hold a tune in a bucket to save his Christian soul. Each morning he sat at his shaving mirror and sang hymns, each phrase in tune within itself yet the next always in a different key. Astonishing! I have tried to do this but with very limited success. Mother had a very good voice but, as was the custom of the Old Order Mennonite, grade eight was as far as she could go. Opera star in a black bonnet. She sure could sing.

When I was 10, I lobbied for and miraculously received a trumpet. It was a tarnished old battered up piece of junk tin and, even though I pretty much blew my guts out into that horn, nothing much of a positive nature came out the other end. In point

of fact I'm pretty sure that most large mammals within the sound of that horn either fled the neighborhood or alternately curled up and died and were glad to go. It did not go well.

Somebody said that perhaps we should clean it. And so it was taken apart and the whole mess was dumped into a washtub with warm soapy water. The water quickly turned into a murky soup. A piece of sponge was attached to a wire and passed through the apparatus. Pretty soon it was clearly evident that the lack of music emanating from the bell of that trumpet was not only attributable to my lack of expertise, but also to the matter of a chunk of cloth which had lodged itself in the main tubing. With the demon rag exorcised and the device reassembled with the assistance of suitable lubrication, it suddenly was possible to produce a trumpet tone.

I took lessons from the high school bandmaster, one Mr. Chizlet, whose expertise was in the violin. Two years later I was in grade 9 and was admitted to the high school band. The new bandleader was Richard Reidstra. He was a highly skilled and experienced musician in wind instruments and had some very definite ideas about *how to play* and *how not to play* music. He was not everybody's cup of tea but he and I got along quite well. He also taught me private lessons. The school band went to Expo 67 in Montréal and also to Expo 70 in Osaka Japan.

I clearly remember the Osaka airport. The flight out of Toronto had been at seven a.m. and many of us had not gotten much, if any, sleep the night before. Then there was the nine-hour flight to Anchorage, Alaska, where we stopped for an hour to refuel, and then another nine hours to Japan. You do the math – we had been up for a long time. So there, in the Osaka airport, one of our number, Brenda Sauder, retired to the ladies room to accomplish such invitations of nature now dictated by her gastrointestinal circumstances. Very quickly she came rushing out and pointed over at the door. Her mouth was going up and down but no sound was coming out – she was that hysterical. Eventually she was able to croak out, *It's just a hole in the floor!*

After high school, and after I got back from wandering around the globe trying to avoid such mischief as I was busy creating for myself, I was approached by Mr. Reidstra to play trumpet in the Kitchener-Waterloo Symphony Orchestra. It seems that they were shy on trumpeters at that time. Mr. Riedstra, who played French horn in the orchestra and whose wife Maria was the concertmaster as well, had convinced the new conductor, Maestro Raffi Armenian, that I was just the man for the job.

I will hasten to explain that my book of classical music was a very slim volume indeed. There was only one secular record in our house. It was music by Tchaikovsky with the *1812 Overture* on one side and the *Slavonic March* on the other. I loved it and played it to death, but that was the only game in town. However, in my great and glorious ignorance on the matter, I soon found myself at Mr. Riedstra's house trying to learn my part in Beethoven's *Seventh Symphony*. I had heard the word Beethoven but knew absolutely nothing about what he wrote or how it should sound. Mr. Riedstra patiently taught me how it was supposed to go. To this day I have no clue how I survived past that first concert, but somehow I muddled through.

I have done very few clever things in my life, to which fact anybody who knows me at all will attest with great vehemence. Nevertheless, this one time I did a clever thing. In the school band, we went to band practice to learn the music. However, the symphony orchestra was a professionally paid position and everybody was obligated to know their music before the first rehearsal. Then the conductor, the generalissimo of music planning his war campaign for that concert, would dictate in no uncertain terms as to how it was supposed to be stuck together. The problem was I had no idea how the music was supposed to sound. In the school band I was the lead trumpet and played the melody. No brain surgery there. In the orchestra, I played second trumpet and there was not a whole pile to do for long periods of time, and yet I had to know when to come in – and get it right.

The music for each concert was given to us about a month in advance. So the clever thing that I did was to take the music down to Sam the Record Man and buy it all. Then I took it home and put it on the turntable and listened to it while I had my portion of the score on the music stand in front of me. That way I could figure out what it was supposed to sound like and when I was supposed to play. Yet still, looking back on it, it is clearly evident that I am no professional musician. I got by via the double happenstance of not overly embarrassing myself together with the fact that, seemingly, there was nobody else around to take my place. I enjoyed it immensely and look back with very fond recollection of those times. In retrospect it was one of the most terrific honors and privileges that I have ever had.

In those days I also sang in the Kitchener-Waterloo Philharmonic Choir under the baton of Howard Dyck. Not sure how I arrived there but I loved singing and auditioned in Mr. Dyck's studio in his house. I always thought I was a bass but he declared me to be a baritone, and that was fine by me. I was starting to learn classical music from the perspective of both voice and instrumentation, a matter for which I will never have any regret.

Once upon a time, there was a joint production of Beethoven's *Ninth Symphony* and, as you all know, it is orchestra and choir at the same time. I was in both organizations, and it needed to be determined whether I sat in the orchestra or stood in the choir. I am not exactly positive of the method involved in the determination of my position, but I am pretty sure that Maestros Armenian and Dyck might have flipped a coin, whereupon Howard lost the toss and I ended up singing in the choir. It was an amazing experience and, again, one which I shall never forget.

You see, whether in a choir or an orchestra or band or just by yourself, without you singing or playing, the music doesn't happen. Therefore, *you are the music*. For example, in a symphony orchestra, everybody has to tune their instruments so that they can harmonize properly. Prior to the start of a concert, the oboe plays the note A, and everybody tunes to that note. However, when a piece of music is in full swing, the players tune off an unspoken entity called the *Center of the Sound*. This is not able to be properly defined in words, but as near as I can, there is a concept which I will try to define as the heart of the orchestra and everybody aims for the center of the heart of that sound. Also I learned to harmonize and join in the wavelength of the first trumpeter next to me. Before long I found that our two trumpet bells were often sort of leaning towards each other as we listened to each other. We aimed for the center of each other's sound, as well as that of the entire orchestra. There were many times when we played octaves, my notes being one octave lower than his and, if I found his wavelength, then my tone would disappear and his would sound like a million bucks. I was the music. We are the music. We are all music. And maybe if we listened to each other a little more there would be greater harmony.

Perhaps the most terrifying experience of my entire life occurred when we played Bizet's *Carmen*. I had never heard of this before, but I was probably the only one in the orchestra and the 1500 people or so in the audience who didn't know pretty much every note of it. Big names came to town, names like Maureen Forrester and so forth. It was a great set of tunes and I was enjoying it very much. Then came the minor matter of me having to go backstage and play the army onto the stage. The army was coming, and I was to play a certain tune as a fanfare from deep in the wings, to make the soldiers sound further away. Normally the trumpets, the second trumpet in particular, can pretty much hide a multitude of minor sins behind all the other the instruments which are playing simultaneously. But not this time. This time I was the only game in town, about as naked as one can tonally get, and in the presence of a lot of people.

So I practiced and practiced and practiced it some more until I thought I had it right. However, at dress rehearsal the nerves got hold of me, and when I saw Raffi's finger stab at me on the monitor I let fly. It did not go well. I knew it, everybody else knew it, and I slunk back to my chair in the pit. I figured I had gotten away with it until, at the end of the rehearsal when everybody was packing up to go, Mr. Armenian looked at me and said, *Herr Brubacher, I will see you in my chambers immediately!* So I shuffled head down into his office and he said, *Herr Brubacher, that did not go well tonight!* Yes sir. *Herr Brubacher, tomorrow it will be perfect!* There were chains and heated steel in that voice, and it was perfect.

That was 40 years ago, and I am nearly recovered.

CHAPTER 🐝 🐝 🐝 🐝 🐝

𝕸𝖆𝖑 𝖉𝖊 𝕸𝖊𝖗⁺

There was not a lot of sickness in our house when I was growing up. There were the usual measles and flu, coughs and sniffles, and other matters requiring the tender administrations of a handkerchief, but aside from my father's polio and brother Gordon's rheumatic fever, I can't remember any significant disease-oriented matters in our household.

Sore throats were not too bad an issue, because we got to drink concoctions of warm something or other laced with honey, and honey was sweet so that was pretty much a treat. I don't think I ever heard anybody complain of a headache. Maybe they were around, but they certainly did not affect me in any material manner. I did not like getting a cold because that led to coughing, and coughing had to be dealt with in what was to me, at least at the time, a spectacularly nasty method. Mother had this brown bottle of medicine which was supposed to be the universal specific for anything concerning strange noises that came out of the respiratory and mouthing systems of small children. It was an evil smelling liquid which appeared to be made out of equal parts ammonia and janitor-in-a-drum. I was forced to swallow a tablespoonful of this perfidious fluid, and it was such a powerful demon that I would run up and down the hall shaking my head at high rates of speed until I thought my neck might snap. But it seemed to work.

Once in a while, I would get the flu and was confined to bed. Influenza, or whatever cousin of same happened to lurk in our household at the time, was determined by the administration of the thermometer under the tongue. I am pretty sure that mother could tell from the flush of the face and the lack of proper rambunctious activity level of a small boy whether something was amiss, but the thermometer was unlimbered to prove it. If my body temperature was above a certain level, then to bed it was. The only bright side was that mother would bring my meals and I could actually eat food in bed, a matter otherwise not even considered. However, the portions were not very big. Feed the cold and starve the fever. Well, when there really was a fever I wasn't very hungry anyway.

A much more common malady would be stomach flu. From time to time some kind of bug would come around and things would start to turn loop-de-loops in our tummies. It was hoped by all and sundry that the patient afflicted with a malady of this nature would be able to find a suitable repository for what might fly out of the speaking end of that small child. Mostly this occurred, and all of the stuff that came out would find the toilet and was thus disposed of with the pull of a lever. I never was much of a fan of praying to the toilet gods, and I still have an aversion to same. But sometimes the matter to hand did not make it all the way to the bathroom, and then it was incumbent upon mother to rise in the night and do what mothers universally do, which is, of course, clean up after the mishaps of their offspring.

I am given to understand that the closest I ever came to any sort of catastrophic health circumstance occurred when I was 16 and I evidently came down with appendicitis. I had been working at a church camp north of Bancroft all summer, where I was employed as a casual laborer. It was obviously evident to the Powers That Be that I was not Christian counselor material, and so I got to collect the garbage, mow the lawn, do such odd jobs around the establishment that needed fetching after, and helping the people who were erecting a new concrete block building which was to be the future home of the boys' sleeping department. My job was to mix mortar and carry it up to the people who were laying blocks.

This was hard work. I say *carry it up* because, as the building grew and they laid blocks on the second floor, those working on scaffolding communicated with terra firma by ordinary ladders. So I mixed the mortar in the cement mixing machine and poured it into two five-gallon pails, each of them half-full. I am not sure what each of those pails weighed but I think something in the order of 50 pounds per. I grabbed the handles of the pails, one in each hand, and ran up the ladders to deposit the mortar on the boards from which the block layers worked. *Look Ma, no hands!* And that was indeed literally the case. I ran up and down the ladders with a pail in each hand with exactly zero hands left over for steadying myself on the ladder. What's more, I did this without even thinking about it, or without any comment or instruction of any kind from the other workers. Looking back on it I think that those in charge of my guardian angels must've sent their biggest and best to look after me, and rotated their shifts approximately every 20 minutes or so. And also, needless to say, I became very strong and very tough, in perhaps the best shape of my life, except maybe when I worked in the feed mill and slugged 100-pound bags around all day.

But I was happy. I was not in my dad's shoe store dusting shoeboxes or worse. I was outside, working hard at this beautiful camp with the lake hard by, and the boats for fishing and the swimming and water skiing. Doesn't get much better than that. The downside of it was that I had to display a continued manifestation of manufactured piety in the form of daily prayer and supplication, which was required of all present. Down on my knees in the presence of my peers thanking the Almighty for my eternal salvation, imploring God's grace in the saving of the souls of the campers who came daily from the ranks of the heathen Lutherans and Presbyterians, not to mention the hell-bound Catholics (those evil people…). We were here to save souls, and the saving of souls was the top of the agenda. They cleverly disguised it with instruction on swimming and canoeing and all manner of outdoor sports, and I suppose they were at least to some degree successful because the camp is still there. Graphite Bible Camp. A great place. But if the truth is known, and God knows what's going on deep down inside so why shouldn't I tell you, while I was imploring God's grace and mercy in the matter of encouraging our missionaries and saving the lost, I was actually heartily wishing that I was at the fishing services on one of those boats down there yonder and reeling in the big one.

However there was one ailment which I would periodically use as a weapon to escape from going to school. This was known as an earache. An earache is not detectable by a thermometer or any other means of normal observation. So if I would complain of an earache, there was no independent arbitration as to whether or not I was telling the truth. I would like to give myself the benefit of the doubt by claiming that I may well have *thought* I had an earache or perhaps felt something akin to one coming on, or even claiming that it was a psychosomatic response to some sort of ridiculous stimulus or other. I suspect pretty much none of that would ever have been true. Yes, there were a few times that I actually did have an earache, and it was pretty miserable and I was right to stay home. But most of the time it was an excuse not to go to school. It wasn't bad enough so that I had to stay in bed the whole time, like if I had the flu, but it was sufficiently potentially serious enough that mother deemed it fit that I stay

home under matriarchal observation. I never abused the privilege by staying home for more than one day at a time, but every so often the boredom of tutelage would set in and it was incumbent upon a small boy to take evasive action, lest I developed some kind of expensive complex or other.

One fine time when I was about 10 years old, I was sick in bed with the flu. It must have been for real because there was no way I was going to be inside on a summer's day unless I was very nearly dead. I also know it was in the summertime because cousin Donnie came around and he only came when it was summer. Donny was allowed to come up to our boys' bedroom to visit. This pepped me right up and pretty soon we were bouncing around on the bed. Nothing so fancy as a thickly padded mattress and box springs in those days. The mattress was about as thick as a dog's tongue and the springs were just that: coil springs of bare steel in a metal frame.

Bouncing up and down on a bed at any time is lots of fun. Bouncing up and down on a bed with your cousin is *much more* fun. We decided that we needed to do a thing called post falling. This occurs where both of us boys would stand up on the foot of the bed with our arms firmly planted at our sides and our bodies stiff while we fell in unison back onto the bed. This caused no small amount of bouncy, screechy, steel bed frame noises and needed to be repeated a considerable number of times. However, with enough repetitive stress, the administrations of even 10-year-old boys proved too much for the strength of the structures of said bed. The bed frame parted, the springs and mattress descended down through and took up residence on the floor below with a resounding crash. Quite soon after that, mother hollered up the stairs, *Boys, boys, shut the window! It sounds like there's a thunderstorm coming!*

But there was one very large shadow which encompassed our entire family. This was, of course, polio. Soon after I was born, and when father was 35, he took the polio. In 1952 the vaccine had not yet been invented and it was still a scourge upon the landscape. Mostly attacking in summer, poliomyelitis was a very serious problem to many communities including our own. I have read accounts of entire large towns and other communities being pretty much shut down on account of the potentially virulent spread of this terrible disease. It attacked the motor nerves of an individual and, if not outright fatal, it could and did render the victim with limited use of limbs and also vitals such as lungs. People took their lives in their hands to go to the bank or the grocery store. Public institutions were shut down, such as schools, playgrounds, and swimming pools. Many died.

In December 1952, father felt a strange weakness in his legs and very soon thereafter was hospitalized. The cause of the problem was discovered to be poliomyelitis and he spent about nine months in the Kitchener-Waterloo Hospital on the ninth floor, which was pretty much entirely devoted to polio victims. He never made it to the iron lung (Google it – it will scare the hell out of you) but it was a near thing. When all was said and done and he had gone through physiotherapy at Lyndhurst Lodge in Toronto, he was confined to a wheelchair for the rest of his life. He was able to walk for very short distances with the help of serious leg braces and crutches, but by and large he was in a wheelchair.

When I was a kid there was no such thing as wheelchair accessible buildings. Our house at the top of the hill east of Elmira was no longer suitable to a wheelchair, and so father caused to be built in the west end of town a domicile which was more suitable. By this I mean that the doors were a little wider than most and that access to the main floor required no stairs. The bathroom on the main floor also had some hand bars which allowed dad to use the tub and toilet with greater ease, but still a far cry from today's hydraulic lifts and accessibility items that are common to homes with disabilities. We went to church where strong men picked up him and his chair and bodily hefted both to the main floor of the sanctuary. His shoe store was never properly fitted with accessibility items, so he simply made things work as best he could.

Thus he never played baseball or hockey or any of the street sports which were common to our town. Once in a while he would take us fishing at the Conestoga Dam. He sat in the car and read his Bible while we boys did the fishing. This was great sport indeed, and much appreciated. But at the time it was never even considered by me, at least, what life might have been otherwise, if dad were able to get around in the normal fashion. He was in the wheelchair. And that's just the way it was.

CHAPTER 🥪 🥪 🥪 🥪 🥪
𝕾𝖆𝖓𝖉𝖜𝖎𝖈𝖍𝖊𝖘 𝖆𝖓𝖉 𝕾𝖚𝖈𝖍

This chapter is dedicated to the 4th Earl of Sandwich

SANDWICHES

According to Wikipedia, the first written usage of the English word *Sandwich* appeared in Edward Gibbon's journal, in longhand, referring to *bits of cold meat*. It was named after John Montagu, 4th Earl of Sandwich, an 18th-century English aristocrat. It is said that he ordered his valet to bring him meat tucked between two pieces of bread and others began to order, *the same as Sandwich!* It is commonly said that Lord Sandwich was fond of this form of food because it allowed him to continue playing cards, particularly cribbage, while eating without using a fork and without getting his cards greasy from eating meat with his bare hands. Our thanks to the Wiki fellas for that.

I love sandwiches. Always have and always will.

We almost never got sandwiches at home. The farm boys and those who lived quite a distance away from our school brought lunch that consisted of lots of sandwiches and apples and cookies and other foodstuffs that one could eat by hand in a hurry then go out and play in the schoolyard. We, on the other hand, who lived about a block away from the school, had to go home every noon to eat our mother's nutritious home-cooked meals. Generally there was soup or fried eggs, or perhaps potato patties made from the leftovers of last night's supper or whatever. But almost never sandwiches.

There were two notable occasions which allowed us to take lunch to school. One circumstance occurred where, once a month for a number of years, mother would go and look after one of our parishioners who was bedridden with severe arthritis. Her name was Mrs. Martin Bauman. I don't know if she had a first name – probably did, but I never heard it. In Mennonite culture the wife was known as an extension of her husband; my mother was Mrs. Urias Brubacher. She would pick up the telephone every Saturday morning and connect with one of the four grocery stores in town. *This is Mrs. Urias Brubacher, and I would like some things sent out please.* Never, *this is Sarah Brubacher and…*

The other time, once per year, that let us take lunch to school occurred when mother hosted her annual quilting bee. Mother loved to quilt and did so nearly to her dying day. In anticipation of her quilting bee, all the furniture in the living room had to be either removed or repositioned in such a manner that her quilting frame, which I discovered much later had belonged to her grandmother, could position itself in the center of the room and be surrounded by chairs. Mother would prepare the base cloth and cotton batting on the frames, followed by the patterned quilt top she had spent so many laborious hours manufacturing. Nary a piece of cloth or rag escaped mother's attention. Any fabric remotely cloth-like or woven was potential fodder for her quilt cannon. Her principal form of entertainment was designing, cutting, and sewing together the cloth pieces into patterns. It was a lot of work and she loved it.

On the appointed day the women involved to do the quilting would appear shortly after breakfast. Some were from our church, while others came from the ranks of friends and relatives, of which she had many. Often they were not yet done with the quilt by the time we got home from school. The quilters always talked up a storm. If there were 10 quilters, it would appear to me and my little sister Lorraine that there would be at least seven conversations going simultaneously. One of the reasons for this interpretation of the matter was that they spoke Pennsylvania Dutch and we understood pretty much nary a word of it. Other times, one person, usually a Frey (who were considered to be very good talkers), would be recounting at length some matter of great pitch and moment, while all the rest would add cogent comment in the form of oooooooooooooOOOOOOOOOOOOOOOOooooooooooooo with triple G (great glee and gusto). It sounded for all the world like exuberant chickens in a henhouse. We would sneak in and park our little butts on the stairs next to the living room door and copy them, oooooooooooooOOOOOOOOOOOOOOOOooooooo ooooo etc. Repeat. If however our oooooos and our OOOOOOOOOOOs would be opposite to the volume of the up-and-down of the hens behind the living room door,

then mother would pick up on this and come out and whack us and tell us to go outside and play.

But in both of the cases above, I got to take sandwiches and apples to school and eat them with the farm boys and then go out and play baseball or in the sandbox or whatever the outdoor joyousness du jour dictated on that particular occasion.

I suppose if I had to choose a desert island sandwich, it would be Baloney and Cheez Whiz. I capitalize Baloney because I *really like* Baloney. Oh I know I know, it's supposed to have all manner of demons lurking therein, but I love it. Dad railed against the evils of too much Cheez Whiz. *It's concentrated – don't put so much on!* which is, of course, a load of that which commeth forth from the south end of a north-bound horse. What he was badly truly saying is, *It's expensive! Lay off the slathering up already!*

A close second would be leftover roast beef, soft cheese, lettuce or tomatoes, and mayonnaise. Why these above? Well, because in both cases the repast is flavorful and slides down easily. Also quick to make. And as there was a lot of pretty dry food in our household and not much in the line of added spices or flavors other than that which mother had been taught in the Mennonite traditions, baloney and Cheez Whiz was pretty racy stuff. Dad decreed that it was unnecessary, and probably non-Christian, to have two kinds of protein in one sandwich, so normally either one or the other had to be surreptitiously ensconced between the slices of bread.

To this day, my refrigerator rejoices in all manner of foodstuffs which can be applied between chunks of the loaf. I have experimented, and nearly any combination will do. There are, of course, various exceptions such as peanut butter and Cheez Whiz or peanut butter and ketchup. Slide down, but no go. I fully realize that if I had intimate acquaintance with the materials from which baloney or macaroni and cheese loaf are manufactured, I may well have second thoughts. I suppose that the principal ingredients are fat and salt and sweepings off the butcher floor, but they taste wonderful and slide down.

No matter. I choose to gird up my loins, leap over these obstacles and enjoy sandwiches. Home-cooked ham with Havarti, sliced tomatoes with salt and pepper, mayo and lettuce, and fry the bacon crisp until she snaps. All imprisoned between thick slices of pumpernickel. Hold ye not the butter, and lay out pickles on the side. Creamy potato salad with slices of hard cooked egg on top. Paprika. A cold German stein of beer to the top right of the plate. A little lederhosen music. Next flight for Munich anyone?

Not at all sure that life gets a whole lot better. Not, at least, with clothes on.

AND SUCH

Baloney and Cheez Whiz sandwiches. Macaroni and cheese. Shepherds pie. Gravy Fleisch (Swiss steak) with mashed potatoes. Rice and cheese. Head cheese with mustard beans or schnibledy bona. Roast beef with gravy and cooked grated turnips with mashed potatoes. Bledlin grumbaada. Cod fillets with creamed peas. Salmon loaf with creamed peas and mashed potatoes. Wieners with pork and beans and buttered bread. Wieners with creamed corn and potatoes. Last, and my gallows repast, hamburger meat loaf with creamed corn and mashed potatoes. No ketchup needed.

So what do all of the above have in common? They all slide down!

I call them trombone food. All of the above foodstuffs go down the hatch with the ease of a tone descending the scale under the tender ministrations of an accomplished trombone player. They all sing a joyful tune on the palate, swirl and co-mingle like a well-tuned symphonic offering amid the taste-buds, appreciated in the same manner as an ovation after the pause of the last chord, and, with a minimum of mastication, make their loving descent, a glissando, into those regions ruled by gastrointestinal fortitude. A fitting and loving transmogrification from plate to satisfying fuel.

Unfortunately while growing up in our household in Elmira it was not all that often that trombone food was served. My father which art in heaven believed in chewing food. Lots and lots and lots of chewing. This, he explained to us, was necessary to promote the secretion of saliva which in turn was an excellent asset in the digestive process. And while all of the hypotheses as proclaimed by our dad were by and large true, it made for some pretty tough and boring eating.

Mostly for dinner it was plain boiled potatoes in their jackets, and those potatoes were not generally all that young and often had skins on them which were becoming pretty tough. I am certainly not blaming mother for not wanting to peel potatoes, because there were nine hungry mouths to fill and she did not need to have a lot of extra work to keep her busy. She never planted potatoes in her garden, but they came in burlap bags and went down into the root cellar, there to sit beside the bags of carrots and turnips and other root vegetables which certainly kept for a fairly long time but also developed some fairly interesting changes, especially to their skins. I never remember mother ordering potatoes from the grocery store.

Before mother got the freezer, she put large quantities of vegetables from the garden into crown jars, steamed them, sealed them up, and put them down on the shelves in the cold cellar. In the wintertime these most often served as the vegetables on our plate. It was always so great to have peas and beans and lettuce and cabbage and best of all corn directly from the garden while those were in season. Along about when I was 12 or 13 years old, one of the neighbors around the corner moved away and we became the proud possessor's of a deep freeze. This was a great blessing to mother because she could not only put up her own corn and other vegetables with much greater ease but also watch for the specials and get other items of a similar nature for good prices.

I think the dinner table meat which we ate the most often was farmer's pork sausage. It was easy to come by and easy to prepare as mother would simply brown it in the frying pan, dump in some water, cover it all with a lid and pretty soon we had fried pork sausage. Nothing wrong with that. I liked it then and I like it now. It was very traditional to have the Sunday main meal at noon after we got home from church, and this often consisted of either Swiss steak or a roast of beef of some kind. We left for church on Sunday mornings at nine o'clock, by which time mother had most of this meal in the oven. She would brown the beef in the roasting pan on the stove top, dump in the amount of water that she thought was going to be needed together with potatoes and carrots and onions. We got home from church sometime between 12:30 and 1 o'clock, by which time the meal was ready. This was a very good thing, due to the fact that stomachs by that time were growling up a pretty good set of rumblings. Mother would pour the juices off the roast into a sauce pot wherein to produce gravy.

Now let there be a word about gravy. Gravy was (and still is) the Ambrosia of the Blessed. God's Gift to the Palate. The Facilitation of Trombone Food. It was the nectar provided as proof positive that the Almighty is merciful and gracious and allows even us sinners to enjoy a wonderful meal. To this day I love gravy. I will pour it onto any sort of meat or make it a sauce for fish, certainly put some onto the potatoes and probably the vegetables too. I can remember many a time on Sunday noon, with my plate now empty and, having poured as much gravy onto the repast without it spilling out onto the tablecloth, the contents of the gravy pitcher still beckoned. On Sunday noon there was often company, guests from the church or beyond, and it was incumbent upon mother to serve bread, a matter which never occurred in the standard course of culinary events otherwise. So it was permitted a slice of bread on the plate, and supplies permitting, inundated with gravy. And if there was cooked turnip and a few bits of beef left over as well, it was allowed to add that to the feast. It doesn't get a whole lot better than that.

But gravy did not appear very often. Many times, especially after the advent of the freezer, the meat would be beef. Dad would contract with one of the local farmers for a quarter of a cow. I am convinced that many of these animals met their legal demise via the tender administrations of whatever implement of destruction was employed in reducing them to hors de combat, generally I think about 20 minutes or so before they would have died a natural death of old age. That is not to criticize the tenderness or otherwise of the resulting contents of our freezer, except I learned to hate steak (that is, the few times that mother tried to prepare it other than slow cooked in the oven) because as opposed to a foodstuff, it appeared palpably designed to grace the bottom of a work boot. It was tough sledding, and in dad's mastication religion, well, it appeared to be a groovy thing to chew your food until your jaws hurt. Down with saliva.

One time we had company for Sunday noon from Lancaster County, PA, who were buddies of dad and mom. We had roast beef with all the trimmings, including horse radish. Mom put it in a little glass dish and the Man From PA helped himself lavishly. On his first fork-full of beef, he piled on a dollop of this white grated radish an amount pretty much on par with the roast. Evidently where he came from they cut their horse radish with a lot of creamy mayo or some such, and it was nowhere nearly as powerful as our raw goods.

Very quickly after he wolfed down this heaping forkful we were treated to a grown man red-eyed, weeping, coughing, choking, sputtering, and with copious quantities of effluent emanating from his nose. I thought his entire head might explode, or at the very least see steam fly out of his ears. It was seriously cool. Mom bypassed the napkins and headed straight for a big towel.

Six days a week, breakfast was always exactly the same. After we read the Scriptures and offered up the appropriate words of prayer, it was porridge. Red River Cereal to be precise. You can still get it at Walmart. It was a concoction of miscellaneous grains which may well have been rejected from any other process used in the creation of bread or Cheerios or what have you. Dump it into the pot with the appropriate amount of water, bring it to a boil, and let it simmer until it is mush. Don't forget to dump in the leftover porridge from yesterday. This goop was then ladled into a soup bowl, on top of which went a generous helping of Kellogg's All Bran, a good dollop of honey, and then all doused in about half a cup of milk. This was followed by a raw apple and the rest of your cup of milk. A breakfast of champions. I am pretty sure that any form of robust health that I enjoy now is a tribute to that breakfast. I have little doubt that most of the world would be a better place if everybody started off the day thusly fortified.

Sunday breakfast was different. We got cold cereal, such as cornflakes or Cheerios, but never Sugar Pops or any of the other cereals that had sweetener overtly added to them. Again with honey and milk. Then there was bread with peanut butter and honey or perhaps peanut butter and jam. Never toast. There were nine of us and the toaster was an ancient contraption which, when it was exhumed, appeared to be good for little else than the production of black smoke and carbonized bread. So we were happy with ordinary bread; after all, it was not often that we had it except perhaps at lunchtime. Sunday breakfast was always also very special because there was exotic fruit such as California grapes. This was seriously good eating. Also from time to time, fruit juice would appear. One such was called Ping, a concoction of pineapple and grapefruit juices. This was a wonderful fluid because pineapple was very sweet and grapefruit was very tart and the two complemented each other very well. I'm not sure when I have ever seen that combination in stores in any sort of recent history. Then off to the onslaught of church.

For lunch we did not take sandwiches to school because we lived just down the street and had to go home to mother's delicious hot lunches. What a drag. She often made soup, from the leftovers from last night's supper, or corn from the garden or perhaps fried eggs. Sometimes there would be potato pancakes, onto which we could spoon her homemade chili sauce. I believe there was precious little chili powder involved, but it tasted very good and it was trombone food. I think she broke a few eggs into it as well and maybe added some finely chopped onion. But the farm boys brought sandwiches to school and played baseball. I kept hoping that we would move out of town so that I could do that too.

There was generally some form of desert involved with each meal. For breakfast of course an apple or other fruit on Sundays. At lunchtime it was probably a cookie or some leftover pie. At suppertime it was often fruit preserves. Sunday for dinner there would pretty much always be pie with fresh fruit in season, such as strawberries, apples, pears, or peaches, and sometimes cherry pie or judacascha pie.

This little round berry is also known as *ground cherries* (physalis coztomatl) and looks much like an amber marble. It is a ground creeper perennial, which kept on crawling around the garden. It did not matter that you plowed it under with the rest of the garden every fall; it would come up again in the spring as a creeping vine. It just merrily made its way around the cabbages and the corn and anywhere else that you let it grow. Some people called them paper bag cherries because the fruit formed in small papery-like sacks. In the early summer they were green, and the berry inside was small and hard and also green. As the summer waxed, the sacks started to turn brown and the berries became larger as well. I think it was probably towards the middle of September or so when the berries were ripe. You could tell this because the sacks now had turned into a sort of porous cheesecloth and were nearly falling off the berries, now translucent amber.

We children were sent out with six-quart baskets to pick these berries. We removed the remainders of the paper bags and then they were ready for pie. And what glorious pie that was indeed. In the manner of pies of Waterloo County, a bottom crust was prepared, the berries went in, sugar on top, cover with more pie dough, bake and enjoy. Very often however, mother would cut the berries about one half with apples. Not only was this a very delicious combination, but also stretched the ground cherries by 50%. Apples were far more available than judacasha.

There were of course, special meals for special occasions. Every time there was a birthday there was ice cream and cake. In those days, the milk came five days a week up the street in the horse drawn wagon under the direction of Mr. Holling. The milk was provided in glass bottles, generally one quart in size. Colored tokens of metal were purchased and placed in the top of one of the empty bottles waiting to be picked up. In this manner Mr. Holling would make the correct exchange, and mother would fetch in the milk. This was in the days before homogenization. Milk came in quart bottles, and whole milk had the cream rise to the top. Mother poured off the cream, which was reserved for dressings and ice cream.

Ice cream! What a treat – and reserved for birthdays only. She made her own in that tiny freezer compartment suspended from the ceiling of the fridge, and it went wonderfully with the inevitable chocolate cake with peppermint icing. The cake was always round and cut like a wheel, with the round hub in the middle and the spokes radiating out. The birthday boy/girl always got the hub, a matter highly prized. Not sure why, the round piece in the middle had only a fraction of the icing on the wedges.

Once in a while, we got spaghetti and wieners, a real treat. I remember on one such occasion, there was a lady from our church staying with us for a week or so. She was a maiden lady, rather portly and possessed of somewhat delicate disposition and sensibilities. We boys discovered that if we took the pot of spaghetti and pushed all the remnants to the handle half, we could then set the pot considerably out over the edge of the table and it would not fall. This would then drive our poor dear visitor to a near nervous breakdown. We then surreptitiously pulled several strands of spaghetti up and over the top edge of the pot and called, *Pass the worms please*, at which juncture we were treated to her making a bee-line for the room in which she held close communion with the toilet gods. Antics such as these were invariably followed by much parental whackage, but it was worth it.

CHAPTER ﹩﹩﹩﹩﹩﹩

Our Piano Man

There was a piano in our house. Or rather there was a succession of perhaps three upright pianos, to my recollection, all of them in varying states of vintage and condition. I do not know whence they came, but large strong people would muscle them in through the kitchen door from the garage and install them against the west wall of the living room. A piano was permitted because there was also one in our church. There were a lot of services in which the piano sat silent and the music emanated from our voices alone, without any encumbrance from other instrumentation like heathen guitars and idolatrous drums and such.

Our pianos came and, without exception, pretty soon came the piano tuner. He was blind and, in the manner of many blind people, had a very keen sense of hearing. His wife brought him and he, by touchy-feely and ear alone, busied himself with whatever it took to apply himself to the tuning and minor repair of the mechanism of our piano. For example, if there was a certain key which stuck, he would soon fix it. If a hammer pad or other portion of the mechanics was in need of repair, he would accomplish this as well. It was all at the behest of my mother, who had a very keen ear for musical pitch and insisted that our piano be *in tune.*

The most recent piano that I recall came when I was about 11 or 12 years old. It was a *player piano* which rejoiced in a foot pedal and tube mechanism and a roller system into which large, holey (but not righteous) scrolls were placed. When one activated the pedals it sucked air through the tubes, all 88 of them (one for each piano key). These were connected to holes in a plate, over which corresponding holes in the scrolls passed. When air was allowed into the mechanism via a hole in the paper, the appropriate piano key was depressed automatically and a tune was played without the benefit of anybody actually tickling the ivories. Wonderful – but it didn't work. It looked as though all the guts and workings were there, but the tubes were very old and ratty and full of crumbling holes.

My soon-to-be brother-in-law was a clever fellow. He cleverly deduced that, if we changed out the old rotten tubes for new ones, things would probably work just fine. We did not know where to get tubing of that nature and so soon-to-be bro-law went out and bought a bunch of cheap skipping ropes, which were made from the correct size of hollow tubing. These were then employed in rejuvenating all the old rubber and, *miracle of miracles!* The player piano actually *played!* This was very seriously groovy and cool. With the piano had come a couple of dozen rolls, or scrolls, and a large percentage of these were heathen songs. One such song was *Turkey in the Straw*, which was without doubt my favorite. It really rocked, and the faster one peddled, the faster and louder played the song. Seriously cool indeed.

Otherwise it was my three oldest sisters who played the piano. The oldest two for sure became quite adept at it and went on to accompany congregational singing at church. I don't remember if they ever took private lessons or not. My older brothers and younger sister did not play, and nor did I except for *Chopsticks*. Anything my sisters did I considered to be sissy girly stuff anyway and wanted no part of it. I needed to make more noise and lobbied for, and miraculously received, a beat-up old trumpet. This was a circumstance with which we have already dealt.

As nearly as I can recall there were only two persons besides my sisters who ever played piano in our house. One of them was a suitor for the affections of my second oldest sister and, I think by the standards of our household, was pretty good at it. Playing piano, that is. No clue about the quality of his suiterage except that she married somebody else. However, he played with a different style than the straight up, simultaneous notes of the chords which occurred in our church, which was also the style that my sisters played. He *rolled* his chords, a matter which had hitherto been unheard of in our experience, and was thus deemed somewhat odd due to his strange treatment of the music. Since then I have learned that there is lots of music which lends itself very well to the rolling of chords, and further that there is tons of music which does not. He automatically and always did it and I am pretty sure that is one of the reasons that my sister did not marry him.

But the other chap who played on our piano was seriously cool beyond anything

that we could possibly have imagined at the time He was a preacher of the itinerant sort and from time to time would stay with us in our house. It was the custom of the parishioners to take in and board such a preacher for the duration of his stay. We had no paid ministers of our own because the heathen did that, and we weren't going to be like them. But it was clearly recognized that to have nothing but lay preachers out of our own congregation perform all of the general ministry was a very bad (read *boring*) idea. After all, very few farmers make scintillating preachers fraught with cogent commentary. So amongst our affiliate congregations there were men who went around by invitation to our associate churches and might stay for a week or two and preach pretty much all of the services during that period of time.

One such was named Alfred Wiener and he was German. He was Germanic even above and beyond the call of normally dutifully being German. He spoke with a thick German accent, through which you could drive a Mack truck, and was Germanicly expressionistic in all matters beyond our Mennonite comprehension. He spoke and did everything with *Triple G*! He was *ALIVE!* Blessed with huge horn rimmed glasses and a crop of hair just like Einstein, he was a seriously hairy man with twisted up eagle-like eyebrows and large quantities of hair emanating from his nose and ears. We were afraid that if he sneezed he might flog himself to death. We knew he was hairy all over as well, because tufts of chest hair burst through his shirt between the buttons. And, oh yes, he played the piano.

He played the piano in the exact same manner as he did everything else, which is with Great Glee and Gusto. My sisters and their henchbirdies who played piano at church did so gently and calmly, in exactly the correct timing, and were sort of the wallpaper to the vocalization of the congregational singing. They played with the apologetic humility supposedly all-pervasive in our lives. *Thou shalt be seen and just barely heard.*

But not Herr Alfred Wiener. After supper he would sit down at the piano and fill the entire house with heathen classical music of the most ferocious order. He didn't just play, he banged and hammered on the keys with both hands with his thick strong Germanic sausage fingers, and we thought that the entire mechanism might explode into smithereens. I have since wondered what he was like in bed. Probably gloriously bouncingly joyful as well. Test the limits of the springs. Ask for a bed with twin I-beam suspension and heavy duty shock absorbers. He certainly sought to extricate audio orgasmic delights from our poor old virginal piano. He played things like Mendelssohn's *The War March of the Priests* and the *Toccata and Fugue in D minor* by Johan Sebastian Bach. Once in a while he would play operatic music and bellow out sections in German and Italian or other languages which were totally unintelligible to us. It was a wondrous matter indeed, and I wish I had a video besides that which is in my head.

The really fun deal about this circumstance was that Alfred Wiener was born in Frankfurt Germany on April 1 around 1927. He told us stories about Nazis and Germany and war and how he, a Jew, was imprisoned in a place called Auschwitz but eventually made good his escape and fled to Canada. I did not at the time understand matters of that nature, but one time he rolled up his sleeve and showed us the tattoo marks from the concentration camp. An astonishing fellow.

So here we had a gentleman named Alfred Wiener who was a Frankfurter by birth and name, was born on April Fools' Day, escaped from Auschwitz, and hammered out classical music with Triple G in a normally subdued and muted sort of Mennonite living room. *Tell me that there is not a God in Heaven! And tell me that the God of Heaven does not have a vast eternal sense of humor! Then check out the foibles and idiosyncrasies of your fellows, and take a gander into your own mirror.*

> Alfred Wiener *lived: Really Lived*
> He did so *with Triple G,* and to a ripe old age
> He had much reason to hate, yet forgave his oppressors.
>
> Life is for the living
> How many people do you know
> You would swear to the Almighty
> They get out of bed every day
> Just to save on the funeral expenses?

CHAPTER XX XX XX VIII

Schiteolla Birds

My dad's shoe store was situated on the corner of Church and Arthur streets in Elmira, Ontario. The front door was on the corner, and as one came through that door they were greeted with the women's section on the right and the children's section on the left. Further to the left, at the extremity of the store, was the shoe repair shop. This was manned by one Robert, a gentleman of German extraction who repaired the shoes in whatever manner it appeared wisdom to him. Whence his training came I don't know, but it may well have been from the Old Country across The Pond.

As a small boy I loved to watch him work. He was a big beefy man who sported a leather apron, in which there were several pockets. After a period of time, I discovered that this was the belly cash register of the shoe repair establishment. This was in the days before sales tax; people came in to pick up their repairs, paid the price required, and left with their goods without the impediment of taxation.

The other section of the store was the men's department. This was a room rented from father's cousin, from the ISB market next door. It was a grocery store which had the initials Isaac S. Brubacher after the name of the proprietor. One of the farm boys next to town told me that ISB stood for International Shit Barn. I thought that was pretty hilarious then and, on further rumination, still do, especially considering the source of such mirth, which was from one of the big strong farm boys living on the farm where grampa Brubacher resided.

The men's section was about 18 inches higher than the floor of the rest of the store. Thus the door to the area sporting men's shoes was subject to a ramp. My father which art in heaven was wheelchair-bound on account of the polio, and, as the ramp was of necessity rather short and somewhat steep, it was incumbent

upon father to call for help in pushing him up the ramp to fit shoes on the men customers.

If there were no staff in the immediate vicinity to assist him with going up the ramp, he let forth a peculiar whistle. If ever you and I should meet, I can re-enact this whistle with great accuracy because I heard it many times. Somebody would appear, and he would be assisted up the ramp and weave his magic in the matter of selling the most expensive shoes in the store to those men who appeared therein.

At the bottom of the ramp was father's desk. In front of his desk was a common wall with the shoe repair shop. I loved to be in the shoe repair shop because I greatly enjoyed watching Robert at work. I offered great admiration in the matter of fixing shoes, and I suppose I was not much beyond kindergarten before I was allowed to bang around on heels and soles here and there and gain the rudiments of the shoe repair trade. Supposedly this kept me out of trouble otherwise, and it was doubtless clearly evident that I was prone to trouble in fairly large and regular quantity if left to my own devices.

On one particular occasion I was in the shoe repair shop and I heard the whistle of my father which art in heaven signifying his requirement of assistance in being helped up the ramp to the men's department. Robert paused in his work and said, *It's going to rain. What?*, said I, looking out at the blazing blue sky. *Yes*, said Robert, *It's going to rain. Shit birds are calling.*

At that juncture the seeds of doubt were sown. Not all humans held father in the absolute reverence and unquestioned respect demanded of creatures like me. Perhaps there was wiggle-room in the reception of the expostulations of my father which wert at that time not quite yet in heaven. Perhaps a smattering of filtration to be exercised.

I have often wondered what transpired afterwards in the career of our Germanic prophet, St. Robert. Pretty sure he did not go on to a scintillating career in politics.

CHAPTER ❧❧ ❧❧ ❧❧ ❧❧

𝔅𝔞𝔯𝔫 𝔐𝔲𝔰𝔦𝔠

The perfect place to play classical music is upstairs in an old bank barn. I know this because I have one.

When I moved here about 10 years ago, the barn already then was in pretty bad shape, with lots of holes where the siding boards were missing, and lots more holes where chunks of the tin roof had fallen prey to the vicissitudes of the weather. The result of this neglect dictated in no small measure that anything that was to be placed below, or stored in the barn above, was also going to be subject to climactic conditions such as rain and snow. As such, no portion of the old barn was any place to linger, except for the deposit and recovery of such items which, if of any value, needed to be carefully covered.

A few years ago, in the later portion of summer, my daughters came to me and said, *Father you are shortly going to turn 60, and therefore you need to have a big party.* Well, said I to myself, *How can this be? How can it be that I am about to turn 60?* After all it seemed like only yesterday or the day before that I held my darling little daughters in my arms and told them stories, and now they are telling me this strange matter of my age. At what point exactly did their mother teach them to practice such terrible arts of prevarication? Yet on further review I had to respect their judgment as Good Christian People and accept the fact that I was indeed about to cross the barrier to the Big Six Oh.

So where to hold the party? Various venues and halls were tossed about, but then I determined that I would fix up the threshing floor of the old barn and we could get a fair few people to celebrate the matter without leaving my premises.

The first item of business was the repair of the upstairs barn floor itself. It was ragged and rotten in many places and full of holes. I decided that I would take it upon myself to fix the floor. I got a lumber truck to bring in large quantities of plywood and other supportive building materials and went at it. Very quickly I repented of my decision to do this by myself and called in a good friend of mine to help. Pretty sure that he repented himself also of the matter partway through the process, but we persevered and eventually the floor was repaired and supported from below.

This however did nothing to deal with the holes in the roof and the sides. I could not do that myself and eventually hired some people of the Mennonite Faith to come and put the matter in order. I went and fetched the boss man and, after measuring what was needed, he gave a list of the items necessary to put this in proper repair. This was duly accomplished and on the appointed day he and his two helpers came to do the job.

It became clearly evident that we needed some help in the form of a motorized man-lift. Not only was it too time-consuming to do the repairs using just a ladder, but excessively dangerous as well. These old barns need people to accomplish matters high off the ground.

The net result however was a hard day's work and, while not restoring the barn to its original glory, it was restored to a degree of integrity which would easily facilitate a birthday party with a fairly large quantity of people and, in case of inclement weather, keep us all dry.

In preparation for the party there was not only the normal influx of celebratory fluids and the accoutrement which normally accompany matters of that nature, but also I decided that it was going to be a *sausage making party*. When I moved into the old farmhouse it was chopped up into small rooms, in the manner of old farm-houses everywhere, and all heated with electric baseboards. Originally the house had been built in two sections, and in each section was a wood stove. By the time I came along these had long disappeared and electricity was the name of the game.

This, however, proved to be an extremely expensive proposition. In point of fact, that first February the porous old farmhouse had produced an electrical bill of roughly $1400 for only that month! I shudder to think of what that might translate to in today's fees. So I decided that I would heat the old place with wood. To this end I tore out a bunch of the bearing walls and substituted them with old barn posts and beams that I had purchased from a Mennonite farmer just west of Elmira. Thankfully I kept photographs of the entire process because, looking back on it, I'm not sure if even I would today have the unmitigated audacity to attempt an engineering operation like that. Nevertheless I did it with some installation help from one of my clients, a man who had a lot of experience in this field.

A suitable woodstove was procured and installed, with stone surroundings and a chimney which went up the outside of the house, and which cost considerably more than the stove itself. A double-walled hand-packed chimney is not an inexpensive matter but one which, by all accounts, creates chimney draft and smoke exit far better than the old-fashioned variety.

It was the middle of February, and to celebrate the matter of the woodstove I threw a party. And the star of the party was the sausage making machine. As it happened one of my clients with very bad feet was also a beef farmer and, with one thing and another, a large quantity of beef came to reside in my freezer. One can only eat so much roast beef before it becomes very difficult to know how to deal with the leftovers. In our home when I was a kid we had a grinding machine which was screwed to the edge of the dining room table, and chunks of the leftover beef went into the top and came out the bottom all ground up. This was used to make shepherd's pie – a favorite of mine then and still is.

So with a lot of leftover roast beef in my house, I decided I needed to have such a grinder. I went over to one of the big stores in Barrie, perhaps HomeSense or whichever one it was, and bought an electric grinding machine. It came with lots of attachments and indeed proved very useful in turning leftover roast beef into shepherd's pie and other such foodstuffs which rejoice in the grinding up of similar items.

It also came with sausage making attachments. In the normal course of affairs one would ask oneself, *From where does sausage come?* And the answer of course is, *From the store. Stores which sell sausage.* Okay then. *Who makes sausage?* One then supposes it is *People who are in the business of making sausage.*

But in my case, not necessarily so. For my stove-warming party I decided that we would make our own sausage. To that end, I went on to the Internet and downloaded a couple of dozen recipes of stuff that people mix up and run through a sausage maker. Principal among these are of course ground-up pork, beef, chicken, turkey, lamb, and even salmon and other fish. Nearly anything you can name.

I went off to the local butcher and ordered sausage casings. After a few days I was the proud possessor of enough casings to make sausages stretching, in an uninterrupted line, between Chicago and New York. *Just soak them in water overnight to loosen them up and they will stretch out just fine,* spake they who sold me sausage casings. I did not ask from where the material came, but let us just say that if a pig no longer is in possession of this long round material its daily intestinal fortitude would be a very serious problem.

So quite a bunch of people showed up for this party. It was in mid-February and seriously out in the middle of pretty much nowhere. Yet these folk knew that my parties are memorable, and so we got together and partied. Their instruction had been to bring a salad and I would provide the rest.

After a suitable period of lubrication I broached the concept of making sausage. To do this I had laid out, on a table beside the sausage making machine, a whole pile of spices and herbs and the various meat stuffs which would be incorporated in the process. By way of introduction, I got out a mixing bowl and a wooden spoon and dumped a bunch of stuff into it, stirring and molding all the ingredients together. Then I got one of the ladies to strip a bunch of sausage casings onto the exit spout, turned on the machine, spooned material into the entrance, and we all watched the sausage fill the casings on exit. Pretty cool. Several barbecues had been lit and I indicated that everybody now needed to help themselves to the facilities and make their own sausages.

Well. There were now 20+ people with drinks in hand viewing the proceedings with roughly the expression of cows pissing on a flat rock. They had no idea what to make of it. But after a while things started to kick in. In dribs and drabs they came up to the making table and went at it. Pretty soon it was indeed a sausage making party, and a pile of fun it turned out to be. This was in no small measure augmented by the fact that there was a live band in the corner comprised of my daughter Angela and her buddies. Even I was persuaded to unlimber my trumpet and join in with the band. With sufficient lubrication of the listener, nearly any band can sound good, no matter

how bad the spontaneous help. We had a great time and I think that the last of the guests and the band disappeared about two o'clock in the morning.

So for my 60th party I determined that we would seek to repeat this concept. And so we did. One of the matters different this time was that the upstairs of the barn still had a lot of dry straw and we needed to avoid a fire. The barbecues were placed on platforms outside the barn, but still in close enough proximity that I had the barn well water pump primed and fire hoses ready. Even in late September a stray spark can be a big problem, so precautions were taken accordingly. Thanks be there was no trouble in that regard.

It was a great time. Family and many friends. People had come from a great distance, for which I have much appreciation. Two days later I got on an airplane and spent three weeks in Scotland. I had never been to Scotland before, and I now know more about it than most people have a right to, including an intimate relation with many of the libations of the Highlands. When I got back people asked me, *So, how did you leave the condition of Scotch?*, and I replied, *I am not really sure. I'm not sure how much there is left*. Great time indeed.

But after the party in the barn, it was the evening of a beautiful late summer day. The sun was setting over the hills to the west, the big barn doors were open, and we sat there taking in the wonderful sunset sitting on bales of straw. I put some music on the stereo that had been imported for the occasion. I chanced upon Brahms *German Requiem*. It filled the old barn beautifully and was a wonderful complement to the golden orange red of the setting sun over the hills yonder. Beautiful.

Since then, on every possible occasion, I have taken the opportunity to watch the sunset from the threshing floor of my barn. Most times it is beautiful beyond description. And then the music. I now study the music of Mozart and Brahms and Beethoven. While the sun goes down, I fill the barn with the music and have the full score of the orchestration in my hand and wallow in it and memorize it. An audio/visual feast at its very finest.

So one of these days, when you learn that I want to have a party for you all, I will hire a symphony orchestra and a professional choir, and we will all go to the barn and spill out the barn hill down onto the valley below, and I will conduct Brahms or Mozart or whatever it is that strikes my fancy on that day. And you all are invited to enjoy that with me because, while I rarely look in the mirror (too scary) and I see that I only have 70 or 80 good years left, it is high time to get on with it and realize that dream.

I hope not to be remembered as some shaking, slobbering thing in a whitewashed hell hole with tubes and crap hanging out of every orifice. Rather in full bloom and glory, vibrating an old barn on a mid-summer's evening, with a lot of happy people enjoying a really good sausage.

The mustard and sauerkraut are just over there, right beside the cold German beer.

Lock up your daughters... 1971

CHAPTER 🐜🐜🐜

In Fine
(Insomniac Therapy, Part Last)

So what do we take with us from our get-together? What did we learn?

Well, the first thing that we have learned is the veracity of that ancient and honorable adage: *It is generally greater wisdom for a man to stay home and keep his counsel to himself and have most people consider him to be a moron as opposed to him getting up on any sort of stage and opening his mouth, or unlimbering his pen, thus proving it.*

But if for a brief moment we can set that to one side, let us first consider the cobbler. It is not such a bad thing to be a cobbler. In point of fact it is quite rewarding. I do not mean in the monetary sense as you will have observed exactly zero wealthy makers and repairers of footwear. I am no exception to the expression *The Poor Shoemaker*.

Nevertheless, what price is to be put on a life's career of improving the walking and mobility of one's fellows? There are many people who have limped in to my shoemaker's shop and presently strode out. From such are riches and satisfaction to be had in no small measure. I have little earthy coin to show for a life-time of shaping leather, yet mayhap there is wealth laid up for the cobbler in another place, and with coin in a bank of a different nature.

And let us consider what we might learn from the Mennonites. Mennonites have arrived. They've pretty much made it. How is that? Because they never left it in the first place. By and large they have achieved that intangible for which most of us seek. It is called *Quiet Enjoyment*.

Today we have mostly turned into rushians – we rush here and rush there, and when we are done rushing over there, we turn right around and come rushing back again. The Mennonites, on the other hand, have an unspoken and unwritten philosophy taken from that wonderful verse in Scripture which says, *In quietness and confidence shall be thy strength.* Hear ye now the loudest noise of the Mennonite: *clip clop, clip clop, clip clop...* They are a strong, quiet people.

Mennonites have a bunch of excellent Christian values going for them. They know the value of honest labor, and when they bow their heads in front of their dinner plates they know where their food has come from. It came from the sweat of their brow in the field and those that toil in the kitchen, and they exercise faith in the Almighty that by the infinite Grace of God there will be another harvest next year.

They take care of each other. There is no such thing as buying insurance. Their insurance and *assurance* is in community – they are communists in the true sense of the word. If somebody is sick they are taken care of. If a barn burns, pretty soon there is another barn there, complete with hay and straw and cattle and pigs too. They look after each other.

You don't see their names in the police records or the newspapers. There is no such thing as unemployment. There are no Mennonites in our prisons or group homes. The less fortunate are taken care of by family.

But today the Mennonite way of life is under siege. About 100 years ago they were much like everybody else, but just more plain in their approach to life. Then the ground shook under the heavy tread of a Three-Headed Demon, which slowly but surely came up the road. The head on the left roared out, *TRACTOR*, while the head on the right seductively cooed, *AUTOMOBILE*. Then the big head in the middle with flashing eyes crackled out, *ELECTRICITY*. Yet another Demon followed hard by. It had huge ears and the name *TELEPHONE* branded to its forehead. And they didn't know what to do about these Demons.

Some Mennonites parked their cars in the driveway, warmed up the tractor, plugged in the toaster and got on the blower to give instructions to their commodity broker. Others said, *No. We will shut these Demons out.* So they built strong fences around their way of life, and were successful at this for many decades.

But these days the fences have become porous and elastic, with technology slithering

through the cracks and burrowing under the fences. Sure, many still clip clop their way to church, and they have no electricity in the house, but their barns and their manufacturing shops are among the most modern in the world. Maybe that is the answer. Maybe they have gotten it right. Perhaps the balance between the horse and the hurly-burly is well struck at the end of their farm lanes.

And if you take only one point of contemplation from our communion in these pages, consider this: *When the walls of a man's house have no switches on them, he has a far greater opportunity for illumination from within.*

So now receive a sometime Mennonite Cobbler's blessing:

> May you be warmed and filled—from within.
> May you be at peace with your neighbors and with yourself.
> May your horse never come up lame and
> May your chickens always lay eggs with good strong shells.
> Last, when you are old, with your pages nearly all cut,
> May your children and your children's children
> Rise with one accord and pronounce you *Blessèd*.

So be at peace. I thank you for your kind attention.

Kenneth David Brubacher
July XVI Anno Domini MMXV

"Whoa, Baby!!! Double trouble!!
No wonder he looked about ready to croak!"

APPENDICES

𝕴𝖓𝖙𝖗𝖔𝖉𝖚𝖈𝖙𝖎𝖔𝖓

Taken from

The Kenneth David Brubacher
Book Of Truth and Wisdom

If pen were put
To experience and knowledge
Mayhap mine be
A fairly hefty Tome

Of useful skills
Perhaps a score or so
Of pages large of font
Lines well spaced

But wisdom
Alas
That be a slender volume

𝕸𝖊𝖓𝖓𝖔𝖓𝖎𝖙𝖊 𝕽𝖊𝖈𝖎𝖕𝖊𝖘

BLEDLIN GRUMBAADA

Bledlin = sliced up, grum = ground, baada = berries. So it is sliced up potatoes

For Every Day:
Peel the grumbaada and cut in half the long way, then slice ivatsvark (cross ways) about as thick as the end of your little finger. Fill the pot with one handle missing about up to the dent. Put in water up until you know it will be nearly all taken into the grumbaada when they are nearly soft. Add salt about half of that half egg shell left aside from your breakfast. Put a lid on and bring to boil, then put to one side of the heat to let simmer. If you let it stay too hot the lid will chump off. Every so often stir to make sure they don't burn. Don't stir too hard or you mush them.

When almost soft add creamy milk straight from the cow. Then put in the corn you cut off the cob the leftovers from supper. Or peas. Bring to a simmer and take off heat. They'll be done now. Serve with summer sausage, pickled beets, medium cheddar cheese, bread and butter. The bread is good for mopping up the juice too. Your pie doesn't get soggy that way.

For When Company Comes:
Make the grumbaada like you did above, but just the salted potatoes not quite soft. They can be done any time and kept warm with a lid on.

Unwind brotvascht (pork sausage) from the canning jar you fetched up from the root cellar and cut into pieces about as long as your man's … OOPS! Family Show!! … manageable lengths. In hot skillet brown them and fry until done and then set aside. It doesn't matter if they cool. Cut about a good double handful of bacon into little pieces and fry them in the pot until not quite crisp. Throw in chopped onions enough to fill a soup dish heaping and stir. Also garlic some. And pepper.

Add in the grumbaada and extra cream in the milk and stir with the leftover corn and/ or peas like above. Make sure you scrape the brotvascht browning and bacon bits off the bottom – that really makes it schmeck don't you know. Cut the brotvasht into chunks about as long as the end of your thumb and stir in while it all warms up chust almost to a simmer once. Put in a good handful of parsley from beside the stairs out.

If you want to go fancy put about 3 pickled beets in the middle of each plate and arrange around them the bledlin grumbaada. Insert a sprig of parsley in the middle of the beets. Looks nice. Pretty sure the men folk will look at you a bit funny. But they'll eat it no worry. Hunger makes for a good sauce. Serve with cheddar cheese a plate of it passed around and don't forget the bread for the mopping up of the juices once.

BROTVASCHT PRESERVES

To prepare the sausage casings clean the pig intestines real good and then scrub them in brine. Screw the meat grinder to the corner of the kitchen table. Take the cloth back first. Put the medium hole plate into the grinder and get the children to crank. Feed the pork bits left over from the butchering into the top of the grinder and collect the ground pork in a big basin.

Mix in the salt and pepper. Also garlic and onion powder too. Do it by hand. It's messy but best. Take the grind plate out and put on the sausage spout instead. Strip the casings on as much as can go. Then tie off the end. Feed the ground meat into the top and get the children to crank some more. The meat comes out into the casings.

Boil glass canning jars along with lids and collars first. Then wind the brotvascht into the chars until full. Screw the lids down onto the chars. Make sure you put on a new jar rubber ring. Steam the jars from dinner time until the chores are for supper. Take them out of the steamer and turn them upside down on a wood board. Use mitts – they're hot. Let sit over night. In the morning take them down into the root cellar. They will keep until next time to make again. If one of them leaks use up right away once in a day or two. Something wrong with the jar or ring.

BARN RAISING   DINNER TIME

115 lemon pies   500 fet kuchen   15 big cakes   3 gallons applesauce

3 gallons rice pudding   3 gallons cornstarch pudding   16 chickens

3 hams large   50 pounds roast beef   300 light rolls

Red beet pickle and pickled eggs   Cucumber pickle

6 pounds dried prunes, stewed   1 large crock stewed raisins

5 gallons stone jar white potatoes and same sweet potatoes

Feeds 175 men

Taken from a hand-written recipe c. 1900. Would have been made pretty much in one kitchen

Dordrecht Confession of Faith
(Mennonite, 1632)

Adopted April 21, 1632, by a Dutch Mennonite Conference held at <u>Dordrecht</u>, Holland.

I. OF GOD AND THE CREATION OF ALL THINGS

Since we find it testified that without faith it is impossible to please God, and that he that would come to God must believe that there is a God, and that He is a rewarder of them that seek Him; therefore, we confess with the mouth, and believe with the heart, with all the pious, according to the holy Scriptures, in one eternal, almighty, and incomprehensible God, the Father, Son, and Holy Ghost, and in none more, nor in any other; before whom no God was made or existed, nor shall there be any after Him: for of Him, and through Him, and in Him, are all things; to Him be praise and honor forever and ever, Amen. <u>Hebrews 11:6; Deuteronomy 6:4; Genesis 17:1; Isaiah 46:8; 1 John 5:7; Romans 11:36.</u>

Of this same one God, who worketh all in all, we believe and confess that He is the Creator of all things visible and invisible; that He, in six days, created, made, and prepared, heaven and earth, and the sea, and all that in them is; and that He still governs and upholds the same and all His works through His wisdom, might, and the word of His power. <u>1 Corinthians 12:6; Genesis 1; Acts 14:15.</u>

And when He had finished His works, and had ordained and prepared them, each in its nature and properties, good and upright, according to His pleasure, He created the first man, the father of us all, Adam; whom He formed of the dust of the ground, and breathed into his nostrils the breath of life, so that he became a living soul, created by God in His own image and likeness, in righteousness and holiness, unto eternal life. He regarded him above all other creatures, endowed him with many high and glorious gifts, placed him in the pleasure garden or Paradise, and gave him a command and prohibition; afterwards He took a rib from Adam, made a woman therefrom, and brought her to him, joining and giving her to him for a helpmate, companion, and wife; and in consequence of this He also caused, that from this one man Adam, all men that dwell upon the whole earth have descended. Genesis 1:27; Genesis 2:7, 17, 18, 22.

II. OF THE FALL OF MAN

We believe and confess, according to the holy Scriptures, that these our first parents, Adam and Eve, did not continue long in this glorious state in which they were created, but that they, seduced by the subtlety and deceit of the serpent, and the envy of the devil, transgressed the high commandment of God and became disobedient to their Creator; through which disobedience sin has come into the world, and death by sin, which has thus passed upon all men, for that all have sinned, and, hence, brought upon themselves the wrath of God, and condemnation; for which reason they were of God driven out of Paradise, or the pleasure garden, to till the earth, in sorrow to eat of it, and to eat their bread in the sweat of their face, till they should return to the earth, from which they were taken; and that they, therefore, through this one sin, became so ruined, separated, and estranged from God, that they, neither through themselves, nor through any of their descendants, nor through angels, nor men, nor any other creature in heaven or on earth, could be raised up, redeemed, or reconciled to God, but would have had to be eternally lost, had not God, in compassion for His creatures, made provision for it, and interposed with His love and mercy. Genesis 3:6; 4 Esdras 3:7; Romans 5:12, 18; Genesis 3:23; Psalms 49:8; Revelation 5:9; John 3:16.

III. OF THE RESTORATION OF MAN THROUGH
THE PROMISE OF THE COMING CHRIST

Concerning the restoration of the first man and his posterity we confess and believe, that God, notwithstanding their fall, transgression, and sin, and their utter inability, was nevertheless not willing to cast them off entirely, or to let them be forever lost; but that He called them again to Him, comforted them, and showed them that with Him there was yet a means for their reconciliation, namely, the immaculate Lamb, the Son of God, who had been foreordained thereto before the foundation of the world, and was promised them while they were yet in Paradise, for consolation, redemption, and salvation, for themselves as well as for their posterity; yea, who through faith, had, from that time on, been given them as their own; for whom all the pious patriarchs, unto whom this promise was frequently renewed, longed and inquired, and to whom, through faith, they looked forward from afar, waiting for the fulfillment, that He by His coming, would redeem, liberate, and raise the fallen race of man from their sin, guilt; and unrighteousness. John 1:29; 1 Peter 1:19; Genesis 3:15; 1 John 3:8; 2:1; Hebrews 11:13, 39; Galatians 4:4.

IV. THE ADVENT OF CHRIST INTO THIS WORLD, AND THE REASON OF HIS COMING

We believe and confess further, that when the time of the promise, for which all the pious forefathers had so much longed and waited, had come and was fulfilled, this previously promised Messiah, Redeemer, and Savior, proceeded from God, was sent, and, according to the prediction of the prophets, and the testimony of the evangelists, came into the world, yea, into the flesh, was made manifest, and the Word, Himself became flesh and man; that He was conceived in the virgin Mary, who was espoused to a man named Joseph, of the house of David; and that she brought Him forth as her first-born son, at Bethlehem, wrapped Him in swaddling clothes, and laid Him in a manger. John 4:25; 16:28; 1 Timothy 3:16; John 1:14; Matthew 1:23; Luke 2:7.

We confess and believe also, that this is the same whose goings forth have been from of old, from everlasting, without beginning of days, or end of life; of whom it is testified that He Himself is the Alpha and Omega, the beginning and the ending, the first and the last; that He is the same, and no other, who was foreordained, promised, sent, and came into the world; who is God's only, first and own Son; who was before John the Baptist, before Abraham, before the world; yea, who was David's Lord, and the God of the whole world, the first-born of every creature; who was brought into the world, and for whom a body was prepared, which He yielded up as a sacrifice and offering, for a sweet savor unto God, yea, for the consolation, redemption, and salvation of all mankind. John 3:16; Hebrews 1:6; Romans 8:32; John 1:30; Matthew 22:43; Colossians 1:15; Hebrews 10:5.

But as to how and in what manner this precious body was prepared, and how the Word became flesh, and He Himself man, in regard to this we content ourselves with the statement pertaining to this matter which the worthy evangelists have left us in their accounts, according to which we confess with all the saints, that He is the Son of the living God, in whom alone consist all our hope, consolation, redemption, and salvation, which we neither may nor must seek in any other. Luke 1:31, 32; John 20:31; Matthew 16:16.

We furthermore believe and confess with the Scriptures, that, when He had finished His course, and accomplished the work for which He was sent and came into the world, He was, according to the providence of God, delivered into the hands of the unrighteous; suffered under the judge, Pontius Pilate; was crucified, dead, was buried, and on the third day, rose from the dead, and ascended to heaven; and that He sits on the right hand of God the Majesty on high, whence He will come again to judge the quick and the dead. Luke 22:53; Luke 23:1; Luke 24:6, 7, 51.

And that thus the Son of God died, and tasted death and shed His precious blood for all men; and that He thereby bruised the serpent's head, destroyed the works of the devil, annulled the handwriting and obtained forgiveness of sins for all mankind; thus becoming the cause of eternal salvation for all those who, from Adam unto the end of the world, each in his time, believe in, and obey Him. Genesis 3:15; 1 John 3:8; Colossians 2:14; Romans 5:18.

V. THE LAW OF CHRIST, I.E., THE HOLY GOSPEL OR THE NEW TESTAMENT

We also believe and confess that before His ascension He instituted His New Testament, and, since it was to be and remain an eternal Testament, that He confirmed and sealed the same with His precious blood, and gave and left it to His disciples, yea, charged them so highly with it, that neither angel nor man may alter it, nor add to it nor take away from it; and that He caused the same, as containing the whole counsel and will of His heavenly Father, as far as is necessary for salvation to be proclaimed in His name by His beloved apostles, messengers, and ministers -- whom He called, chose, and sent into all the world for that purpose -- among all peoples, nations, and tongues; and repentance and remission of sins to be preached and testified of; and that He accordingly has therein declared all men without distinction, who through faith, as obedient children, heed, follow, and practice what the same contains, to be His children and lawful heirs; thus excluding no one from the precious inheritance of eternal salvation, except the unbelieving and disobedient, the stiff-necked and obdurate, who despise it, and incur this through their own sins, thus making themselves unworthy of eternal life. Jeremiah 31:31; Hebrews 9:15-17; Matthew 26:28; Galatians 1:8; 1 Timothy 6:3; John 15:15; Matthew 28:19; Mark 16:15; Luke 24:47; Romans 8:17; Acts 13:46.

VI. OF REPENTANCE AND REFORMATION OF LIFE

We believe and confess, that, since the imagination of man's heart is evil from his youth, and, therefore, prone to all unrighteousness, sin, and wickedness, the first lesson of the precious New Testament of the Son of God is repentance and reformation of life, and that, therefore, those who have ears to hear, and hearts to understand, must bring forth genuine fruits of repentance, reform their lives, believe the Gospel, eschew evil and do good, desist from unrighteousness, forsake sin, put off the old man with his deeds, and put on the new man, which after God is created in righteousness and true holiness: for, neither baptism, supper, church, nor any other outward ceremony, can without faith, regeneration, change or renewing of life, avail anything to please God or to obtain of Him any consolation or promise of salvation; but we must go to God with an upright heart, and in perfect faith, and believe in Jesus Christ, as the Scripture says, and testifies of Him; through which faith we obtain forgiveness of sins, are sanctified, justified, and made children of God, yea, partake of His mind, nature, and image, as being born again of God from above, through incorruptible seed. Genesis 8:21; Mark 1:15; Ezekiel 12:2; Colossians 3:9, 10; Ephesians 4:22, 24; Hebrews 10:22, 23; John 7:38.

VII. OF HOLY BAPTISM

Concerning baptism we confess that all penitent believers, who, through faith, regeneration, and the renewing of the Holy Ghost, are made one with God, and are written in heaven, must, upon such Scriptural confession of faith, and renewing of life, be baptized with water, in the most worthy name of the Father, and of the Son, and of the Holy Ghost, according to the command of Christ, and the teaching, example, and practice of the apostles, to the burying of their sins, and thus be incorporated into the communion of the saints; henceforth to learn to observe all things which the Son of God has taught, left, and commanded His disciples. Acts 2:38; Matthew 28:19, 20; Romans 6:4; Mark 16:16; Matthew 3:15; Acts 8:16; Acts 9:18; Acts 10:47; Acts

16:33; Colossians 2:11, 12.

VIII. OF THE CHURCH OF CHRIST

We believe in, and confess a visible church of God, namely, those who, as has been said before, truly repent and believe, and are rightly baptized; who are one with God in heaven, and rightly incorporated into the communion of the saints here on earth. These we confess to be the chosen generation, the royal priesthood, the holy nation, who are declared to be the bride and wife of Christ, yea, children and heirs of everlasting life, a tent, tabernacle, and habitation of God in the Spirit, built upon the foundation of the apostles and prophets, of which Jesus Christ Himself is declared to be the cornerstone (upon which His church is built). This church of the living God, which He has acquired, purchased, and redeemed with His own precious blood; with which, according to His promise, He will be and remain always, even unto the end of the world, for consolation and protection, yea, will dwell and walk among them, and preserve them, so that no floods or tempests, nay, not even the gates of hell, shall move or prevail against them-this church, we say, may be known by their Scriptural faith, doctrine, love, and godly conversation, as, also, by the fruitful observance, practice, and maintenance of the true ordinances of Christ, which He so highly enjoined upon His disciples. 1 Corinthians 12; 1 Peter 2:9; John 3:29; Revelation 19:7; Titus 3:6, 7; Ephesians 2:19-21; Matthew 16:18; 1 Peter 1:18, 19; Matthew 28:20; 2 Corinthians 6:16; Matthew 7:25.

IX. OF THE ELECTION, AND OFFICES OF TEACHERS, DEACONS, AND DEACONESSES, IN THE CHURCH

Concerning the offices and elections in the church, we believe and confess, that, since without offices and ordinances the church cannot subsist in her growth, nor continue in building, therefore the Lord Jesus Christ Himself, as a husbandman in His house, has instituted, ordained, enjoined, and commanded His offices and ordinances, how everyone is to walk therein, and give heed to and perform His work and calling, as is meet, even as He Himself, as the faithful, great, chief Shepherd and Bishop of our souls, was sent, and came into the world, not to bruise, break, or destroy the souls of men, but to heal and restore them, to seek the lost, to break down the middle wall of partition, to make of twain one, and thus to gather of Jews, Gentiles, and all nations, one flock, for a church in His name, for which -- that no one should err or be lost-

He Himself laid down His life, thus ministering to their salvation, and liberating and redeeming them, (mark) wherein no one else could help or assist them. Ephesians 4:10-12; 1 Peter 2:25; Matthew 12:19; Matthew 18:11; Ephesians 2:14; Galatians 3:28; John 10:9, 11, 15; Psalms 49:8.

And that He, moreover, before His departure, left His church supplied with faithful ministers, apostles, evangelists, pastors, and teachers, whom He before, through the Holy Ghost, had chosen with prayer and supplication; that they might govern the church, feed His flock, and watch over, protect, and provide for it, yea, do in all things, as He had done before them, had taught, by example shown, and charged them, to teach to observe all things whatsoever He had commanded them. Luke 10:1; Luke 6:12, 13; John 2:15.

That the apostles, likewise, as faithful followers of Christ, and leaders of the church, were diligent in this respect, with prayer and supplication to God, through the election of brethren, to provide every city, place, or church, with bishops, pastors, and leaders, and to ordain such persons thereto, who would take heed unto themselves, and unto the doctrine and flock, who were sound in faith, pious in life and conversation, and of good report without as well as in the church; that they might be an example, light, and pattern in all godliness and good works, worthily administering the Lord'sordinances – baptism and supper – and that they might everywhere (where such could be found) appoint faithful men who would be able to teach others also, as elders, ordaining them by the laying on of hands in the name of the Lord, and provide for all the wants of the church according to their ability; so that, as faithful servants, they might husband well their Lord›s talent, get gain with it, and, consequently, save themselves and those who hear them. 1 Timothy 3:1; Acts 23:24; Titus 1:5; 1 Timothy 4:16; Titus 2:1, 2; 1 Timothy 3:7; 2 Timothy 2:2; 1 Timothy 4:14; 1 Timothy 5:2; Luke 19:13.

That they should also see diligently to it, particularly each among his own over whom he has the oversight, that all places be well provided with deacons (to look after and care for the poor), who may receive the contributions and alms, in order to dispense them faithfully and with all propriety to the poor and needy saints. Acts 6:3-6.

And that also honorable aged widows should be chosen and ordained deaconesses, that they with the deacons may visit, comfort, and care for, the poor, feeble, sick, sorrowing and needy, as also the widows and orphans, and assist in attending to other wants and necessities of the church to the best of their ability. 1 Timothy 5:9; Romans 16:1; James 1:27.

Furthermore, concerning deacons, that they, especially when they are fit, and chosen and ordained thereto by the church, for the assistance and relief of the elders, may exhort the church (since they, as has been said, are chosen thereto), and labor also in the Word and in teaching; that each may minister unto the other with the gift he has received of the Lord, so that through mutual service and the assistance of every member, each in his measure, the body of Christ may be improved, and the vine and church of the Lord continue to grow, increase, and be built up, according as it is proper.

X. OF THE HOLY SUPPER

We also confess and observe the breaking of bread, or Supper, as the Lord Christ Jesus before His suffering instituted it with bread and wine, and observed and ate with His apostles, commanding them to observe it in remembrance of Him; which they accordingly taught and practiced in the church, and commanded that it should be kept in remembrance of the suffering and death of the Lord; and that His precious body was broken, and His blood shed, for us and all mankind, as also the fruits hereof, namely, redemption and eternal salvation, which He purchased thereby, showing such great love toward us sinful men; whereby we are admonished to the utmost, to love and forgive one another and our neighbor, as He has done unto us, and to be mindful to maintain and live up to the unity and fellowship which we have with God and one another, which is signified to us by this breaking of bread. Matthew 26:26; Mark 14:22; Acts 2:42; 1 Corinthians 10:16; 1 Corinthians 11:23.

XI. OF THE WASHING OF THE SAINTS' FEET

We also confess a washing of the saints' feet, as the Lord Christ not only instituted, enjoined and commanded it, but Himself, although He was their Lord and Master, washed His apostles' feet, thereby giving an example that they should likewise wash one another's feet, and do as He had done unto them; which they accordingly, from this time on, taught believers to observe, as a sign of true humility, and, especially, to remember by this feet washing, the true washing, whereby we are washed through His precious blood, and made pure after the soul. John 13:4-17; 1 Timothy 5:10.

XII. OF THE STATE OF MATRIMONY

We confess that there is in the church of God an honorable state of matrimony, of two free, believing persons, in accordance with the manner after which God originally ordained the same in Paradise, and instituted it Himself with Adam and Eve, and that the Lord Christ did away and set aside all the abuses of marriage which had meanwhile crept in, and referred all to the original order, and thus left it. Genesis 1:27; Mark 10:4.

In this manner the Apostle Paul also taught and permitted matrimony in the church, and left it free for every one to be married, according to the original order, in the Lord, to whomsoever one may get to consent. By these words, *in the Lord*, there is to be understood, we think, that even as the patriarchs had to marry among their kindred or generation, so the believers of the New Testament have likewise no other liberty than to marry among the chosen generation and spiritual kindred of Christ, namely, such, and no others, who have previously become united with the church as one heart and soul, have received one baptism, and stand in one communion, faith, doctrine and practice, before they may unite with one another by marriage. Such are then joined by God in His church according to the original order; and this is called, marrying in the Lord. 2 Corinthians 7:2; 1 Corinthians 9:5; Genesis 24:4; Genesis 28:2; 1 Corinthians 7:39.

XIII. OF THE OFFICE OF THE SECULAR AUTHORITY

We believe and confess that God has ordained power and authority, and set them to punish the evil, and protect the good, to govern the world, and maintain countries and cities, with their subjects, in good order and regulation; and that we, therefore, may not despise, revile, or resist the same, but must acknowledge and honor them as the ministers of God, and be subject and obedient unto them, yea, ready for all good works, especially in that which is not contrary to the law, will, and commandment of God; also faithfully pay custom, tribute, and taxes, and to render unto them their dues, even also as the Son of God taught and practiced, and commanded His disciples to do; that we, moreover, must constantly and earnestly pray to the Lord for them and their welfare, and for the prosperity of the country, that we may dwell under its protection, earn our livelihood, and lead a quiet, peaceable life, with all godliness and honesty; and, furthermore, that the Lord would recompense unto them, here, and afterwards in eternity, all benefits, liberty, and favor which we enjoy here under their praiseworthy administration. Romans 13:1-7; Titus 3:1; 1 Peter 2:17; Matthew 22:21;Matthew 17:27; 1 Timothy 2:1.

XIV. OF REVENGE

As regards revenge, that is, to oppose an enemy with the sword, we believe and confess that the Lord Christ has forbidden and set aside to His disciples and followers all revenge and retaliation, and commanded them to render to no one evil for evil, or cursing for cursing, but to put the sword into the sheath, or, as the prophets have predicted, to beat the swords into ploughshares. Matthew 5:39, 44; Romans 12:14; 1 Peter 3:9; Isaiah 2:4; Micah 4:3; Zechariah 9:8, 9.

From this we understand that therefore, and according to His example, we must not inflict pain, harm, or sorrow upon any one, but seek the highest welfare and salvation of all men, and even, if necessity require it, flee for the Lord's sake from one city or country into another, and suffer the spoiling of our goods; that we must not harm any one, and, when we are smitten, rather turn the other cheek also, than take revenge or retaliate. Matthew 5:39.

And, moreover, that we must pray for our enemies, feed and refresh them whenever they are hungry or thirsty, and thus convince them by well-doing, and overcome all ignorance. Romans 12:19, 20.

Finally, that we must do good and commend ourselves to every man's conscience; and, according to the law of Christ, do unto no one that which we would not have done to us. 2 Corinthians 4:2; Matthew 7:12.

XV. OF THE SWEARING OF OATHS

Concerning the swearing of oaths we believe and confess that the Lord Christ has set aside and forbidden the same to His disciples, that they should not swear at all, but that yea should be yea, and nay, nay; from which we understand that all oaths, high and low, are forbidden, and that instead of them we are to confirm all our promises and obligations, yea, all our declarations and testimonies of any matter, only with our word yea, in that which is yea, and with nay, in that which is nay; yet, that we must always, in all matters, and with everyone, adhere to, keep, follow, and fulfill the same, as though we had confirmed it with a solemn oath. And if we do this, we trust that no one, not even the Magistracy itself, will have just reason to lay a greater burden on our mind and conscience. Matthew 5:34, 35; James 5:12; 2 Corinthians 1:17.

XVI. OF THE ECCLESIASTICAL BAN, OR SEPARATION FROM THE CHURCH

We also believe in, and confess, a ban, Separation, and Christian correction in the church, for amendment, and not for destruction, in order to distinguish that which is pure from the impure: namely, when any one, after he is enlightened, has accepted the knowledge of the truth, and been incorporated into the communion of the saints, sins again unto death, either through willfulness, or through presumption against God, or through some other cause, and falls into the unfruitful works of darkness, thereby becoming separated from God, and forfeiting the kingdom of God, that such a one, after the deed is manifest and sufficiently known to the church, may not remain in the congregation of the righteous, but, as an offensive member and open sinner, shall and must be separated, put away, reproved before all, and purged out as leaven; and this for his amendment, as an example, that others may fear, and to keep the church pure, by cleansing her from such spots, lest, in default of this, the name of the Lord be blasphemed, the church dishonored, and offense given to them that are without; and finally, that the sinner may not be condemned with the world, but become convinced in his mind, and be moved to sorrow, repentance, and reformation. Jeremiah 59:2; 1 Corinthians 5:5, 13; 1 Timothy 5:20; 1 Corinthians 5:6; 2

Corinthians 10:8; 1 Corinthians 13:10.

Further, concerning brotherly reproof or admonition, as also the instruction of the erring it is necessary to exercise all diligence and care, to watch over them and to admonish them with all meekness, that they may be bettered, and to reprove, according as is proper, the stubborn who remain obdurate; in short, the church must put away from her the wicked (either in doctrine or life), and no other. James 5:19; Titus 3:10; 1 Corinthians 5:13.

XVII. OF SHUNNING THE SEPARATED

Concerning the withdrawing from, or shunning the separated, we believe and confess, that if any one, either through his wicked life or perverted doctrine, has so far fallen that he is separated from God, and, consequently, also separated and punished by the church, the same must, according to the doctrine of Christ and His apostles, be shunned, without distinction, by all the fellow members of the church, especially those to whom it is known, in eating, drinking, and other similar intercourse, and no company be had with him that they may not become contaminated by intercourse with him, nor made partakers of his sins; but that the sinner may be made ashamed, pricked in his heart, and convicted in his conscience, unto his reformation. 1 Corinthians 5:9-11; 2 Thessalonians 3:14.

Yet, in shunning as well as in reproving, such moderation and Christian discretion must be used, that it may conduce, not to the destruction, but to the reformation of the sinner. For, if he is needy, hungry, thirsty, naked, sick, or in any other distress, we are in duty bound, necessity requiring it, according to love and the doctrine of Christ and His apostles, to render him aid and assistance; otherwise, shunning would in this case tend more to destruction than to reformation.

Therefore, we must not count them as enemies, but admonish them as brethren, that thereby they may be brought to a knowledge of and to repentance and sorrow for their sins, so that they may become reconciled to God, and consequently be received again into the church, and that love may continue with them, according as is proper. 2 Thessalonians 3:15.

XVIII. OF THE RESURRECTION OF THE DEAD,

AND THE LAST JUDGMENT

Finally, concerning the resurrection of the dead, we confess with the mouth, and believe with the heart, according to Scripture, that in the last day all men who shall have died, and fallen asleep, shall be awaked and quickened, and shall rise again, through the incomprehensible power of God; and that they, together with those who then will still be alive, and who shall be changed in the twinkling of an eye, at the sound of the last trump, shall be placed before the judgment seat of Christ, and the good be separated from the wicked; that then everyone shall receive in his own body according to that he hath done, whether it be good or evil; and that the good or pious, as the blessed, shall be taken up with Christ, and shall enter into life eternal, and obtain that joy, which eye hath not seen, nor ear heard, neither hath entered into the heart of man, to reign and triumph with Christ forever and ever. Matthew 22:30, 31; Daniel 12:12; Job 19:26, 27; Matthew 25:31; John 5:28; 2 Corinthians 5:10; 1 Corinthians 15; Revelation 20:12; 1 Thessalonians 4:15; 1 Corinthians 2:9.

And that, on the other hand, the wicked or impious, as accursed, shall be cast into outer darkness, yea, into the everlasting pains of hell, where their worm shall not die, nor their fire be quenched, and where they, according to holy Scripture, can nevermore expect any hope, comfort, or redemption. Mark 9:44; Revelation 14:11.

May the Lord, through His grace, make us all worthy and meet, that this may befall none of us; but that we may thus take heed unto ourselves, and use all diligence, that on that day we may be found before Him unspotted and blameless in peace. Amen.

These, then, as has been briefly stated before, are the principal articles of our general Christian faith, as we teach and practice the same throughout in our churches and among our people; which, in our judgment, is the only true Christian faith, which the apostles in their time believed and taught, yea, testified with their life, confirmed with their death, and, some of them, also sealed with their blood; wherein we in our weakness with them and all the pious, would fain abide, live, and die, that we may afterwards obtain salvation with them through the grace of the Lord.

Thus done and finished in our united churches, in the city of Dordrecht, the 21st of April, 1632, new style.

Brubacher Genealogy

Hans Brubacher who died (also presumably lived) in Europe, date unknown.
Son Abram.

1. Abram M. Brubacher was born in 1695 in Switzerland and married Maria
   Herr. Abram died in Europe 1753 in Mannheim, Germany. Maria died 1756.
   They had 11 children.

2. Abraham H. (for Herr, they took their middle initial from the first letter of
   their mother's maiden name, and still do) Brubacher, born 1731, was 6th of
   the 11 children, and emigrated with his cousin John, and married Magdalena
   Eschleman 1749. They travelled by ship to Lancaster County PA, and
   bought 174 acres of land on Middle Creek near Clay. They had 10 children of
   which Johannes was the firstborn. He died in 1811.

3. Johannes E. (Eschleman) Brubacher was born 1758 and died 1831. He
   married Veronica Hess and they moved to Monroe Township, Juniata County
   PA. They had 10 children of which Abraham H. (Hess) is the second oldest.

4. Abraham H. Brubacher was born 1784 and died 1827. He married Mary
   Sherk in 1867 and they had 10 children, of whom son Jacob S. was the 5th.
   They lived in Monroe Township and then Walker Township, Juniata County,
   PA at the time of his death. He changed the spelling of his name to Brubaker
   as it now appears on his grave marker.

5. Jacob S. (Sherk) Brubacher was born 1813 and died 1875. He married
   Magdalena Shelly and they had 6 children of which Jacob S. was the
   youngest. When M. Shelley died 1846 he married Anna Kurtz and they had
   7 more children. They lived close to the Brick Church west of Richfield, PA.

His grave marker also spells the name Brubaker.

6. Jacob Shelley Brubaker was born 1846 and died 1915. He married Anna Martin 1869 and they had 7 children of which Josiah M. (my Grampa) was the youngest. Jacob came to Canada with his brother John in August 1864. In Canada everybody spelled the name Brubacher so they switched back as well. In 1869 he married Anna Martin and they lived on a farm 3 ½ miles west of St. Jacobs just past Three Bridges where David Martin now lives. In 1888 they moved to Osceola County, Iowa (!! A seriously cool story, that). In 1913 they moved to Snyder County, PA, and he made the mistake of spelling his name Brubacker. This was pointed out to him, but he was a strong-willed man and insisted it was to be that way. This may well account for his offspring variously being Brubacher, Brubaker, or Brubacker. They were a family widely scattered.

7. Josiah Martin Brubacher (my Grampa B.) was born 1885 in Snyder County PA and died 1977 in St. Jacobs, ON. He married Annie Brubacher in 1884 and they had 13 children, of which my father Urias B. was 6th on the list. Three died very young and the second oldest died at 24 (not sure of what). They farmed next to Balsam Grove School east of Elmira, ON. It was in the Great Depression and times were tough. Annie Brubacher died 1940 and they are both buried in the Elmira Mennonite Cemetery behind the white church chust up the grade west of town don't you know.

8. Urias Brubacher Brubacher was born 1919 and died 2000. He married Sarah Bauman Bowman (1921 – 2008), daughter of Daniel M. Bowman of Floridale (my other grampa) on January 1, 1940. They spawned 7 children of which Kenneth David is the second youngest.

9. Kenneth David Brubacher was born 1952 and married Geraldine Francis Bauman 1974. They have 2 children, Angela Rose (1977) and Genevieve Rebecca (1980).

10. Genevieve married David Hiller and they have 6 children (in order), Micah Moses, Elyse Rose, Julia Lily, Isaac ...., Benjamin ..., Josiah .... Angela married Noe Ishaka and they have 3 children, Elija ..., Safi ..., and Caleb (not) .... and .... zzzzzzzz ...

About the Author

Kenneth David Brubacher was born into a large family of sort of Mennonites in Elmira, ON, through no fault of his own. He was encouraged to make an attempt at becoming a normal human being, but with clearly with limited success. To the surprise of nearly everyone he graduated from secondary school in 1970.

From there he traveled the world extensively, turning his hand to many kinds of jobs, and eventually returned to Elmira having accomplished very little. He got work as a millwright, but it was soon evident that he was a millwrong. After being mercifully fired from that job he went trucking and almost immediately distinguished himself (Summa Cum Laude with Oak Leaf Cluster and Silver Star) by destroying the truck.

He married and begat two lovely daughters who took after their mother in many wonderful ways, and turned out normal. It was considered a blessing that he had no sons because there was a high degree of probability that they might well grow up to be like their dad.

Knowing little about shoes, and even less about feet, he then took over his father's shoe repair shop and started to make shoes by hand along about April Fools' Day 1978. Very few people caught on. It was obvious that people whose feet were so bad that they sought out the services of a cobbler were not very fussy. The business prospered in spite of its inherent inadequacies.

He also applied himself to many varieties of sport, establishing a universal mediocrity in their pursuit seldom seen. When his body was sufficiently trashed he took up umpiring baseball, where it was observed that his training must have occurred under the tender administrations of the CNIB.

Currently he makes his home on a rented farm near Creemore, ON, and repairs a few shoes in his small shop in Collingwood. The farmhouse will soon become a gravel pit, whereupon it was his intent to establish institutions where Mennonites could go to seek quiet enjoyment. This, of course, until it was pointed out to him that they had already done it. These establishments are known as Mennonite Farms.

The author heartily recommends that any reader who takes a notion to write and produce a book or a play, then to lie down on the couch and watch videos of fawns gamboling in a sun-splashed meadow full of butterflies - until the feeling goes away.

It is hoped that you enjoy the book, and that its contents and presentation may provide therapeutic assistance in the remedy of your insomnia.

Printed in the United States
By Bookmasters